The President as Economist

The President as Economist

Scoring Economic Performance from Harry Truman to Barack Obama

Richard J. Carroll

 PRAEGER

AN IMPRINT OF ABC-CLIO, LLC
Santa Barbara, California • Denver, Colorado • Oxford, England

Library of Congress Cataloging-in-Publication Data

Carroll, Richard J.
  The president as economist : scoring economic performance from Harry Truman to Barack Obama / Richard J. Carroll.
     p. cm.
  Includes bibliographical references and index.
  ISBN 978–1–4408–0181–5 (hard copy : alk. paper) — ISBN 978–1–4408–0182–2 (ebook)
1. United States—Economic policy. 2. United States—Economic conditions. 3. Budget—United States—History. 4. Government spending policy—United States—History. 5. President—United States—History. I. Title.
HC103.C35   2012
330.973—dc23   2012009290

ISBN: 978–1–4408–0181–5
EISBN: 978–1–4408–0182–2

16 15 14 13 12   1 2 3 4 5

This book is also available on the World Wide Web as an eBook.
Visit www.abc-clio.com for details.

Praeger
An Imprint of ABC-CLIO, LLC

ABC-CLIO, LLC
130 Cremona Drive, P.O. Box 1911
Santa Barbara, California 93116-1911

This book is printed on acid-free paper (∞)

Manufactured in the United States of America

Contents

PART I. GENERAL ECONOMY: THE PRESIDENT'S INFLUENCE ON THE PRIVATE SECTOR

PART II. FISCAL ECONOMY: THE PRESIDENT'S INFLUENCE ON THE PUBLIC SECTOR

PART III. COMBINING PUBLIC AND PRIVATE INDICATORS: OVERALL PRESIDENTIAL PERFORMANCE RANKINGS

Figures and Tables

FIGURES

TABLES

Preface

> If all the economists were laid end to end, they'd never reach a conclusion.
>
> —George Bernard Shaw

Economics is a lot like psychiatry; you can make things up and they often sound sensible. It is possible to critique an administration's economic policy without any knowledge of economics at all. The more ideological a person is, the easier it is to be an economist. And the risks are minimal. After all, it's not as if something can go wrong if you don't know what you're doing in economic policy. It's not like flying an airplane or transplanting a kidney or building a bridge. Anybody can be an economist.

Maybe the reason people feel uninhibited about their economic opinions is that they see reputable economists disagreeing about how to solve economic problems. But it would be wrong to infer from this disagreement that the field of economics is illegitimate, that "winging it" is just as good as policy based on empirical facts, data, and theoretical underpinnings for economic behavior. Trained, experienced economists tend to know these things better than a noneconomist, just as an airline pilot tends to fly a plane better than a passenger.

But economic expertise can be corrupted by ideology. Look at the costly mistakes by the financial geniuses on Wall Street (e.g., AIG and Goldman Sachs) with their credit default swaps, at the Fed (e.g., Alan Greenspan) with their model of "self-regulation," and at the Treasury (e.g., Henry Paulson) with their faith in the subprime mortgage market even after it began to collapse, which led to the 2008 financial crisis. Economics knowledge cannot overcome the corrupting influences of ideology and greed. Still, for the average person to contribute positively to the public debate, he or she has to have some basic idea what she is talking about, and this book will help in that regard—more hard data and less ideology.

Economic data, if not steered by ideological motivations, are good at disinfecting economic policy from bad premises. Data define the record of economic policy performance, and that record carries lessons with it. But if one is an ideologue, then data will be used simply to support the ideology. I confess that I have little respect for ideologues. I marvel at how they throw away everything that is important to good policy. The context of the issue; the contributions of other disciplines like science, psychology, and history; and their very own maturity about life are all cast aside just to maintain their ideological approach to economics.

With the high level of partisanship in our country, I am surprised at the lack of attempts to rank presidential performance in a systematic way. Previous efforts to assess presidents' or political parties' economic performance tend to overlook one or another major element of economic performance. Some are limited only to gross domestic product, which neglects unemployment and inflation and many other important aspects of performance. Some exclude the entire public-sector side of performance (debt, deficits, and taxes), which is the area where the president, arguably, has most control over what happens economically. Other analyses focus only on the averages during the administration, which ignores what a president inherited from his predecessor and what he left behind. Such an analysis omits the central element of performance, which is how much a president improved or damaged the economy. Assessments also seem to omit the reality that there is some lag in the effect of a new president's policies and that the legacy of the previous president lingers a while, such as the cases of Bush 43 to Obama and Carter to Reagan to name prominent examples. All of these aspects of performance need to be taken into account. Still, there is no perfect way to assess presidential economic performance, just better ways and worse ways.

PRECURSOR TO *THE PRESIDENT AS ECONOMIST*

The precursor to this book, *An Economic Record of Presidential Performance from Truman to Bush* (Praeger 1995), took into account all of these elements and produced rankings on individual indicators and overall performance from the Truman administration to the George H. W. Bush (Bush 41) administration.

The President as Economist has updated and expanded the analysis in a number of areas. The update includes two additional, eight-year presidential administrations, Bill Clinton's and George W. Bush's, plus a partial record for Barack Obama. The presentation in the earlier book was almost entirely data driven and stopped short of linking policies to the performance indicators. In that sense, it was a pure scorecard. In the earlier book, I referred to avoiding an "ideological treatise that sets out to prove ideological hypotheses." The book was a neutral presentation of the data with the intent to provide a resource to the "individual to process economic information from new reports more critically, and, therefore, more effectively."[1]

The President as Economist presents the data as they are but also makes connections between policy choices and performance indicators. With the current economic debate mired in ideology, we desperately need a stronger positive statement of what works and what doesn't and under which circumstances.

The methodology for the overall ranking of presidents has been expanded to include two additional statistical methods. If similar rankings can be produced through multiple methods, then the conclusions about performance are sturdier. A review of the indicators and the weighting scheme from the previous book supported the deletion of several indicators that were not sufficiently related to presidential economic performance.

NOTE

1. Richard Carroll, *An Economic Record of Presidential Performance from Truman to Bush* (New York: Praeger, 1995), xiii–xiv

Acknowledgments

I want to thank the many analysts working in the U.S. Government who are responsible for maintaining the data that are necessary not only for analyzing presidential economic performance, but also for monitoring our economy and developing effective economic policy. The agencies central to this effort include the Bureau of Economic Analysis at the U.S. Department of Commerce, the Bureau of Labor Statistics at the U.S. Department of Labor, the U.S. Census Bureau, the Federal Reserve and the Office of Management and Budget. These agencies provide the data and analysis that help policy-makers decide whether taxes should go up or down, whether interest rates should be raised or lowered, where federal revenues should be spent and where not, and how to sustain critical government programs like Social Security and Medicare. Whether policy-makers actually comprehend and fully consider the data is another matter.

Individuals who were particularly helpful at various stages of the book include, Tiffin Shewmake, David Cieslikowski, Nils Junge, Linda Karr, Keith Alger, Eric Bell, and Aart Kraay. I also want to thank my acquisitions editors, David Paige and Valerie Tursini, who were responsive to questions and gave excellent advice as I developed the book, and my production coordinators, Michelle Scott and Subaramya Nambiaruran.

Introduction

Economic depression cannot be cured by legislative action or executive pronouncement. Economic wounds must be healed by the action of the cells of the economic body—the producers and consumers themselves.

—Herbert Hoover

The main purpose of this book is to use the exercise of ranking presidents to learn lessons from the economic successes and failures of presidents and to show the circumstances when specific economic policies work and when they do not. The book also provides a statistical portrayal of presidential administrations with the intent to reduce the spurious claims that are frequently made about presidents' records in political debates. For example, detractors of President Obama point out that the unemployment rate that George W. Bush left behind was 7.8 percent in January 2009 and that Obama made it worse. The reality is that the economy was still plummeting as Obama took office and could not be stabilized until the unemployment rate peaked at 10 percent in October 2009 before declining steadily to below 8.5 percent. (A one-year performance lag captures this reality.) Having a historical record at hand helps guard against misrepresentations.

Having the recent historical context also helps with understanding economic news and putting it into perspective. The reader will have a better idea of the elements of economic performance and of what constitutes a good performance. As voters, we implicitly make these evaluations all the time. Lastly, the book strongly challenges some popularly held views about economic policy and performance that, frankly, have harmed the United States' conduct of economic policy, particularly in recent years.

The value of an economic policy depends on the results it produces. The data will confirm these results. If the president chooses the right policies or is fortunate to be president in good economic times, then his record, if accurately measured, will reflect both the good policy and the luck. This book presents a data-based score of economic performance for each president from Harry Truman to Barack Obama as well as the narrative of his policies and fortunate or unfortunate historical circumstances.

In an assessment of presidential administrations we want to know how our favorite president performed and find evidence of what we believe to be true about presidents and their policies. We might also like to discover, for example, evidence of poor performance about presidents we do not like. The real usefulness of presidential rankings is not just how presidents performed relative to each other; it is rather which presidents' policies performed better as suggested by their ranking. When we know which policies performed best and in which circumstances, we are in a good position to lay discredited policies aside and to focus on policies that have worked in the past in similar circumstances.

We tend to be most interested in more recent presidents, particularly the one currently in office, and especially if he is seeking reelection. Yet there are examples of circumstances and policies from earlier administrations that are strikingly similar to more recent administrations. Seeing how earlier presidents dealt successfully with these circumstances can help with today's challenges. The time period we cover in this book—from 1946 to 2011, 66 years—has many examples of policies that work in some situations but not in others. This provides a good clue about what policies will work in today's economic conditions.

HIGH STAKES AND RECENT ECONOMIC CONDITIONS

The United States faces serious short- and long-term economic problems with little maneuvering room for policy. Even before the economic crisis that hit in 2008, the U.S. deficit was on the rise, the trade deficit was at record levels, the dollar was weak, and the United States had done worse than nothing to deal with rising energy and health care costs. Policymakers have complicated our predicament by continuing to hold outdated debates about which economic policies work. Some influential policymakers adopt rigid ideological approaches, appearing oblivious to lessons learned as far back as the Great Depression in the 1930s (Annex 2).

We continue to experience the fallout of a laissez-faire (unregulated free market) policy that permitted the private sector to make pervasive and costly mistakes leading up to the 2008 economic crisis. As a result of the crisis, in 2009, gross domestic product (GDP) declined 3.5 percent, unemployment increased from 4.9 to 10.0 percent, federal government revenue fell by almost half a trillion dollars, and the deficit exceeded $1 trillion. Behind these data lie the suffering and frustration of millions of American families who lost their homes and who watched their savings dwindle. As a country, we have to do a better job of analyzing our economic decisions of the past in order to find the right path forward.

Relevance of Presidential Rankings to Current Policy

Ranking the performance of U.S. presidents can easily become politicized. Performance rankings will indicate that one approach to policy is better than another, at least in a given context. These conclusions will not be palatable to economic ideologues, particularly because performance rankings show that no policy will work in every circumstance. For example, a president who followed a philosophy of deregulation who also had a low presidential ranking probably demonstrated that his approach was inappropriate for the circumstances in which he governed. Extending this example, a policy of less financial regulation in the wake of Wall Street's crisis in 2008 would seem a particularly ill-advised policy approach.[1] Describing the context in which certain policies work will help identify the appropriate economic policies in the present context.

GOOD PRACTICE IN MEASURING PRESIDENTIAL PERFORMANCE

Because of the potential for politicizing presidential rankings, the methodology to evaluate administrations has to be transparent to ensure that it can be inspected for statistical mischief. The credibility of the analysis is also strengthened if we can arrive at the same conclusion using several different approaches. The analysis in this book employs a number of safeguards in evaluating presidential administrations (Annex 1 contains a more detailed discussion of approach and methodology):

1. Official government data that provide comprehensive and consistent coverage of economic performance
2. Simple and transparent methodology using several approaches to rank the presidents and compare the results

3. Transparent weighting structure

4. Linking indicator results to policies and economic context

Official Government Data that Provide Comprehensive and Consistent Coverage

Official government data have their limitations, but they provide the best and perhaps the only way, to compare presidential administrations over the entire time period, 1946 to 2011. There are many good performance indicators, but only a limited number are available for that full time period.

A comprehensive approach in this case using 17 indicators (Table I.1) allows the score to capture more aspects of performance than just the "Big Three" of GDP, employment, and inflation. It allows a president to get credit for good achievements that might not have translated immediately into, say, GDP growth. For instance, a president who had mediocre GDP growth but who recorded high investment and savings rates deserves to have that reflected in his score even though the fruits of the higher savings and investment may not be realized during his administration.

Table I.1   Economic Indicators Used in the Analysis

Indicator	Description	Source
Gross domestic product (GDP) growth rate	Growth of GDP adjusted for inflation as measured by the consumer price index for all urban consumers (CPI-U)	Department of Commerce (DOC), Bureau of Economic Analysis (BEA)
Productivity growth rate	Growth rate in the index of productivity for the nonfarm business sector	DOC, BEA
Inflation	Consumer price index for all urban consumers (CPI-U)	Department of Labor (DOL), Bureau of Labor Statistics (BLS)
Real interest rate	Bank prime rate adjusted for inflation	Board of Governors of the Federal Reserve
Gross private investment rate share of GDP	Gross private investment divided by GDP	DOC, BEA
Personal savings rate	Total personal savings divided by total disposable income	DOC, BEA

Table I.1   (continued)

Indicator	Description	Source
Unemployment rate	Total number of unemployed persons divided bythe total labor force	DOL, BLS
Employment growth rate	Growth rate in the number of employed persons	DOL, BLS
Growth in the stock market	Dow Jones Industrial Averages, adjusted for inflation	Dow Jones historical data
Percent of the population below the poverty line	Number of people falling below the poverty income threshold divided by the total population	Bureau of the Census
Exports as a share of GDP	Total exports divided by GDP	DOC, BEA
Trade balance as a share of GDP	Net exports (exports minus imports) divided by GDP	DOC, BEA
Federal budget growth	Growth rate of federal budget outlays adjusted for inflation	Office of Management and Budget (OMB)
Federal budget as a share of GDP	Federal budget outlays divided by GDP	OMB
Federal deficit as a percentage of federal budget	Total federal budget deficit divided by the total federal budget	OMB
National debt as a percentage of GDP	Total federal debt (publicly and privately held) divided by GDP	OMB
Taxation	Federal taxes as a percentage of GDP	OMB

Simple and Transparent Methodology and a Variety of Approaches

For each performance indicator, we include both averages and trends in the ranking. Each indicator compensates for the other's weaknesses. For example, a president, such as Reagan, inheriting either high unemployment or high inflation from his predecessor, such as Carter, will probably not have better than a mediocre average for both indicators, even if he succeeded in lowering inflation and unemployment. However, the economic improvement is captured by the indicator trend change. The trend change for each administration is the difference between endpoints of the administrations, which describes what a president inherited versus what he left behind. Similarly, a president (George W. Bush) who inherited a strong and improving fiscal balance from his predecessor (Clinton), but who then racked up huge debts, is penalized for the fiscal deterioration.[2,3]

For Chapters 1 through 9, no statistical methodology is required. The ranking of presidents is based simply on the presidents' averages and trends for each indicator. It is in Chapter 10, the synthesis chapter, where statistical methods are needed. Three methods are used to bring all the indicators together: (1) standard deviations from the mean, (2) the min-max method, and (3) a simple average of each president's rankings for all of the indicators. Each of these methods is described briefly in Chapter 10 and in greater detail in Annex 1.

Transparent Weighting Structure: Accounting for the Relative Importance of Indicators

Also in Chapter 10, we account for the fact that some indicators are more important than others. For each of the methods above a set of weights is selected where each indicator is placed into one of four categories of importance: Most important, Important, Less important, and Least important. Again, more detail is provided in Chapter 10 and Annex 1.

The weighting structure considers a number of factors in assessing the importance of an indicator: the degree of influence a president has on the indicator (higher weight), the degree to which the indicator is correlated with one or more other indicators (lower weight), the degree of volatility of the indicator (lower weight), and whether the indicator represents intermediate success (e.g., real interest rate; lower weight) or ultimate success (e.g., GDP or employment growth; higher weight).

If the indicator is volatile, then its average is much more important to measuring performance than its trend. This is generally true of growth-rate indicators like GDP growth and stock market growth that fluctuate a lot. For example, stock market growth rates fluctuate wildly compared to other indicators. So whether a president had a good growth rate at the beginning of his administration and a bad one at the end does not matter much because, historically, stock market growth could easily go strongly in the opposite direction the very next year without indicating a significant or lasting change in the economic health of the country.

So, the *change* in these indicators' growth rates from the first year to the final year of the administration does not usually say as much about performance as does the *average* growth rate for the indicator that was achieved under a presidential administration. In contrast, for share-of-GDP indicators like debt as a percentage of GDP or the unemployment rate, which do not fluctuate as much, the trend is often more important than the average.

Linking Indicator Results to Policies and Economic Context

In each chapter we look at the policy choices of the presidents to identify plausible links between policies and indicators. In this way, we build a stronger performance narrative for each president that goes beyond the pure indicator to the actual attribution of the economic results measured by the indicator. We also emphasize the context for each policy and indicator to better draw out lessons for current economic challenges.

When attributing results to policies, we have to think about how much influence, and therefore responsibility, a president really has with respect to the economy. The U.S. economy is primarily a market economy that is driven by the actions of hundreds of millions of people, by economic cycles, and by world events which may be mostly beyond the control of policymakers. However, the president does have varying levels of influence on different aspects of the economy. For example, with respect to the federal deficit, the president has a substantial influence—that is, unless he has inherited a war, a recession, or both. Further, the president has a lot to say about the size of the federal budget and whether taxes go up or down.

GDP is another matter because there are so many additional factors that drive it, including demographics, the health of the financial sector, global market conditions, and a host of other private-sector factors that are largely beyond the control of the president. That is a major reason why indicators are included that underlie economic equity and growth, such as savings and investment, interest rates, and inflation and employment. The ultimate question of economic performance is not just what was achieved but what was achievable, given the circumstances.

OTHER ASPECTS OF EVALUATING A PRESIDENT'S ECONOMIC PERFORMANCE

When rating presidents, a lot of decisions have to be made as to what is important to performance and what is not. We have already discussed the selection of indicators and the possibility of assigning weights to each, the context for policies, and the different levels of influence a president has over different indicators. But there are other aspects to consider.

Persisting Effects of Presidential Policies

This analysis asserts that a president's policies have lagged effects. We account for this by assigning a one-year lag. In other words, the year in which the president leaves office is part of his record even though he typically leaves in January. Why? Because the effects of the departing president's policies have much more of an effect on the economic results during that year of departure than do the policies of the new president. The new president does have influence over the economy in his first year, but not nearly as much as does his predecessor.

For example, Jimmy Carter's last year of record is 1981, not a good year for the economy. In another case, Bush 43's first year of record is 2002 (he escapes the recession of 2001, which was no fault of his), and his last year of record is 2009 (he does not escape the impact of the 2008 financial crisis). It is only appropriate and just that a president who leaves behind an economy in shambles is held responsible for the associated results, at least for one year, and that a president with a strong performance is given credit for the positive results of his administration.

In some cases a one-year lag is insufficient to capture the lingering effects of previous policies. For example, the effects of the Vietnam War on the economy persisted years after its official conclusion in early 1973. Likewise, the damage caused by extending subprime loans to people who were not creditworthy (and then building stacks of derivatives upon them) has been profound and will also take a number of years to decant from the financial system. Unfortunately, there is no reliable method to customize the lag for each indicator. The one-year lag does protect presidential records to an important extent from negative impacts from preceding administrations.

Real versus Nominal

Growth rates in this analysis are always adjusted for inflation to produce the real growth rate of an indicator. That way, the president is neither penalized nor rewarded for indicator changes that are caused by inflation. For example, the stock market graph that is adjusted for inflation looks very different from the one that is not adjusted (Chapter 4). The stock market graph using actual end-of-year Dow Jones values shows a constant rise, but the one adjusted for inflation has an oscillating pattern. Inflation is considered by itself in the assessment of presidential performance in Chapter 2.

Economic Volatility after World War II

The first year after the war, 1946, was the first year of a major economic and political transition for the United States. The U.S. military was demobilizing, many countries' infrastructures were destroyed by the war, and federal government expenditures were 41.9 percent of GDP in 1945. During the transition, federal expenditures fell to 24.8 percent in 1946 and to 14.8 percent in 1947. By comparison, in recent years—before the financial crisis—federal expenditures have been around 20 percent of GDP. After the war, the United States emerged as the leading economic power in the world and worked to establish new rules for international trade and commerce. These changes are reflected in some of the indicators, which are quite volatile. This volatility poses some issues for Truman's record. Should these volatile years be counted on Truman's record, or should we record his performance after the economy settled down in 1949 or 1950?

To have a fair assessment, we cannot trim away the negatives and leave just the positives, or vice versa. For example, WWII was a huge stimulus to the economy, and economists on the left and the right generally agree that this stimulus is what finally vaulted the U.S. economy out of the Great Depression (1929–1941). So when that stimulus is rapidly removed by reducing government expenditures from 41.9 percent to 14.8 percent of GDP during 1945 through 1947, the obvious effect on GDP is a substantial decline. In fact, GDP fell by 10.9 percent, which was more than three times the next largest recession (3.5 percent in 2009). That really does not seem fair to Truman. However, the GDP growth rates were very high in 1950 (8.7 percent) and 1951 (7.7 percent). In addition, Truman gets credit for lowering federal outlays as a percentage of GDP. In the final analysis, we decided to present Truman's economic data record straight up, that is, including the volatile postwar years of 1946 through 1948.

STRUCTURE AND FEATURES OF THE INDIVIDUAL CHAPTERS AND OVERALL BOOK

Each chapter of Parts I and II is organized in the same way. First the indicator(s) is defined (including identifying the agency responsible for the indicator) and critiqued to establish its value in measuring economic performance. The indicator's correlation with other indicators is also discussed, which impacts the weight given to the indicator. If the indicator is highly correlated with other indicators, then it might not be as important to give that indicator a high weight. (There is further discussion of weights in Chapter 10 and in Annex 1).

Next we review how each indicator performed on each president's watch. Major presidential policy choices, particularly of the more recent administrations, and their impact on the indicators are discussed. The chapter includes a table that ranks the 12 presidents from best to worst for both the average and the trend of the indicator. Each chapter concludes with a summary of findings and special issues relating to the indicator.

The book's chapters are based on specific indicators rather than individual presidential administrations. This approach places more focus on what the indicator is actually capturing and its reliability. The reader gains an analytical advantage by becoming more familiar with the indicators' strengths and weaknesses. Basing chapters on indicators also allows the composite performance of each president to develop gradually over the course of the entire book. The disadvantage of basing chapters on indicators is that it requires some repetition of the discussion of events and policies that affected multiple indicators. We have made attempts to discuss these policies and events each time in a new light that is relevant to the indicator. The final synthesis chapter summarizes the overall performance of each administration.

Graphs of indicators are selectively used. Some graphs show when the indicators have distinct patterns that can be traced to specific administrations and policies. Some indicators behave differently in the earlier half of the time period (pre-1978) from the later half of the time period. This behavior is an important consideration in the narrative about a president's performance. For example, GDP growth rates tended to be higher and unemployment lower in the early period compared with the later period. Presidents like Truman, Eisenhower, Kennedy, and Johnson benefited, while presidents like Carter, Bush (both 41 and 43), Clinton, and certainly Obama had a tougher challenge.

The final chapter, Chapter 10, summarizes the overall performance of each administration. This chapter uses an overall measure of how the U.S. economy performed during each presidential administration, the Presidential Performance Index (PPI). The PPI is the basis for the overall ranking of presidential performance and combines all of the indicators used in the analysis.

PRESIDENTS AND THEIR TERMS OF OFFICE

The presidents covered in this analysis and their actual terms of office are listed below. Note that for presidents who served partial terms, we round the length of their records to the nearest year. For all presidents who completed a full term, the end date is January 20.

1. Harry S. Truman, 1945 (April 12)–1953
2. Dwight D. Eisenhower, 1953–1961
3. John F. Kennedy, 1961–1963 (November 22)
4. Lyndon B. Johnson, 1963 (November 22)–1969
5. Richard M. Nixon, 1969–1974 (August 9)
6. Gerald R. Ford, 1974 (August 9)–1977
7. James E. Carter, 1977–1981
8. Ronald W. Reagan, 1981–1989
9. George H. W. Bush, 1989–1993[4]
10. William J. Clinton, 1993–2001
11. George W. Bush, 2001–2009[5]
12. Barack H. Obama, 2009–Present

The Affect of the Length of Administration on Economic Performance

Some presidents served a full two terms (Eisenhower, Reagan, Clinton, and Bush), others served more than one term but less than two terms (Truman: seven years, nine months; Johnson: five years, two months; and Nixon: five years, seven months), some one term (Carter and H. W. Bush), and some less than one term (Kennedy: two years, ten months; and Ford: two years, five months). There is a difference between serving eight years versus four years. In one instance, the president has more time to improve the economy, lower the debt, lower poverty, and improve the stock market. On the other hand, eight years is plenty of time to experience one or more recessions, and that will hurt a president's averages. If there is a short term, like those of Ford or Kennedy, then the president may luck out by being part of an economic improvement (Ford) or a strong economic period (Kennedy).

Note that Barack Obama's record is partial. With the one-year lag, his first-term record will not be available until the data are published after the end of 2013. For this book, we are able to include most indicators for only the first half of his administration. It is important to include his partial record because, as the current president, he is the one most relevant to economic performance in the future.

KEY THEMES

A number of important messages are developed in this book:

Ideology and Effective Economic Policy Do Not Mix

Economic policy is all about the context. The same prescription, whether it is cutting tax rates, cutting government spending, erecting trade barriers, or another action, will not produce positive results in every economic context. Ideology does not consider different contexts because it is based on principles, not contextual realities. Principles may be good to have, but without a contextual basis they are very risky to the economy. For instance, one's ideological stance may be that a smaller and weaker government is universally better. Therefore, reducing taxes is always good because it moves toward that goal of a smaller government. However, as we will see, tax cuts do not guarantee higher employment or income and may damage the fiscal health of the nation.

It May Take Time to Get Out of an Economic Mess, and the Way Out Is Not Always Clear

As we have recently learned, when an economy is in a deep recession and the room to maneuver has been constrained by other weaknesses in the economy, it can take a long time for the economy to recover. Moreover, policymakers, particularly when they do not have much room to maneuver, have no clear path out of the recession. Different approaches have to be tried: tax cuts, targeted investments (infrastructure, renewable energy, education) and more general stimulus expenditures (unemployment compensation, tax rebates, etc.). We really are not sure which ones will work—or if they will work—and we have to be cautious not to go too far with any one policy because we just do not have that much capacity to take on debt.

Performance Is Based on a Wide Variety of Economic Indicators, Not Just One or Two

Some presidents did well in areas that produce benefits beyond their administrations. Clinton may have benefited from some of Reagan's policies, and Kennedy and Johnson from Eisenhower's. To capture these longer lags we include savings and investment, poverty line, and taxation data.

Be Careful When Contemplating Financial Deregulation; Financial Crises May Not Be Far Behind

Sometimes policy makers deregulate because they think that it will make U.S. enterprises more competitive. However, policy makers are often naïve about other motivations behind companies' desire for deregulation. We saw a number of disastrous mistakes in the Reagan (savings and loan deregulation and the subsequent crisis), Clinton (repeal of Glass-Steagall and deregulation of derivatives, and later the 2008 financial crisis), and Bush 43 (weak enforcement and poor management of the financial system) administrations.

THE ECONOMY IN A BROADER CONTEXT

Politicians see economic success as the key to getting reelected, and it is therefore almost always the top policy area for them, particularly on a national level. Increasing or steady growth, low inflation, and low or falling unemployment virtually guarantee political success. In focusing on these important indicators we should not lose sight of the broader context. The economy is not the only important policy area for the United States, or for any country. In fact, war and peace, social order, and the sustainable use of the physical environment are vital to the nation and to a president's performance. Yet the popular media and the political world seem to treat the environment and other policy areas as a subset of the economy.

The environment, for example, is something we address only when all the economic variables are good—strong growth, low inflation and unemployment. But perhaps it should be the other way around. A president can make many economic policy mistakes, and those mistakes will make us poorer and less comfortable, but if he make too many environmental policy mistakes, then we may find ourselves poisoned, starved, or warring over supplies of energy or even clean water. So the analysis in this book needs to be seen in that context as well. If the president's economic performance was weak, but he did, or tried to do, the right things for the long haul, for war and peace, the social order and environmental science, then his legacy should reflect that contribution.

NOTES

1. Yet Wall Street has been fairly effective in staving off financial regulation that would be strong enough to prevent a repeat of the 2008 financial debacle.

2. To go further with the example, Reagan inherited a high unemployment rate from his predecessor, Jimmy Carter. He is likely, therefore, to have a high average overall unemployment rate, which he did, at 7.2 percent. However, that high rate also provided an opportunity for a large drop in unemployment, which would also be credited to the president's performance record. Reagan did achieve a 2.3 percentage point drop in the unemployment rate. In contrast, Truman and Eisenhower inherited very low unemployment rates and got credit for keeping the average low, but both raised the unemployment rate to some degree, and their scores were lower as a result.

3. Note that indicator trends are the difference in endpoints, not the difference in averages for two successive presidential administrations. For example, it might be confusing to the reader that President Clinton had a higher *average* debt rate than his predecessor (Bush 41), 63.0 versus 61.7 percent, but that Clinton also lowered the debt as a percentage of GDP compared with Bush 41 by a substantial 9.7 percentage points. How was this possible? It was possible because Clinton inherited a debt level from Bush equal to 66.1 percent of GDP, but by the time Clinton left office, the debt had fallen to 56.4 percent of GDP. Bush 41, on the other hand, had inherited a much lower debt-to-GDP ratio of 53.1 percent from Reagan. Thus, while Clinton's average debt share of GDP was higher than Bush 41's, the debt was falling. Under Bush 41, it was rising (a total of 13.0 percentage points of GDP). Whose record was better on the debt? Clearly, Clinton's was, even though he had a worse average debt level. So in this case, the indicator trend tells us more than does the indicator average.

4. Referred to as "H. W. Bush" or "Bush 41" in the text.

5. Referred to as "W. Bush" or "Bush 43" in the text.

Abbreviations

ACA	Affordable Care Act of 2010
AFDC	Aid to Families with Dependant Children
ARRA	American Recovery and Reinvestment Act of 2009
BEA	Bureau of Economic Analysis *or* Budget Enforcement Act
BLS	Bureau of Labor Statistics
CBO	Congressional Budget Office
CERCLA	Comprehensive Environmental Response, Compensation and Liability Act of 1980
CFMA	Commodity Futures Modernization Act of 2000
CPI-U	Consumer Price Index—All Urban Consumers
DJIA	Dow Jones Industrial Average
DOC	Department of Commerce
DOD	Department of Defense
DOE	Department of Energy
DOL	Department of Labor
EGTRRA	Economic Growth and Tax Relief Reconciliation Act of 2001
EPA	Environmental Protection Act of 1970
ERTA	Economic Recovery Tax Act of 1981
FDIC	Federal Deposit Insurance Corporation
FIRREA	Financial Institutions Reform Recovery and Enforcement Act of 1989
FSLIC	Federal Savings and Loan Insurance Corporation

G.I. (Bill)	Government Issue
GATT	General Agreement on Tariffs and Trade of 1947
GDP	gross domestic product
GM	General Motors
HHS	Health and Human Services
IMF	International Monetary Fund
NAFTA	North American Free Trade Agreement of 1994
NASDAQ	National Association of Securities Dealers Automated Quotation
NIPA	National Income and Product Accounts
NOAA	National Oceanic and Atmospheric Administration
OBRA	Omnibus Budget Reconciliation Act (1990 and 1993)
OMB	Office of Management and Budget
OPEC	Organization of Petroleum Exporting Countries
OSHA	Occupational Safety and Health Administration
OTS	Office of Thrift Supervision
PRC	People's Republic of China
PRWORA	Personal Responsibility and Work Opportunity Reconciliation Act of 1996
S&L	savings and loan
S&P	Standard and Poors
TALF	Term Asset-Backed Securities Loan Facility of 2009
TANF	Temporary Aid to Needy Families
TARP	Troubled Asset Relief Program
WIN	Whip Inflation Now
WWII	World War II

Timeline of Events

HARRY S. TRUMAN

Truman becomes president	April 12, 1945
End of WWII	August 1945
Bretton Woods system of international exchange	December 27, 1945
Strikes in steel, coal, auto, and railroad industries	1945–1946
Employment Act of 1946	1946
General Agreement on Tariffs and Trade	1947
Fair Deal	1949
Marshall Plan	1948–1952
Korean War	1950–1953
Federal government seizure of steel mills	June 1952

DWIGHT D. EISENHOWER

Creation of the Department of Health, Education and Welfare (HEW)	1953
National Interstate and Defense Highways Act	1956
Expansion of the Social Security Program to include disability insurance	1957
Military industrial complex farewell speech	January 17, 1961

JOHN F. KENNEDY

New Frontier presented	1960
Peace Corps	1961
Trade Expansion Act	1962
Cuban Missile Crisis	October 1962
Clean Air Act	1963
Nuclear Test Ban Treaty	October 1963
Assassination	November 22, 1963

LYNDON B. JOHNSON

Kennedy-Johnson tax cut	1964–1965
Civil Rights Act	1964
War on Poverty	1964
The Great Society	1965
Creation of Medicare and Medicaid programs	1967
Vietnam War	1965–1973
Surtax for war	1968

RICHARD M. NIXON

Creation of the Environmental Protection Agency (EPA)	1970
Creation of the National Oceanic and Atmospheric Administration (NOAA)	1970
Creation of the Occupational Safety and Health Administration (OSHA)	1970
Collapse of Bretton Woods and the gold standard	1971
Wage and price controls	1971
Opening relations with China	February 27, 1972
Watergate break-in	1972
Endangered Species Act	1973
End of Vietnam War (U.S. involvement)	January 1973
Arab oil embargo	1973
Resignation	August 9, 1974

GERALD R. FORD

Pardon of Richard Nixon	September 8, 1974
Whip Inflation Now (WIN)	October 8, 1974
Tax Reduction Act	1975
Helsinki Accords	August 1975

JAMES E. CARTER

Creation of the Department of Energy	August 4, 1977
Oil shock	1979
Egypt-Israel Peace Treaty	1979
Hostage crisis in Iran	1979–1981
Creation of Superfund	December 1980

RONALD W. REAGAN

Firing of air traffic controllers	1981
Reagan tax cuts	1981–1983
Social Security reform and tax increase	1983
Tax Reform Act	1986
Iran-Contra Scandal	1986–1987
Intermediate-Range Nuclear Forces Treaty	December 1987
S&L crisis	1986–1989

GEORGE H. W. BUSH

Resolution of the S&L crisis	August 1989
Fall of the Berlin Wall and end of the Cold War	November 1989
Omnibus Budget Reconciliation Act (OBRA-1990)	1990
Operation Desert Storm against Iraq	1991

WILLIAM J. CLINTON

Family and Medical Leave Act	1993
OBRA-1993	1993

North American Free Trade Agreement (NAFTA)	1994
Welfare reform	August 1996
Asian financial crisis	1997–1998
Impeachment	December 19, 1998
Dot.com bubble	1995–2000
Deregulatory measures[1]	1999–2000

GEORGE W. BUSH

Terrorist attacks	September 11, 2001
Bush tax cuts	June 2001
Afghanistan War	October 7, 2001–Present
No child left behind education reform	January 2002,
Iraq War	March 19, 2003– December 20, 2011
Prescription drug benefit program	2003
Real estate/financial/subprime mortgage crisis	2008
Troubled Asset Relief Program (TARP)	2008

BARACK H. OBAMA

Term Asset-Backed Securities Loan Facility (TALF)	2009
Stimulus program	2009
Auto industry bailout	March 2009
Affordable Care Act	March 2010
Dodd-Frank financial reform bill	July 21, 2010
Payroll tax cut and extension of Bush tax cuts	December 2010
Osama bin Laden killed	May 2011
Debt ceiling battle	July–August 2011
Ending of Iraq War	December 2011

NOTE

1. Gramm-Leach-Bliley Act, November 1999, which included the repeal of the Glass-Steagall Act; also the Commodity Futures Trading Modernization Act of 2000.

PART I

General Economy: The President's Influence on the Private Sector

Part I covers economic events, policies, and results in the private sector. The private sector is the main source of income, employment, and innovation but also of resource exploitation and environmental degradation. This analysis is based on key economic indicators that capture policy goals that are largely determined in the private sector. The president has little control over many variables affecting private-sector performance. Still, he is responsible for using the tools at his disposal to promote economic growth and employment and to ensure that as many citizens as possible are part of that growth. Part I begins with a chapter on the most prominent of economic indicators, GDP growth. It also covers the closely related growth of labor productivity, which drives, or should drive, the standard of living of a country. Chapter 2 reviews presidential performance with respect to inflation and real interest rate indicators. Chapter 3 covers savings and investment, which are ingredients for growth and employment and which in turn are affected by inflation and interest rates.

In Chapter 4, we discuss performance of the stock market during presidential administrations, which gives an indication of how markets received a president's policies and reacted to economic conditions of the time. Chapter 5 reviews presidential performance with respect to employment indicators and the percentage of the population that is more or less left out of the economy—those who fall below the poverty line. Chapter 6 captures presidential performance with respect to trade—in particular, the balance of trade and the growth of exports.

ONE

GDP and Productivity: Presidential Influence on Economic Production

Our gross national product ... if we should judge America by that ... counts the destruction of our redwoods and the loss of our natural wonder in chaotic sprawl ... Yet the gross national product does not allow for the health of our children, the quality of their education, or the joy of their play ... it measures everything, in short, except that which makes life worthwhile. And it tells us everything about America except why we are proud that we are Americans.

—Robert F. Kennedy, address at University of Kansas, Lawrence, March 18, 1968

VALUE AND CRITIQUE OF THE INDICATORS

Gross Domestic Product (GDP)

Every economic move a president makes is aimed, one way or another, at increasing GDP. Whether it is tax policy, expenditures on education, choosing a chairman of the Federal Reserve, or regulatory policy, the president wants to increase and sustain the nation's economic growth. He knows that other objectives, such as employment growth, poverty reduction, and even resources to run the government, depend on the growth of GDP. Thus, GDP is often seen as the bottom line of economic performance. It is the main measure of all that we produce in our national economy over a given time period. If GDP falls, it means that the nation has less income, fewer jobs, and less revenue for government programs.

News organizations are fixated on GDP growth as the primary goal of public policy and fill considerable amounts of airtime with continuous speculation on the future path of GDP growth. The monthly GDP report published by the U.S. Commerce Department affects the stock market and other private investment decisions by influencing expectations about the economy. We also define *recession* as a decline in GDP over two straight quarters.

GDP is defined as the market value of the goods and services produced by labor and property located in the United States.[1] GDP is valuable as a measure of the total production of an economy, which is a key aspect of performance. The GDP is not the actual sum of all production but rather an estimate derived from a number of detailed surveys from many agencies of the U.S. government. It is not feasible to record every single item and service that is produced in the United States. These surveys, however, measure the economic activities of tens of thousands of companies and individuals that approximate the actual GDP of the nation.[2] It is perhaps the largest sample, other than the population census, taken regularly in the United States. GDP and its components are part of the U.S. National Income and Product Accounts (NIPA), which is compiled by the Bureau of Economic Analysis of the U.S. Department of Commerce.[3]

GDP is commonly described in economics textbooks by the equation

$$C + I + G + (X - M) = GDP$$

where C is private consumption, I is private investment, G is government purchases, and X minus M is exports minus imports. Note that G is not the total federal budget but only what the government actually buys. For example, Social Security expenditures by the government are not added to GDP because the government is not buying anything; it is just transferring money.[4] Investment is the total expenditure in the economy on all types of (nonfinancial) investments (e.g., equipment and training).

Goods and services that are part of consumption, investment, and government purchases must be produced in the United States or a foreign country. All of the production from other countries that the United States buys (imports) is subtracted from GDP, while all of the goods and services that the United States sells to other countries (exports) are added to GDP. That is why it is called gross *domestic* product. NIPA data for all of these components of GDP are used in subsequent chapters.

If Something Is Good for GDP Growth, Is It Necessarily Good for the United States?

Based on the high priority placed on increasing GDP, it would seem that anything that raises GDP must be good for the nation. However, there are some serious caveats about GDP. For one, GDP counts as good many things in society that are actually bad. Say that Americans all of a sudden decided that they were going to drink half as much soft drinks (half of the 9.92 billion cases that they drink annually[5]). With annual sales at $72 billion, this would mean a drop in GDP of $36 billion. Although consumers would lose the pleasure of sipping sweetened, artificially flavored water, the overall net benefits to Americans would be substantial. The benefits of healthier weight, a lower incidence of diabetes, and perhaps fewer behavioral issues in kids would not be measured by GDP as positive. In addition to the drop in GDP from reduced soda sales, GDP would count the benefits as negatives because health care expenditures would be lower!

Environmental impact and economic efficiency are two areas where GDP gives a positive value to the negative aspects of an activity. For example, to produce one pound of red meat, 2,500 gallons of water are needed along with 10 pounds of grain. It is both costly to the environment and a resource-intensive and inefficient way of producing food.[6] So here is another contradiction in GDP. If we protect the environment and become more efficient, we will be better off, but we will also lower GDP. Another example is highway toll booths, where drivers may sit in idling cars (spewing carbon monoxide and guzzling gas) for long periods to pay a couple of dollars in tolls. If toll booths were eliminated, it would lower GDP but would improve our lives. The list goes on.

Economic Limitations of GDP in Capturing Performance

On the purely economic side, GDP growth is also an incomplete measure of performance. Other indicators are needed to supplement it to more accurately depict the economic performance of presidents. A president might have done many things right, such as promoting higher levels of savings and investment, that will produce benefits in the long run. He might have pursued a sensible fiscal policy and so on, but GDP growth may not have materialized during his tenure. Shouldn't we try to capture good policies that improved other indicators so that a president's performance is not punished for factors that may be well beyond his control? These caveats are not meant to discredit GDP growth as a performance indicator, but we need to temper our enthusiasm for this indicator. Too many news outlets uncritically view GDP as the *exclusive* bottom line of economic policy and miss out on the deeper aspects of performance.

In this chapter we will look specifically at GDP during presidential administrations. The pattern of GDP growth shows the booms and the busts on the presidents' watches and defines their record with respect to this important economic indicator. It will also allow us to begin to build a statistical record of presidents' performances that will also depend on other economic indicators.

Correlation of GDP with Other Performance Indicators

GDP is correlated with many of the other performance indicators, such as investment, productivity, and employment. And the correlation is usually two-way. For example, GDP growth provides more resources for investment, which in turn generates higher GDP in the future. Also, with higher GDP, the demand for labor is greater. When more people are working to produce goods and services, GDP is also higher. On the public-sector side, because tax revenues are higher in a growing economy, the debts and deficits tend to be lower. So, in this analysis, with the many indicators covered, GDP weighs heavily in a president's overall performance, both directly and indirectly.

Productivity

We also look at productivity, which is how much the United States produces with a given amount of labor. In theory at least, productivity should determine the amount of income we receive. It is a goal of economic policy to raise productivity because it is generally recognized as a good thing to produce more output with fewer resources. The official Bureau of Labor Statistics (BLS) definition of the productivity indicator is *the GDP divided by total hours worked in the nonfarm business sector during one year.*[7] The formula for productivity is:

$$\frac{\text{GDP for the Nonfarm Business Sector}}{\text{Hours Worked by Persons in the Nonfarm Business Sector}}$$

With GDP in the numerator, the productivity indicator has much the same strengths and weaknesses as does GDP. An additional limitation of the productivity indicator is that it can increase when something bad happens. For example, when unemployment goes up, the number of hours worked (the denominator) falls. So, in the short run at least, productivity as measured by this indicator rises. It looks like we are counting something as good that may not be good. To compensate for this weakness, we also incorporate employment data in our analysis (Chapter 5), and if unemployment rises, that counts against the president's record. If productivity rises because GDP does not fall as fast as do hours worked, then productivity really is higher, just not for the reasons that we would prefer. In most cases in our historical period (1946–2011), productivity rises because GDP is rising.

The types of policies that a president can pursue to increase the productivity of labor include expenditures on education that are geared to market demands for workers with specific expertise, investment in capital so that workers have better equipment to work with, and investment in health to enhance the quality and longevity of workers' efforts.

The Bureau of Labor Statistics, which publishes this indicator, measures productivity only from 1947, so it omits 1946, the first year of the Truman administration. For both GDP and productivity indicators, the average growth rate better captures presidential economic performance than does the change in growth rates from the beginning to the end of the administration because growth rates have a high degree of fluctuation.

REVIEW OF ADMINISTRATIONS' GDP PERFORMANCE—TRUMAN TO OBAMA

As part of the first chapter in the book and the first review of presidential administrations, we will briefly discuss some of the key events and legislative accomplishments during each administration that had an impact on economic performance. This review helps establish the historical context for each president's performance and illustrates some of the linkages between presidential decisions and performance indicators—in this case, GDP and productivity. We also emphasize the lessons from earlier administrations for present-day economic policy. Subsequent chapters will focus more specifically on the performance indicators but will cite relevant events and policies as appropriate to the indicator in each chapter.

It is not possible to fully attribute particular economic results to specific presidential decisions. It is possible to identify actions that were consistent with what actually happened, and, in some cases, to link what happened with what an administration intended. In these days of political polarization, these are already major steps forward in improving the public debate. Tables 1.1 and 1.2 rank presidential administrations by GDP and productivity growth, respectively.

Figure 1.1   GDP Growth Rates, 1946–2010

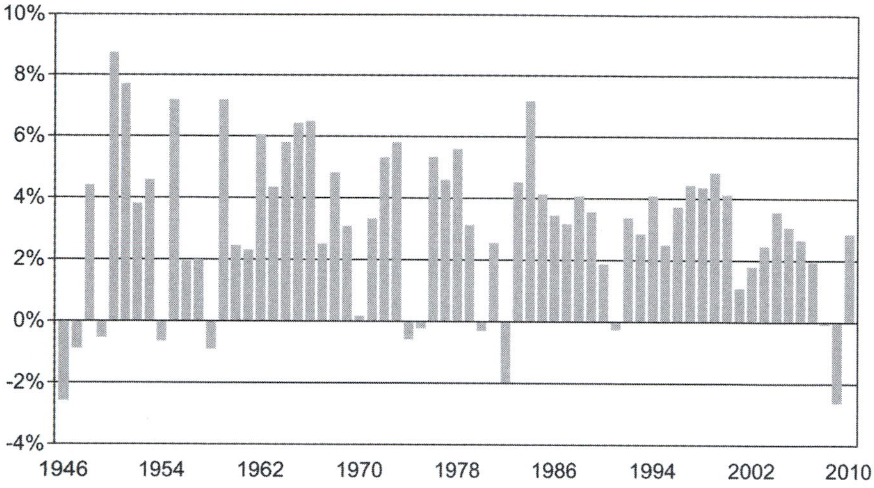

GDP Growth Patterns

In 1946 the GDP per capita in the United States was $12,675 adjusted for inflation. By 2010, GDP per capita had risen to $43,389, also adjusted for inflation, an increase in the standard of living, at least as measured by GDP, of 242 percent. It was a bumpy road, however, to achieve that increase in national output. Figure 1.1 shows the volatility of the GDP growth rate, particularly in the earlier part of the period up to the early 1960s. GDP growth rates tended to be a bit higher in the first half of the period (1946–1977) but experienced more frequent recessions than in the second half (1978–2011). Also, recessions for the entire period tended to be mild and brief, in contrast to the Great Depression (1929–1941; see Annex 2). With the exception of the recessions in 1946, 1982, and 2009, growth declines in the other eight recession years were no worse than a 0.9 percent decline in GDP on an annual basis. Between 1983 and 2008, there was only one negative growth year, 1991, in which growth was −0.2 percent, an extraordinarily good run for the economy. Perhaps this expansion created an aura of invincibility of the free market leading up to the economic crisis in 2008 and 2009, which could explain why policymakers who were in charge in the years leading up to the crisis did so little to avert it.

Harry S. Truman

Harry S. Truman became the 33rd president of the United States upon the death of Franklin D. Roosevelt on April 12, 1945, shortly before the end of WWII. He had been Roosevelt's vice president for only 82 days. Against the political conventional wisdom of the time, he won the election in 1948 and completed his term on January 20, 1953. His main economic task was to manage the transformation from a world war economy to a stable peacetime economy, which the United States had not seen since the 1920s. For this analysis, his record runs from 1946 through 1953, the equivalent of a full two-term president.

Major Events

- G.I. Bill, 1944[8]
- Atomic bombing of Hiroshima and Nagasaki, end of WWII, August 1945
- Bretton Woods system of international exchange, December 27, 1945 (see Chapter 6)
- Strikes in steel, coal, auto, and railroad industries, 1945–1946 (see Chapter 5)
- Price controls implemented during WWII lifted
- Employment Act of 1946
- General Agreement on Tariffs and Trade (GATT), 1947 (see Chapter 6)
- Taft-Hartley Act (Labor-Management Relations Act), 1947 (see Chapter 5)
- Recognition of Israel, May 14, 1948
- Fair Deal (1949) included increases in the minimum wage, the Housing Act of 1949, expansion of the Social Security program, and civil rights for African Americans. It also called for, but did not achieve, national health insurance and the repeal of the Taft-Hartley Act.
- Marshall Plan, 1948–1952 (see Chapter 6)
- Korean War, 1950–1953
- Federal government seizure of steel mills, June 1952

Some of these events are discussed in this chapter and some in other chapters, as indicated, where they are most relevant.

Truman had two advantages in achieving a successful transition. One was that Americans were desperate to consume. They had been essentially consumption-starved for 17 years, from the onset of the Great Depression in 1929 until the end of WWII in 1945. This "pent-up demand," as economists call it, could be translated into substantial economic growth, especially when U.S. industry was configured toward consumers rather than the military. The second main advantage was that at the end of the war, the United States faced no significant competitors for either its domestic market or the global market.

The challenge for the Truman administration was to manage the transition of 12 million people from the armed forces into the economy.[9] The G.I. Bill was an important tool in carrying out this transition. With the end of the war, there was also the risk that the economy would not be able to compensate for the rapid decrease in government war expenditures. In 1945 U.S. government expenditures were $92.7 billion or 41.9 percent of the total economy. By 1948, government expenditures were only $29.8 billion or 11.6 percent of the economy. That was a lot of stimulus for the private sector to make up. The mid- to late 1940s was a radically different context from today's economy, but it shows that the economy was resilient enough at least at one time in history both to incur the costs of a massive stimulus and to adapt to the withdrawal of that stimulus.

Postwar Economic Volatility

GDP did drop precipitously in 1946 (-10.9 percent) but stabilized by the following year with only a 1.6 percent decline. The total GDP decline, therefore, was 12.5 percent. Compared with the budget decline of 27.1 percentage points of GDP during 1946 and 1947 (from 41.9 percent in 1945 to 14.8 percent of GDP in 1947), it was not that bad of a performance. Again, the consumer demand compensated for most of the decline in federal outlays. By 1950, the GDP growth rate reached 8.7 percent, and 7.7 percent the following year. Statistically, the tricky thing in evaluating Truman's record is dealing with the transition year of 1946. It certainly was not his fault that the economy lost massive public-sector stimulus when the federal budget had to adjust to peacetime levels. But to be fair in evaluating his performance, we cannot very well delete that negative growth year from his record and then credit him with the boomerang of the economy a few years later.

A statistical method to deal with this effect is to simply replace the extreme -10.9 percent decline in GDP with the next highest value for declining GDP during our period of analysis, 1946 to 2011. That value is -3.5 percent, which occurred in 2009 following the 2008 financial collapse. There is also the option of including 1946 as it is or simply omitting the year from Truman's record. Here are the three resulting average GDP growth rates for the Truman administration:

- Including 1946 without any adjustment: 1.9%
- Including 1946 with top coding adjustment: 3.1%
- Deleting 1946 from Truman's record: 3.9%

Because we use a one-year lag and because Franklin Roosevelt died in the first half of 1945, our convention is to extend Roosevelt's record to the end of 1945. For this analysis we chose to record all indicators for 1946 on Truman's record without adjustment, even though there is some justification for top coding because 1946 was an outlier year. The negative growth rate of 1946 does damage Truman's record, but Truman benefits from including 1946 in his record with respect to other indicators. Thus, there are performance advantages and disadvantages from the extraordinary transition from a world war to peacetime.

Early Postwar Economy

Wartime price controls began to disappear after mid 1946, and the Office of Price Administration lost its power. The Congress also wanted to take measures to ensure that there was no repeat of the Great Depression. Congress passed, and Truman signed, the Employment Act of 1946. The act turned out to be more of a symbolic measure, but it did create the Council of Economic Advisors to ensure that the president received regular expert briefings on the economy. Chapter 5 discusses the Employment Act of 1946 in more detail.

In 1949, as the economy stalled, Truman shifted his approach to the economy. He decided that balanced budgets would have to be sacrificed for improved growth. Thus, he moved away from the high-tax approach and agreed to lower taxes on businesses to perk up economic growth. Along with the stimulus of the Korean War, GDP growth accelerated, as mentioned earlier, to 8.7 percent and 7.7 percent in 1950 and 1951, respectively.

Korean War, June 1950–July 1953

In June 1950, Soviet-supported North Koreans crossed the 38th parallel and invaded South Korea. President Truman gained a UN Security Council resolution to challenge the invasion. The fiscal significance of the war for the United States was the budget expenditures ($18 billion) required to fund U.S. forces under UN command. Most of the fighting occurred in the first year, June 1950 to mid 1951. There were wide swings in the war, with the UN troops driving the communist North Koreans to the border with communist China before the Chinese helped the North Koreans push the

UN forces far down the Korean peninsula before being pushed back again. Thereafter, there was a stalemate with lengthy truce talks. In the end, the combatants ended where they started, the 38th parallel, which divides North and South Korea to this day. In addition to economic growth, the war brought a degree of inflation: 7.9 percent in 1951. An interesting sidelight to the war was that the United States ordered thousands of military trucks from a relatively unknown Japanese company named Toyota, which proved to be an important boost in the company's early years as a vehicle manufacturer.

Comparison of Truman and Obama

The Truman and the Obama administrations, though more than half a century apart, have some interesting parallels: both were Democrats dealing with a hostile Congress (in Truman's case including members of his own party), both were presidents trying to make progressive headway in a number of areas (including civil rights and health care), and both were dealing with Republicans who were desperately trying to get back into power after having been voted out of power for poor economic performance.

Americans today might be surprised to learn that Truman faced hostility as bad as, and possibly even worse than, what Obama has faced. The phrase "To err is Truman" became popular in Republican circles, and there were reasons for his high degree of unpopularity—the Korean war did not go well, involving a large loss of American life with not much gained; Truman also fired WWII hero General Douglas MacArthur from command in Korea; the economic transition was not always smooth; and there was significant labor unrest. For Obama, though not his fault primarily, the United States is still mired in Afghanistan, though Iraq involvement has ended, two military operations that have been extremely costly in money and lives, but neither of which has accomplished much for U.S. interests. Under Truman, there was the specter of Joseph P. McCarthy alleging that the State Department was overrun with communists. It might be a stretch to liken some of Obama's opponents to McCarthyites, but there is a similar element of exaggeration and bitterness that they share. At the end of the day, Truman was reelected and had what is widely viewed as a successful presidency.

Summary of Truman's GDP and Productivity Record

Truman's average GDP growth rate averaged 1.9 percent (11th overall) with a 5.7 percentage point improvement in the GDP growth rate (best overall). The impact of the 10.9 percent GDP decline in 1946 on Truman's record is significant. Without 1946, Truman would have averaged 3.0 percent, a ranking of sixth overall. For productivity, Truman averaged a growth rate of 3.2 percent (second overall) with a slight decline in the index of −0.5 percent.

Dwight D. Eisenhower

After serving a career in the military and becoming a five-star general and supreme commander of Allied forces in Europe in WWII, Dwight Eisenhower was drafted by the Republican Party to run as its nominee in 1952. He easily defeated governor of Illinois Adlai Stevenson II and became the 34th president of the United States. He defeated Stevenson again in 1956 and served two full terms as president from January 20, 1953, to January 20, 1961.

Major Events

- Creation of the Department of Health, Education and Welfare (HEW), now the Department of Health and Human Services (HHS), 1953
- Expansion of the Social Security Program to include disability insurance and increase of the minimum wage, 1957
- Infrastructure investments: National Interstate and Defense Highways Act (also known as the Federal Aid Highway Act) of 1956 and St. Lawrence Seaway (with Canada)
- Farewell speech raising concern about the military industrial complex and its impact on the defense budget, January 17, 1961

Eisenhower, as the list of major events indicates, used the government for major economic and social gains. He was not an activist as was Truman, but he had major differences with the right wing of his own Republican party. In particular, he did not support their position to repeal much of Roosevelt's New Deal programs. Rather, the signature events of his presidency prove that he was politically a moderate. Under his administration, the Department of Health, Education and Welfare was created to more systematically address and enforce policies in those areas. The Social Security Program was expanded in 1957 to cover persons who could not work because of a disability. This program has delivered substantial benefits to millions of Americans but has also been costly to the budget, accounting currently for $130 billion annually.

Interstate Highway Program

While in Germany during WWII, Eisenhower observed the country's high-speed highway system (the Autobahn, which had been constructed in the 1930s) and saw the potential benefits of such a highway system for the United States. In 1956, Eisenhower signed the Federal Aid Highway Act, which launched the Interstate Highway Program, a 41,000-mile highway system connecting major cities in the United States. The program took more than 40 years to complete and was also extended by several thousand miles. This program is an example of a major infrastructure investment to which the president was willing to commit federal resources and which has produced inestimable benefits to U.S. commerce. According to one study of the economic impact of the highway[10] that was published on the 50th anniversary of the program's launch, the highway program realized a social rate of return of 35 percent in the 1950s and 1960s, which moderated to about 10 percent during the 1970s and beyond. The study described some of the advantages of the program:

> The Interstate Highway System replaced a lower capacity, lower speed, less safe, and more expensive (per mile of travel) highway system. The Interstate System provided a new envelope of space, time, and cost, in which our economy could reorganize. A safer, 65 mile per hour system was overlaid onto a less safe, less well-maintained 20 to 40 mile per hour system which previously existed in urban and rural areas.

Eisenhower also supported the building of the St. Lawrence Seaway (with Canada), which opened in 1959 and allowed access for ships from the Atlantic Ocean to reach the Great Lakes and ultimately the central United States.

Farewell Speech and the Military Industrial Complex

In his farewell speech to the nation, Eisenhower delivered an eloquent admonition to future presidents. Among the themes of his speech, the former five-star general of the army in WWII warned of the growing influence of the "military industrial complex":

> In the councils of government, we must guard against the acquisition of unwarranted influence, whether sought or unsought, by the military-industrial complex. The potential for the disastrous rise of misplaced power exists and will persist.

We must never let the weight of this combination endanger our liberties or democratic processes. We should take nothing for granted. Only an alert and knowledgeable citizenry can compel the proper meshing of the huge industrial and military machinery of defense with our peaceful methods and goals, so that security and liberty may prosper together.[11]

This admonition was prescient in an economic sense. The military component of the federal budget has claimed vast resources in peacetime. In addition, the four wars fought since that time have, arguably, not been either wars of survival nor of self-defense, as was the case with WWII.

Summary of Eisenhower's Record on GDP and Productivity

Eisenhower's record on growth had more stability than Truman's and averaged a higher rate although the GDP growth rate was reduced by several recessions (1954, 1958, and 1960). The 1954 recession is explainable, in part, by the end of the Korean War and the resulting reduction in government expenditures. The 1958 recession is somewhat less understandable because it occurred during the period when the interstate highway system, one of the great infrastructure investments in our history, was launched. The act authorized $850 million in fiscal year 1958 alone. The 1960 recession was brief, and there was overall positive growth for the year. The chronic recessions of the Eisenhower administration provided a strong rationale for the tax rate reductions pushed by John F. Kennedy (passed in 1964).

Eisenhower's average GDP growth rate was 2.6 percent (seventh overall), slightly less than the period (1946–2011) average of 2.9 percent. There was a 2.3 percentage point decline in the growth rate as Truman closed with a 4.6 percent growth rate and Eisenhower ended with a 2.3 percent growth rate in 1961.

On productivity, Eisenhower ranked sixth, with a growth rate of 2.3 percent and an increase in the growth rate of 0.8 percentage points.

John F. Kennedy

John F. Kennedy was the 35th president of the United States. He governed from January 20, 1961, until his assassination on November 22, 1963. Kennedy's record comprises only three years, yet he had a record of significant legislative accomplishments. He is credited with one of the most notable economic policy measures in the postwar era, the Kennedy-Johnson tax cut of 1964 (passed after his assassination).

Major Events

- New Frontier—1960 acceptance speech
- Peace Corps, March 1961
- Trade Expansion Act (to reduce protectionism), 1962 (see Chapter 6)
- Cuban Missile Crisis, October 1962
- Clean Air Act, 1963
- Nuclear Test Ban Treaty, October 1963
- Assassination, November 22, 1963
- Kennedy-Johnson tax cut (posthumous), February 1964 (see Chapter 9)

The New Frontier programs expanded New Deal programs and created new antipoverty programs. He started the Peace Corps for young Americans to contribute their services and to learn about foreign cultures by volunteering overseas. Kennedy navigated through several Cold War events including, luckily, a peaceful conclusion to the Cuban Missile Crisis (1962) and the (not so fortunate) "Bay of Pigs" invasion of Cuba. He also signed the Nuclear Test Ban Treaty (1963) to halt testing of nuclear weapons. On the economic front, Kennedy was a strong ally of organized labor and helped strengthen collective bargaining rights of labor unions, which were considerably larger and more politically powerful than they are today. He also launched the Trade Expansion Act in 1962, which helped reduce protectionism (see Chapter 6).

Kennedy inherited an economy in weak shape. Bankruptcy was high, farm income had declined, and there had been four recessions since the end of WWII. Kennedy believed it was necessary to lower tax rates in order to get the U.S. economy on a more sustained path of economic growth.

Summary of Kennedy's GDP and Productivity Record

The Kennedy administration recorded the highest average GDP growth rate of any president, at 5.3 percent, for his three-year record. There was also an improvement of 3.5 percentage points in the growth rate. Obviously his high growth rate cannot be attributed to the tax cuts, as they were passed only during the last year of his record. The tax cuts rather benefited Johnson's GDP growth rate and possibly those of presidents after him.

Kennedy's growth may be traced in part to the typical springboard effect of an economy emerging from a recession as well as to an expansion of benefits programs, particularly for the poor and unemployed, and an emphasis on elevating minorities' economic status.

Kennedy ranked first in average productivity growth at 3.6 percent, but with a small decline of -0.2 percentage points in the rate of productivity growth.

Lyndon B. Johnson

Lyndon Johnson became the 36th president of the United States on November 22, 1963, when John F. Kennedy was assassinated. He won the election in 1964 in a landslide over Republican rival Barry Goldwater. Observing the unpopularity of the Vietnam war and the strength of potential opposition in the Democratic primaries, he decided not to run for reelection in 1968.

Major Events

- Kennedy-Johnson tax cut implemented during 1964 and 1965
- Civil Rights Act, 1964
- War on Poverty launched in 1964, including Medicaid, legal services for the poor, and the Head Start program for preschool learning in economically disadvantaged areas
- The Great Society, a formalization of the War on Poverty, 1965; included the Medicare program, which provided major medical benefits to Americans at retirement age
- Vietnam War, 1965–1973
- Surtax imposed to pay for Vietnam War, 1968

Johnson successfully followed through on Kennedy's tax, civil rights, and assertive Cold War initiatives. He pursued his Great Society programs, which produced enormous benefits for millions of Americans but also enormous costs to the federal budget.

The Great Society

In his State of the Union Address on January 4, 1965, President Johnson presented his plan for the Great Society. It was not just to move toward "the rich society and the powerful society, but upward to the Great Society."[12] The difference, Johnson explained, was that the Great Society would also be defined by its ability to "end poverty and racial injustice."

The Great Society included Medicare and Medicaid to ensure health care for the most vulnerable groups in America, the elderly and the poor. Medicare is funded by a specific payroll tax like Social Security. Initially, the expenditures on these programs were too small to affect the budget and GDP, but over the decades, as the American population aged and health costs increased, Medicare expenditures increased rapidly. Certainly, the benefits were substantial in terms of improving people's lives and health outcomes, but at a cost. Today, total national health care costs, public and private, are about one-sixth of GDP ($2.5 trillion), about half of which is funded by the public sector (see Chapter 7).

These policy initiatives are highly relevant to today's public policy debate because these very programs are at risk of being dismantled in reaction to their admittedly shaky financial condition. This predicament has been created by a combination of Democratic refusal to acknowledge fully the financial problems of the programs and the Republicans' active efforts to underfund the programs with the ultimate agenda of eliminating them in their current form. This issue will be discussed further in Part II on the public sector.

Vietnam War, March 1965–January 1973

Although there was a significant U.S. troop presence in Vietnam when Johnson took office, the Vietnam War was clearly Johnson's war. When Johnson assumed office in November 1963, there were 17,000 U.S. troops in Vietnam, mainly serving as "advisors" to South Vietnamese army units. In August 1964, the North Vietnamese reportedly attacked a U.S. ship in the Gulf of Tonkin, after which the Gulf of Tonkin Resolution was passed by Congress, paving the way for military action. After several escalations, Johnson sent the first combat troops in March 1965. What started as a few skirmishes and tens of millions of dollars evolved into a troop presence of 540,000 soldiers and tens of billions of dollars of budget expenditures by 1968. Government expenditures on the war reached 13 to 14 percent of the total U.S. budget for fiscal year 1969–1970.

As the war became increasingly expensive, Johnson initiated a change in how the war costs were presented to the public. The on- and off-budget totals of the federal budget were combined into one larger overall budget total. This move had the effect of making the war expenditures seem smaller, at least as a percentage of the federal budget. The war was a significant additional stimulus for an economy that was already growing and performing well. (The continued course of the war is reviewed under Nixon later in the chapter.)

The Revenue and Expenditure Control Act of 1968, signed by Johnson on June 28, 1968, imposed a 10 percent surcharge on individual and corporate income. Low-income taxpayers were exempt. Individual taxpayers calculated their total tax due on Form 1040 and then were prompted to refer to a special surcharge table and add the appropriate amount to their regular tax liability. Corporations also paid the tax. In 1969 Congress renewed the surcharge through the middle of 1970 but reduced it to 5 percent.

By paying the surcharge, all Americans who could afford it were contributing to the war effort. The surcharge was also a reason that debt as a percentage of GDP did not rise despite the costs of the war (see Chapter 8). This fiscal approach stands in stark contrast to that of the Bush 43 administration, which actually reduced taxes before entering two wars (Afghanistan and Iraq). The Bush 43 administration made no subsequent efforts to generate revenue to pay for these wars.

Summary of Johnson's GDP and Productivity Record

Johnson had the third-highest average GDP growth rate at 4.6 percent with a 2.7 percentage point drop in the growth rate. When added to Kennedy's impressive growth rate of 5.3 percent, an average GDP growth rate of nearly 5 percent was achieved during the combined eight years of the two administrations. Growth in the 1960s was the strongest of any postwar decade, often exceeding 5.5 percent, though it moderated to a 3.2 percent average for 1967 through 1969. This growth can be attributed in part to the double stimulus of the Kennedy-Johnson tax cuts of 1964 and 1965 (see Chapter 9 on taxation for details) and to expenditures for the Vietnam War, which began in 1964 (and concluded at the beginning of 1973).

On productivity, Johnson ranked fourth at 2.4 percent with a decline in the productivity growth rate of −2.7 percentage points.

Richard M. Nixon

Richard Nixon became the 37th president of the United States on January 20, 1969, after a narrow victory over Democrat Hubert Humphrey and Independent George Wallace. Leading up to his reelection bid, Nixon had highly favorable news for his administration, both politically and economically. Troops and prisoners of war from Vietnam came back to the United States in a steady stream, which was continually in the news. In the election year, 1972, the economy grew at 5.3 percent, inflation was only 3.2 percent, and unemployment was a reasonable 5.6 percent. As a result, Nixon was reelected in a landslide over South Dakota senator George McGovern, winning 49 of 50 states. Given the good economic and political news and the resulting margin of victory, it seems incredible in retrospect that people in Nixon's administration saw the need to gain additional (and illegal) advantage over his Democratic opponent. Two years after his landslide reelection, Nixon was implicated in a cover-up of the illegal activities known as the Watergate scandal, and pressure mounted for him to resign the presidency, which he did on August 9, 1974. Nixon's record is, therefore, six years, with his appointed vice president, Gerald R. Ford, filling out the remaining two years of his second term.

Major Events

- Creation of the Environmental Protection Agency (EPA) and the National Oceanic and Atmospheric Administration (NOAA), 1970
- Creation of the Occupational Safety and Health Administration (OSHA), 1970
- Collapse of Bretton Woods and the gold standard, 1971
- Wage and price controls, 1971
- Opening of China, Shanghai Communique, February 27, 1972
- Environmental legislation including the 1972 Marine Mammal Protection Act, the 1973 Endangered Species Act, and amendments to the 1967 Clean Air Act
- Vietnam War continuing and concluding in 1973
- Watergate break-in, 1972
- Arab Oil Embargo, 1973
- Resignation from the presidency, August 9, 1974

The 1970s were sometimes, but not always, troublesome for the U.S. economy. Stagflation, a combination of weak growth and high inflation, dominated about one-third of the decade. However, in 4 of the 10 years, GDP growth exceeded 5.0 percent, and in three other years it exceeded 3.0 percent. There was a recession in 1970 and a deeper one during 1974 and 1975.

Although Nixon inherited a low unemployment rate of only 3.3 percent, inflation was on the rise. The long-run economic boom of the 1960s finally subsided, with a GDP growth rate of only 0.2 percent for 1970. The system of international payments, the Bretton Woods system, which was based on a gold standard,[13] broke down (see below). Nixon removed the United States from the gold standard, which meant that the U.S.

government was no longer obliged to redeem U.S. dollars for gold. Nixon also responded to growing inflation with wage and price controls (see Chapter 2), but they were not effective in reducing inflation.

In 1973, energy prices shot up when the Organization for Petroleum Exporting Countries (OPEC) embargoed oil shipments to the United States to protest the Nixon administration's decision to support Israel in the Yom Kippur War. The "misery index," which was the sum of the unemployment rate and the inflation rate, was created to measure the stagflation economy.

Despite these economic woes and a shameful, premature end to the administration over the Watergate crimes, the Nixon era was one of the most legislatively progressive periods in American history, rivaling that of his predecessor. Though Nixon may not have initiated much of the progressive agenda, he did sign it into law. This marks a strong contrast to today's dynamic between the Congress and the executive branch, where the president has been setting the agenda and having to do extraordinary maneuvering to gain passage of bills. A few of the more important events and their effects on the economy during the Nixon administration are briefly discussed below.

Vietnam War (Nixon Phase, 1969–1973)

In 1969, President Nixon changed the character of the war by pursuing a policy of "Vietnamization," which would shift the burden of ground combat from the U.S. forces to those of South Vietnam. U.S. troop levels were steadily reduced along with the number of U.S. casualties. Troop levels continued to decline, although the administration waged a vigorous bombing campaign in Vietnam as well as an incursion into Cambodia (with disastrous consequences for the people of Cambodia). In January 1973, a peace agreement was signed with the North Vietnamese government, and the remaining U.S. troops and prisoners of war returned to the United States. In the end, the Vietnam war had cost almost 58,000 lives and over $100 billion. Throughout the war, the U.S. economy was characterized by sustained economic growth and low unemployment but also larger budget deficits and increasing inflation. The full economic price of the Vietnam war was to be paid for years to come.

Dismantling the Bretton Woods System

In August 1971, Nixon eliminated key features of the Bretton Woods system, which had been established during the Truman administration but which no longer reflected economic reality. Bretton Woods was a fixed-exchange-rate system that no longer worked in a world where economic forces required exchange rates to adjust constantly. Different inflation rates between countries as well as fluctuating trade balances and other factors made it impractical to maintain a constant (fixed) value of one currency with respect to another. The United States could support its fixed exchange rate only by selling gold. With U.S. gold reserves falling, Nixon temporarily took the United States off the gold standard, which prevented other nations from cashing in U.S. dollars for more American gold. By 1973 the dollar-gold link was abolished entirely, as was the system of fixed exchange rates. Although the Bretton Woods system was largely dismantled, two institutions from the original Bretton Woods Agreement in 1945, the International Monetary Fund (IMF) and the World Bank, remained in operation and continue to this day.

Shanghai Communique

Nixon's outward-looking foreign policy led him to the People's Republic of China (PRC) in February 1972 where he met Chairman Mao Tse Tung. His goal of eventually normalizing relations with China began with the Shanghai Communique on February 27, 1972. The agreement addressed the PRC's long-term objection to U.S. relations with Taiwan. The move was necessary to begin trade relations with China. In 2011, the United States was exporting US$100 billion to China while importing about US$400 billion from China.

The Oil Crisis of 1973

In the 1950s and 1960s most industrialized countries had become dependent on oil imports for much of their energy consumption. The 1973 crisis was precipitated by OPEC's oil embargo of countries supporting Israel in the Arab-Israeli war of that year. The embargo was in effect against the United States from October 1973 to March 1974 and led to long lines at gas stations. The embargo also quadrupled the price of oil from about $3 to $12 per barrel, equivalent to an increase of $10 to $40 per barrel in today's dollars, which contributed to the recession in the following year. A number of measures were taken in the United States to manage the scarcity, including voluntary lowering of thermostats, restrictions on gasoline purchases, and a standby authority for rationing. The United States also began to produce smaller, more fuel-efficient cars.

Watergate and the End of the Nixon Administration

The Watergate scandal was an example of largely a political and legal event that arguably had a debilitating effect on the economy. The stock market declined steadily as the scandal played out, and the economy entered a deep recession about the time of Nixon's resignation. The Dow Jones Industrial Average (DJIA) was 1,020.02 at the end of 1972 and plummeted to 616.24 by the end of 1974. It was comparable to the economic effects of the 9/11 terrorist attacks in 2001, which also had a profoundly depressing effect on the stock market.

Summary of Nixon's GDP and Productivity Record

With all of these strains on the economy and the resulting weak economic growth years, Nixon's average GDP growth rate was 2.3 percent, below the period average performance of 2.9 percent and only half of Johnson's rate. There was a -3.3 percentage point drop in the GDP growth rate. Nixon's productivity growth rate was 2.1 percent, close to the period average of 2.2 percent. There was a 2.6 percentage point increase in the productivity growth rate.

Gerald R. Ford

Gerald Ford became the 38th president of the United States upon Richard Nixon's resignation on August 9, 1974. He had been appointed by Nixon to replace Nixon's previous vice president, Spiro Agnew, who had resigned because of criminal conduct. Ford was the only president who was not elected on a presidential ticket. He ran for election against Jimmy Carter in 1976 but lost a competitive race. As a result, his economic record spans only two years. With the one-year lag, Ford's record covers 1976 and 1977.

Major Events

- Pardon of Richard Nixon, September 8, 1974
- Whip Inflation Now (WIN) speech, October 8, 1974
- Tax Reduction Act of 1975
- Helsinki Accords, August 1975

There were not really any significant economic legislative measures during Ford's tenure. Other than the battle against inflation, his administration seemed mainly concerned with healing after the Watergate scandal and with Cold War and Middle East foreign policy issues. To ease tensions on the Cold War front, President Ford signed the Helsinki Accords, which were signed by 35 nations, including all European nations and the Soviet Union, and which gave the Soviet Union recognition of post–WWII frontiers in Europe. All signatories pledged to respect human rights and fundamental freedoms and to cooperate in economic, scientific, humanitarian, and other areas.

Ford took over from Nixon during a recession, and his record mainly includes the recovery from that recession. So Ford was fortunate in that his economic trends were positive, and his overall record reflects this timing. When Ford took office in 1974, inflation had risen to 11.0 percent, and that became his number-one economic priority. Unemployment that year was only 5.6 percent but was rising fast (reaching 8.5 percent the following year).

On October 8, 1974, Ford launched his Whip Inflation Now (WIN) campaign, which was largely a voluntary call to American households to battle inflation by producing more and wasting less. His approach to economic policy was to trim federal expenditures and levy temporary tax increases on individuals and corporations, elements that were presented in the WIN speech. In the following year, Ford reckoned that a tax rebate was a better approach to the unemployment problem, and he signed the Tax Reduction Act of 1975, which gave a temporary tax cut to individuals (see Chapter 9).

Summary of Ford's GDP and Productivity Record

Ford had the second-highest GDP growth rate among presidents, though his was only a two-year administration, at 4.9 percent with a 4.8 percentage point increase in the growth rate. Productivity grew at 2.4 percent, third highest among presidents. Again, this good record stems more from the fact that his presidency was timed at the end of a recession rather than any significant policy initiative. That said, Ford's efforts to reduce deficits and inflation at least did not derail the recovery.

James E. Carter

James E. ("Jimmy") Carter became the 39th president of the United States on January 20, 1977, after defeating Gerald Ford. A former governor of Georgia, Carter's good economic beginning dissolved into stagflation by the end of his administration. Adverse external factors compounded the economic woes. In 1979, there was another energy shock with spiking gas prices, a takeover of the U.S. embassy in Iran followed by a 444-day hostage crisis, and a Soviet invasion of Afghanistan. These events seemed to depress the U.S. economy further, and in 1980 it went into recession. Carter was soundly defeated in his reelection bid in 1980 by Ronald Reagan. Thus, Carter's record consists of one term.

Major Events

- Creation of the Department of Energy, August 4, 1977
- Oil shock, 1979
- Egypt-Israel Peace Treaty, 1979
- Appointment of Paul Volcker as Federal Reserve Chairman, August 1979
- Hostage Crisis in Iran, 1979–1981
- Comprehensive Environmental Response, Compensation, and Liability Act (CERCLA), also known as Superfund (toxic waste site clean-up), December 1980

Economically speaking, Carter began well but finished poorly. He inherited an economy in recovery, but that lasted only through 1978 (which had a 5.6 percent growth rate, 6.1 percent unemployment, and 7.6 percent inflation). The economy deteriorated rapidly in 1979 and, in 1980, economic indicators were poor: GDP growth sank to −0.3 percent, unemployment was 7.1 percent, and inflation averaged 13.5 percent for the year. During Carter's term, the actions of the OPEC oil cartel resulted in an increase in oil prices, from $13 a barrel to over $34. As occurred earlier in the decade, with the United States still heavily dependent on imported oil, the oil price increase resulted in a substantial increase in inflation, which increased every year of Carter's presidency and was in double digits during 1979 through 1981. Carter's inflation policy and appointments to the Federal Reserve are discussed in Chapter 2.

Early in his presidency, Carter aggressively tackled the challenges of energy cost and supply, which were his main short- and long-term priorities. Carter created the U.S. Department of Energy (DOE) by signing the U.S. Department of Energy Act in 1977. The DOE was established to regulate existing energy suppliers and fund research on new sources of energy, particularly renewables (wind and solar power). In terms of increasing the share of renewable energy in the mix of the U.S. energy supply, the DOE has not lived up to Carter's hopes.[14] Carter signed his first energy package into law on November 9, 1978, which deregulated oil and natural gas prices. That deregulation led to an increase in the supply of energy in the 1980s and consequently a lowering of prices.

Carter also had environmental accomplishments, one of which was "Superfund," which he signed into law in December 11, 1980. This law created a tax on the chemical and petroleum industries and provided broad federal authority to respond directly to releases or threatened releases of hazardous substances that may endanger public health or the environment. The tax went to a trust fund for cleaning up abandoned or uncontrolled hazardous waste sites.

Carter had other successes in energy policy, particularly in nuclear energy policy, with which he had experience in his naval career. He was able to influence Congress to abolish the powerful Joint Committee on Atomic Energy, a step that would make it easier to block breeder reactors and move toward light-water reactors of the kind favored by the administration.

Summary of Carter's GDP and Productivity Record

Despite leaving office with a weak economy, Carter recorded a GDP growth rate of 2.7 percent, not far from the 1946–2011 period average of 2.9 percent, and sixth overall. There was a 2.1 percentage point drop in the growth rate, consistent with ending the administration in a sluggish economy. Productivity grew at only 0.5 percent, which was last place among the 12 presidents.

Ronald W. Reagan

Ronald Reagan became the 40th president of the United States by defeating incumbent Jimmy Carter in a landslide. Reagan brought a philosophy of governing to the presidency that preached lower taxes and smaller government, as well as a build-up of national defenses to more assertively prosecute the Cold War. At other times his administration's policies were largely pragmatic and balanced rather than ideologically pure, even in tax policy. He won reelection in an even bigger landslide in 1984, defeating former vice president (under Jimmy Carter) Walter Mondale, taking 49 of 50 states. Reagan served two full terms as president, giving him an eight-year economic record.

Major Events

- Firing of air traffic controllers, 1981
- Economic Recovery Tax Act (income tax cut), 1981 through 1983 (see Chapter 9)

- Social Security reform, 1983 (see Chapter 7)
- Iran-Contra Scandal, 1986–1987
- Tax Reform Act of 1986
- Appointment of Alan Greenspan as Federal Reserve Chairman, August 11, 1987
- "Black Monday" stock market plunge, October 19, 1987 (see Chapter 4)
- Intermediate-Range Nuclear Forces (INF) Treaty, December 1987
- Savings and Loan (S&L) crisis, 1986–1989

Ronald Reagan inherited one of the weakest economies in the postwar era. Although 1981 had seen some improvement over 1980, with GDP growth rising from −0.3 percent to 2.5 percent and the inflation rate falling from 13.5 percent to 10.3 percent, the economy was still weak and vulnerable to another downturn. In fact, in the first year of Reagan's record (with the one-year lag), 1982, there was a severe recession, with GDP falling by 1.9 percent. This second recession in two years was partly the price of extinguishing the high inflation that had begun at the end of the 1960s, which had persisted and worsened in the 1970s. Along with inflation, the Reagan administration was concerned about rising tax rates. U.S. federal taxes paid had climbed from 17.1 percent of GDP in 1971 to 19.6 percent in 1981 largely because nominal (not adjusted for inflation) income increases were forcing Americans into higher marginal tax brackets. This phenomenon was called "bracket creep" (see Chapter 9).

Reagan adopted his own version of the Kemp-Roth tax-reduction plan, named after Republican congressman Jack Kemp of New York and Republican senator William Roth of Delaware. The tax cut was implemented over three years and amounted to about a 25 percent reduction (10 percent in 1981, 10 percent in 1982, and 5 percent in 1983) during 1981 through 1983. With the lowered tax rates and the reduced inflation rates, GDP recovered and achieved a 4.5 percent growth rate in 1983 and 7.2 percent in 1984, the highest since 1959. Reagan made a number of other significant changes in tax rates and policies, including tax increases, which are detailed in Chapter 9.

Reagan's free-market philosophy backfired in the savings and loan industry. Though industry deregulation had begun under Carter in 1980, it was under Reagan that the most expensive abuses and moral hazard took place in the industry. Reagan's 1986 tax reform placed further pressure on S&Ls by limiting the amount of losses from real estate investments that could be subtracted from an investor's gross income. In December 1986, the Federal Savings and Loan Insurance Corporation (FSLIC) went insolvent. The S&L crisis was not resolved until the administration of Bush 41. Union power declined under Reagan as well. One of Reagan's first tests as president was the air traffic controllers' strike in 1981. When the controllers refused to go back to work, Reagan fired all of the strikers, and the air traffic controllers' union was busted.

Another important event in the Reagan presidency was the appointment of Alan Greenspan to replace Paul Volcker as Federal Reserve chairman in August 1987. Greenspan was to serve five terms as chairman under four different presidents (including Bush 41, Clinton, and Bush 43, each whom reappointed Greenspan at least once). Greenspan was a strong proponent of financial deregulation and continued as chairman until January 2006, several years into the development of the subprime mortgage phenomenon.

Summary of Reagan's GDP and Productivity Record

Overall, Reagan achieved a growth rate of 3.4 percent for his administration (fifth overall), with a 1.0 percentage point increase in the growth rate. Productivity grew at only 1.6 percent (next to last), with a −0.6 percentage point drop in the rate.

George H. W. Bush (Bush 41)

George H. W. Bush became the 41st president of the United States on January 20, 1989, easily defeating Democratic candidate Michal Dukakis and taking 43 of 50 states. Bush benefited from being the "heir apparent" to popular outgoing president Ronald Reagan as his sitting vice president. In the course of Bush 41's administration, the economic expansion that began in 1983 slowed down. Moreover, Bush 41 had to reckon with the costs of some of Reagan's economic policies, which placed an additional drag on growth. Though his approval rating reached as high as 90 percent during the Desert Storm operation in Iraq, economic realities whittled away at his popularity, and his reelection bid against Bill Clinton and independent H. Ross Perot was unsuccessful. Therefore, Bush had a one-term, four-year record.

Major Events

- Resolution of the S&L crisis—Financial Institutions Reform Recovery and Enforcement Act (FIRREA), August 1989

- Fall of the Berlin Wall and end of the Cold War, November 1989
- Omnibus Budget Reconciliation Act (OBRA), 1990
- Operation Desert Storm against Iraq, 1991

After seven years of above-average growth, the economy slowed down in 1990 and 1991 under the George H. W. Bush administration. Part of the reason for this slowdown is that the Bush 41 administration had to deal with some of the negative impacts of Reaganomics, which Bush 41 had called "voodoo economics" in his 1980 campaign. The Bush 41 administration also had the burden of paying for the S&L crisis, which had intensified under Reagan. At the same time, Bush benefited from the fall of the Soviet Union because defense expenditures could be cut as a share of the federal budget (see Chapter 8). Despite the defense savings, the Reagan structural deficits had left Bush with a difficult challenge. Even with good GDP growth under Reagan, deficits were large.

Once GDP growth rates slowed, deficits became even larger as the growth of tax revenue also slowed. The first year of Bush's record, 1990, had only a 1.9 percent GDP growth rate followed by a 0.2 percent decline in GDP in 1991. In 1992, the GDP growth rate was 3.4 percent, but the recovery was too late for Bush's reelection hopes, and Bill Clinton won the presidency mainly on economic issues.

To a significant extent, George H.W. Bush's economic legacy can be viewed as a partial cleanup of the negative aspects of Reagan's economic policies, in particular the deficits and the S&L crisis. The budget deficits put Bush under such pressure that he was forced to violate his campaign pledge not to raise taxes (see Chapter 9). The S&L crisis should have served as a lesson for preventing future financial malpractice and how to deal with it if it occurred. There were similarities between the S&L crisis and the financial meltdown from subprime mortgages in 2008. Both crises involved the real estate market, but the main similarity was that in both cases, as long as certain people were making money, there was little incentive to manage the risk that was being piled up at financial institutions. The main difference is that the 2008 financial crisis turned out to be many times more pervasive and costly.

In February 1989, George H. W. Bush presented his S&L bailout plan. In August 1989, the Financial Institutions Reform Recovery and Enforcement Act (FIRREA) was passed, which replaced the Federal Home Loan Bank Board and FSLIC with the Office of Thrift Supervision (OTS). The deposit insurance function shifted to the Federal Deposit Insurance Corporation (FDIC). The Resolution Trust Corporation was created to deal with failed S&Ls. The FIRREA also included $50 billion of new borrowing authority, higher net worth requirements for S&Ls and regulation by the OTS and FDIC, and allocation of funds to the Justice Department to help finance prosecution of S&L crimes. The following quote from the FDIC Banking Review succinctly summarizes the financial costs and historical significance of the S&L crisis.

> The savings and loan crisis of the 1980s and early 1990s produced the greatest collapse of U.S. financial institutions since the Great Depression. Over the 1986–1995 period, 1,043 thrifts with total assets of over $500 billion failed. The large number of failures overwhelmed the resources of the FSLIC, so U.S. taxpayers were required to back up the commitment extended to insured depositors of the failed institutions. As of December 31, 1999, the thrift crisis had cost taxpayers approximately $124 billion and the thrift industry another $29 billion, for an estimated total loss of approximately $153 billion. The losses were higher than those predicted in the late 1980s, when the RTC was established, but below those forecasted during the early to mid-1990s, at the height of the crisis.[15]

With the deficits rising above the Gramm-Rudman-Hollings thresholds[16] (see Chapter 8), Bush had to contend with automatic spending cuts and deficit reduction measures. After negotiations with both Democrats and Republicans, Bush signed the Omnibus Budget and Reconciliation Act (OBRA) on November 5, 1990, which included some tax increases and which violated his 1988 campaign pledge not to raise taxes (see Chapter 9 on taxation for further discussion).

Summary of Bush 41's GDP and Productivity Record

Bush 41 had the third lowest average GDP growth rate of all 12 presidents at 1.9 percent, with a 0.7 percentage point drop in the rate. Under Bush, productivity grew at 1.9 percent annually, also the third lowest, with a 0.2 percentage point drop in the rate.

William J. Clinton

Bill Clinton became the 42nd president of the United States, defeating George H. W. Bush in a three-way race that also included billionaire entrepreneur H. Ross Perot. Clinton's administration could be characterized as both progressive and conservative at the same time. He made a major, if unsuccessful, effort to reform the health care system in the United States, in particular addressing the estimated 27 million Americans without health care coverage. He advanced gay rights and supported a number of environmental initiatives. He also managed an impressive improvement of the nation's finances.

On the other hand, he also signed the North American Free Trade Agreement (NAFTA), signed a conservative reform of the welfare system, and supported financial deregulation. In his reelection bid, Clinton defeated Kansas senator Robert Dole, as well as H. Ross Perot, again. The Republicans pursued Clinton in his second term for false statements about Monica Lewinsky in his deposition for the Paula Jones sexual harassment case. He was ultimately impeached by a vote entirely of House Republicans in 1999, an event that strangely seems only a footnote to his presidency. Despite the impeachment, Clinton left office having served two full terms and, thus, an eight-year record.

Major Events

- Family and Medical Leave Act of 1993
- Omnibus Budget Reconciliation Act, 1993 (see Chapter 8)
- NAFTA, 1994 (see Chapter 6)
- Personal Responsibility and Work Opportunity Reconciliation Act (PRWORA) of 1996, also known as welfare reform, August 1996
- Asian Financial Crisis, 1997–1998 (see Chapter 6)
- Impeachment, December 19, 1998
- Dot.com bubble, 1995–2000 (see Chapter 4)
- Deregulatory measures (Gramm-Leach-Bliley Act, November 1999, which included the repeal of the Glass-Steagall Act; Commodity Futures Modernization Act, 2000)

Clinton took office after the recession under Bush 41 in 1991 and the initial recovery, albeit with still-high unemployment of 7.5 percent. With deficits and debt still threatening to get out of control, Clinton understood (and was compelled to understand) that another round of tax increases would be needed to bring the deficit under control. The Omnibus Budget Reconciliation Act 1993 created two new higher tax brackets, 35 and 39.6 percent. Additional details are in Chapter 9. Despite predictions from the right of economic ruin from tax increases, the economy did begin to grow, and deficits shrank and even turned into surpluses in the latter part of his administration.

Family and Medical Leave Act of 1993

In one of his first acts as president, Clinton signed the Family and Medical Leave Act on February 5, 1993, barely two weeks after taking office. The act signaled a major shift in policy from the preceeding Republican administrations and provided for up to 12 weeks of unpaid leave for medical or family reasons without losing one's job.

Unsuccessful Attempt to Reform the Health Care System

Clinton led an unsuccessful attempt to reform health care in 1994, which Republicans strongly opposed. This was followed by a Republican takeover of the House. In the 16 years following the failure of the health care reform, essentially nothing was initiated on the Republican side to provide an alternative to address the increasing number of Americans without health insurance. During that period (1994–2010), the number of uninsured Americans went from 27 million to 47 million. The rising cost of health care was also not addressed.

NAFTA and Welfare Reform

Clinton succeeded in passing two conservative initiatives, the North American Free Trade Act (NAFTA, 1994) and welfare reform (1996). NAFTA led to expanded trade and trade deficits with Canada and Mexico. Additional details on NAFTA are in Chapter 6 on trade. In August 1996, Clinton signed PRWORA (welfare reform) and fulfilled his 1992 campaign promise to "end welfare as we have come to know it." PRWORA replaced the Aid to Families with Dependent Children (AFDC) program, which had been in effect since 1935, with Temporary Assistance for Needy Families (TANF). The welfare reform put a time limit on how long people could receive TANF benefits. Conservatives hailed the measure as restoring America's work ethic.

Dot.com Bubble (1995–2000)

The dot.com bubble was a speculation-driven surge in stock prices of companies that based their businesses on the Internet. The bubble began roughly in 1995 and peaked on March 10, 2000. Soon afterward, the bubble popped, and the economy entered a mild recession in March 2001. The NASDAQ, the stock exchange on which dot.coms were traded, lost trillions of dollars of stock value. Chapter 4 has additional details.

Impeachment of Bill Clinton (1998)

Though impeachment is a rare and severe form of punishment for a president, the impeachment of Bill Clinton seems to be a strikingly inconsequential part of his legacy. This may be because his impeachment was carried out exclusively by Republican congressmen (only a few Republicans voted against impeachment). In contrast to Nixon (who resigned before being impeached), the march to impeachment did not seem to depress the economy, which grew at a rate of more than 4.0 percent during 1999 and 2000.

Financial Deregulation

During Clinton's administration there were two financial deregulatory measures that later contributed to the 2008 financial crisis. Former Goldman Sachs CEO Robert Rubin, with strong support from Clinton advisor Lawrence Summers and Federal Reserve chairman Alan Greenspan, fought for and secured the repeal of the Glass-Steagall Act. The Glass-Steagall Act was passed in 1933 during Franklin Roosevelt's administration to create a wall of separation between banks and the stock market. Leading up to the Great Depression, commercial banks had used deposits to speculate in the stock market. When the speculative investments failed, so did the banks. The act was repealed during the Clinton administration with nearly unanimous support from Congressional Republicans but also with the strong urging of Clinton's treasury secretary, Robert Rubin.

The second major deregulatory measure was the deregulation of over-the-counter derivatives through the Commodity Futures Modernization Act (CFMA) in 2000. This deregulation made it possible to create difficult-to-value (and to trace) derivatives that were later created with "bets" on subprime mortgages that would inevitably default. We look more closely at Clinton's and Bush 43's roles in financial crises in Chapters 4 and 10.

Summary of Clinton's GDP and Productivity Record

Clinton's average GDP growth rate was 3.6 percent, slightly above that of Reagan, and fourth best overall. The growth rate fell by 1.8 percentage points, which is consistent with Clinton's economic expansion coming to an end. Productivity growth averaged a rate of 2.2 percent, seventh overall, with an increase in the productivity growth rate of 2.3 percentage points between 1993 and 2001.

George W. Bush (Bush 43)

George W. Bush won perhaps the narrowest victory in the history of presidential contests over incumbent vice president Al Gore. After a contentious recount of votes in Florida, the Supreme Court of the United States voted 5–4 against the Florida Supreme Court recount method, stating that it was a violation of the Fourteenth Amendment to the Constitution (the Equal Protection Clause). Thus, despite losing the popular vote by about 500,000 votes, Bush 43 won the electoral college with 271 electoral votes, one more than required, and was declared the 43rd president of the United States. In 2004, Bush 43 faced another close election but was again successful, this time defeating Massachusetts senator John Kerry. Bush 43 was a full two-term president with an eight-year record.

Major Events

- The Economic Growth and Tax Relief Reconciliation Act of 2001 (EGTRRA, also known as the "Bush tax cuts"; see Chapter 9), June 2001
- 9/11 terrorist attacks, 2001
- War in Afghanistan, October 7, 2001, to present
- War in Iraq, March 19, 2003, to December 20, 2011
- Medicare Prescription Drug, Improvement, and Modernization Act of 2003 (Medicare Part D), effective 2006
- Real estate/financial/subprime mortgage crisis, 2008–2009
- Troubled Asset Relief Program (TARP bailout), 2008

Growth under Bush 43

Like his father, George W. Bush came into office after his predecessor's long, successful run of GDP growth. Only two months after taking office, Bush faced an economy in a mild recession (which, with the one-year lag, is assessed against Clinton's record). Bush believed the answer to the sluggish economy was another round of tax cuts (the EGTRRA), which favored mainly the upper income brackets by lowering the top tax rates and phasing out the estate tax (see Chapter 9). Initially, the economy did not respond, growing at only 1.1 percent in 2001 and 1.8 percent in 2002. By 2003, growth picked up to 2.5 percent and 3.6 percent in 2004. Growth then declined to 3.1 percent in 2005, 2.7 percent in 2006, and

1.9 percent in 2007 as the real estate bubble began to deflate. Things got worse—much worse—in 2008 with growth at -0.3 percent before recording a further GDP decline of 3.5 percent in 2009, the worst percentage decline in GDP since 1946.[17]

War and Other Fiscal Burdens

Against this background, Bush waged his "war on terror," which included invasions and prolonged occupations of Afghanistan and Iraq. These operations have cost approximately $1.5 trillion in direct budget costs so far. Unlike the case of Johnson's tax surcharge to pay for the Vietnam War, no additional tax contribution was asked of the American people. Another fiscal burden that was added under the Bush 43 administration was the prescription drug benefit (Medicare Part D), which was passed without provision for additional funding. Once the 2008 financial crisis hit, government revenue plummeted and the TARP bailout was needed to help stabilize financial institutions.

Medicare Prescription Drug, Improvement, and Modernization Act of 2003

The prescription drug benefit went into effect on January 1, 2006. This benefit offers prescription drug coverage to everyone with Medicare. To get Medicare prescription drug coverage, the beneficiary must join a plan run by an insurance company or other private company approved by Medicare. The program has provided benefits to more than 10 million Americans but has been criticized for not being funded by additional revenue and for not negotiating lower prices with pharmaceutical companies. The annual cost of the program has already grown to between $50 and $60 billion net of beneficiary premiums and state transfers (which together account for 17 percent of program costs).

Reappointments of Alan Greenspan

Bush 43 was an admirer of Alan Greenspan to the extent that he reappointed him twice to lead the Federal Reserve, first in June 2000 and second in June 2004. Unfortunately, Greenspan may have been reappointed one, if not two, too many times, as his leadership proved ineffective in avoiding the conditions that led to the 2008 economic crisis. His fifth term ended in January 2006 when Ben Bernanke became Federal Reserve chairman.

The Troubled Asset Relief Program

At the end of his presidency, with the financial crisis in full swing, Bush 43 at the urging of his Treasury Secretary, Henry Paulson, pushed for the TARP in order to slow down the economic decline. The main recipients of TARP included the American Insurance Group (AIG, $69.8 billion), Bank of America ($45 billion), Citigroup ($50 billion), automakers ($85.3 billion), and a number of financial firms, such as Goldman Sachs ($79.3 billion). Most of the money has since been repaid to the U.S. Treasury.

Summary of Bush 43's GDP and Productivity Record

Bush's GDP growth record ranks last at 1.4 percent, with a 4.6 percent reduction in the growth rate from the administration's beginning to the administration's end, also a last place finish. Productivity grew at 2.2 percent annually on average (equal to the period average), but mainly because of the sharp fall in employment when the financial crisis hit at the end of his administration.

This growth record is particularly disappointing when factoring in the massive expenditures for war in Afghanistan and Iraq. Surely these wars should have stimulated higher rates of GDP growth. However, these war expenditures did not propel growth rates even to half the period average of 2.9 percent.

Barack Obama

Barack Obama became the 44th President on January 20, 2009 after defeating Arizona Senator John McCain by a comfortable margin. Obama pledged to repair the economic damage from the financial crisis, end the war in Iraq, reform the health care system and lead toward a more secure energy future based on replacing fossil fuels with renewable and nuclear energy sources. He is currently serving his first term of office and is the first African American to hold the office of President.

Major Events

- Term Asset-Backed Securities Loan Facility (TALF), 2009
- American Recovery and Reinvestment Act (ARRA) of 2009, also known as the economic stimulus program, which aimed at compensating for the slowdown in the private economy from the financial crisis ($787 billion)

- Automobile industry bailout, March 2009
- Affordable Care Act, March 23, 2010
- Dodd-Frank Wall Street Reform and Consumer Protection Act (Dodd-Frank Bill), July 21, 2010
- Extension of Bush tax cuts and institution of payroll tax reduction, 2010
- Debt ceiling battle, 2011
- End of war in Iraq, December 20, 2011

Early Initiatives to Combat the Economic Crisis

Barack Obama took office as the economy was spiraling downward. The TARP bailout had been launched and was providing some reassurance to the financial markets that the government was going to use its power to avoid a financial collapse. Shortly after taking office, Obama launched the Term Asset-Backed Securities Loan Facility (TALF). TALF aimed mainly at restarting the consumer and small business credit markets. TALF had a capacity to spend up to $1 trillion but actually spent about $100 billion. Financial experts viewed TALF as a success in maintaining a consumer credit flow.

The administration followed with an economic stimulus bill. The economic stimulus bill had an original allocation of $787 billion. The composition of the economic stimulus bill was planned as $288 billion in tax benefits (of which $300.1 billion, more than 100 percent, has been paid), $275 billion in project-related contracts (of which $215.3 billion has been paid), and $224 billion in entitlements (e.g., unemployment compensation, of which $213.5 billion has been paid).[18] Proponents of these interventions argued that the economic decline would have been far steeper without them and that unemployment, and ultimately even the national debt, would have been higher.

Fortunately, the economy did find the bottom of the recession in 2009. In all likelihood the economy would have fallen much further were it not for the resources that these interventions injected into the economy as well as the "signaling effects" that the U.S. government was committed to turning the economy around.

Automobile Industry Bailout

With two of the "big three" automakers facing Chapter 11 bankruptcy, the Obama administration, concerned about the loss of hundreds of thousands of jobs and even more in related industries, decided that the auto industry needed an infusion of capital. The auto industry bailout did not require an additional appropriation as it used TARP money. All told, GM and Chrysler used about $85 billion of TARP money. The two automakers recovered to a large extent, and hundreds of thousands of jobs were saved. In 2011, GM was once again the largest manufacturer of cars in the world. The U.S. government is not expected, however, to recover all of the money, and it is estimated that it will lose about $17 billion.[19]

Effects of the 2008 Crisis on Obama's Record

Obama's inheritance from Bush could work either way for Obama's record on growth and overall record. Either the economy could not help but improve during his administration, and his record would be relatively good, or the economy was so badly damaged during Bush's administration that it might take longer than the election cycle to right the economy. In the latter case, Obama could be stuck with weak averages on most indicators and insufficient improvement in the trends, which could lead to failure in getting reelected.

Despite the economy's slow response to a variety of economic initiatives, Obama has had major legislative achievements. The Affordable Care Act (ACA) dealt with several long-neglected problems in U.S. health care; the Act addressed some of the worst abuses by the health insurance companies, such as denial of coverage for pre-existing conditions. Obama signed the Dodd-Frank (financial reform) bill in July 2010. The bill tightens regulations to avoid a repeat of the abuses that led to the 2008 crisis. The main elements of the bill are:

- **Consumer financial protection:** Creates a consumer protection agency housed at the Federal Reserve to ensure that consumers receive accurate information when seeking mortgages, credit cards, and other financial products with the goal of protecting consumers from hidden fees, abusive terms, and deceptive practices.
- **Too big to fail:** Imposes new capital and leverage requirements on large financial firms, updates the Federal Reserve's authority to allow system-wide support but not prop up individual firms, and establishes new standards and supervision practices.
- **Advance warning system**: Creates a council to identify and address systemic risks posed by large, complex companies, products, and activities before they threaten the stability of the economy.
- **Transparency and accountability for exotic instruments:** Eliminates loopholes that allow risky and abusive practices to go on unnoticed and

unregulated—including loopholes for over-the-counter derivatives, asset-backed securities, hedge funds, mortgage brokers, and "payday" lenders.

- **Executive compensation and corporate governance:** Provides shareholders with a say on pay and corporate affairs with a nonbinding vote on executive compensation and "golden parachutes."

- **Credit agencies:** Provides new rules for transparency and accountability for credit rating agencies.

- **Stronger enforcement of regulations:** Strengthens oversight and empowers regulators to pursue financial fraud, conflicts of interest, and manipulation of the system.

Republicans have vowed to repeal this bill.

Summary of Obama's GDP and Productivity Record

In Obama's brief record, growth was 2.3 percent, eighth overall. The growth rate increased 5.2 percentage points from the last year of the Bush record (2009), second overall. Productivity grew at 2.4 percent, which ranked fifth overall.

Table 1.1   GDP Growth Rates by Presidential Administration

Administration	Growth Rate	Administration	Growth Rate Trend
Kennedy	5.3%	Truman	5.7%
Ford	4.9%	Obama	5.2%
Johnson	4.6%	Ford	4.8%
Clinton	3.6%	Kennedy	3.5%
Reagan	3.4%	Reagan	1.0%
Obama	2.3%	Bush 41	−0.7%
Carter	2.7%	Clinton	−1.8%
Eisenhower	2.6%	Carter	−2.1%
Nixon	2.3%	Eisenhower	−2.3%
Truman	1.9%	Johnson	−2.7%
Bush 41	1.9%	Nixon	−3.3%
Bush 43	1.4%	Bush 43	−4.6%
Period Average 1946–2011	**2.9%**		**N.A.**

Table 1.2   Productivity Growth Rates by Presidential Administration

Administration	Growth Rate	Administration	Growth Rate Trend
Kennedy	3.6%	Nixon	2.6%
Truman	3.2%	Clinton	2.3%
Ford	2.4%	Eisenhower	0.8%
Johnson	2.4%	Bush 41	−0.2%
Obama	2.4%	Kennedy	−0.2%
Eisenhower	2.3%	Carter	−0.2%
Clinton	2.2%	Truman	−0.5%
Bush 43	2.2%	Reagan	−0.6%
Nixon	2.1%	Bush 43	−0.6%
Bush 41	1.9%	Ford	−1.2%
Reagan	1.6%	Obama	−1.6%
Carter	0.5%	Johnson	−2.7%
Period Average 1947–2011	**2.2%**		**N.A.**

CONCLUSIONS AND ISSUES FOR GDP AND PRODUCTIVITY

The presidents with the top three GDP growth rates were Kennedy, Johnson, and Ford, all of whom were in the first half of the period, before the 1978 midpoint, while the bottom two growth performers, Bush 41 and Bush 43, were in the recent half of the period. That might lead one to conclude that GDP growth rates were simply higher before 1978. However, the next three highest growth rates belong to presidents in the more recent half of the period: Clinton, Reagan, and Carter. The three below them are all on the first half of the period: Eisenhower, Nixon, and Truman.

On productivity, the more impressive records are those of presidents who had low unemployment but good productivity (Kennedy, Truman, and Johnson, as well as Eisenhower and Clinton). Not as impressive are presidents whose productivity growth was high because unemployment was higher (Obama, Bush 43). In the case of Obama, a higher productivity growth rate says that, although employment may have fallen by a certain percentage, GDP fell by significantly less than that percentage. So there was in fact a productivity increase, just not the one we would have preferred.

NOTES

1. http://www.bea.gov/national/pdf/nipaguid.pdf.

2. *Concepts and Methods of the U.S. National Income and Product Accounts*, Chapters 1–7, Bureau of Economic Analysis, U.S. Department

of Commerce, November 2010, pp. 3-1–3-15. http://www.bea.gov/
national/pdf/NIPAhandbookch1-7.pdf.

3. For an introduction to NIPA, go to http://www.bea.gov/national/
pdf/nipa_primer.pdf.

4. "Government purchases" exclude most of the federal budget,
including government transfer payments such as Social Security, welfare
and unemployment compensation payments, grants to state and local gov-
ernments, net interest paid on the debt, and subsidies to various activities.
These exclusions account for about 70 percent of the budget. To include
expenditures such as Social Security in GDP would amount to double
counting because GDP is counted through the goods and services that people buy when they spend the payments from the government.

5. Martinne Geller, Reuters article, March 12, 2008. http://www
.reuters.com/article/2008/03/12/us-beverage-digest-idUSN122175522008
0312.

6. Americans feed more food to animals than they do to themselves.

7. The nonfarm business sector excludes the economic activities of
the following: general government, private households, nonprofit organizations serving individuals, and farms, but it still accounts for about
three-quarters of GDP. Source: BLS website, http://www.bls.gov/bls/
glossary.htm#N.

8. Note that the Serviceman's Readjustment Act, better known as the
G.I. Bill, was signed into law by Franklin Roosevelt on June 22, 1944,
but had its first real impact during the Truman administration. The G.I.
Bill helped veterans transition into the economy by providing college or
vocational education for World War II veterans (G.I.s), one year of unemployment compensation, and loans to buy homes and start businesses.

9. Later presidents would have the challenge of employing and providing programs for the "baby-boomer" generation, which began under
the Truman administration.

10. National Cooperative Highway Research Program (NCHRP)
Project 20-24(52), "Future Options for the National System of Interstate
and Defense Highways—Technical Memorandum Task 2: The Economic
Impact of the Interstate Highway System," NCHRP Project 20-24 (52),
FY 2006.

11. From Eisenhower's farewell address to the nation, January 17, 1961.

12. Note that the phrase *Great Society* had appeared earlier in
Johnson's commencement address to University of Michigan students on
May 22, 1964.

13. A monetary standard under which the basic unit of currency is
equal in value to and exchangeable for a specified amount of gold.

14. The share of renewables in the U.S. energy supply mix has not increased in the past 20 years. It is worth reflecting on how improved the U.S. energy position would be today had the U.S. government followed through more seriously on Carter's energy initiatives.

15. From Timothy Curry and Lynn Shibut, "The Cost of the Savings and Loan Crisis: Truth and Consequences," *FDIC Banking Review* 13, no. 2 (December 2000), http://www.federalreserve.gov/pubs/bulletin/2009/pdf/scf09.pdf.

16. Officially known as the Gramm-Rudman-Hollings Balanced Budget and Emergency Deficit Control Act of 1985, which placed caps on federal spending to keep federal deficits under control.

17. Bush 43 provides an excellent example of why the one-year lag is an appropriate adjustment. Without the lag, Bush 43's record absorbs the mild 2001 recession, which he obviously had nothing to do with, but he would also not be tarred with the severe 2009 recession, for which his administration bore a great deal of responsibility.

18. Recovery.gov Track the Money: http://www.recovery.gov/Pages/default.aspx.

19. Michigan Automotive News, "TARP panel: Auto bailout success unclear, but rescue extended 'too big too fail' guarantee," March 16, 2011, http://www.mlive.com/auto/index.ssf/2011/03/tarp_panel_auto_bailout_succes.html.

TWO

Inflation and Interest Rates: Incentives and Disincentives for Economic Production

By a continuing process of inflation, government can confiscate, secretly and unobserved, an important part of the wealth of their citizens.

—John Maynard Keynes

VALUE AND CRITIQUE OF THE INDICATORS

Inflation

Inflation would not be a bad thing if it were simply an increase in the price level where wages and interest rates adjust fully and immediately. Investors and workers would be unaffected. For example, if the inflation rate were 10 percent but wages increased also by 10 percent, then the value of wages would be unaffected by inflation. But inflation does not work that way. There are real costs when consumers and investors have to adjust to inflation. One of the costs is increased uncertainty in predicting the future. With rapidly increasing prices, it becomes difficult to accurately allocate expenditures between today and tomorrow because we are less certain about what the value of the dollar will be. Investment decisions cannot be made as easily. Wages usually lag behind inflation, leaving workers with a lower standard of living, at least for a while.

Real interest rates are the (nominal) interest rates we see in the marketplace, which are then adjusted for inflation. Typically, real interest rates also rise when there is inflation. In inflationary periods (double-digit or near-double-digit inflation levels), financial markets are not as certain where prices will be in the future as they are when inflation is low. For example, if inflation is low, say around 1.5 to 2.5 percent, we have a pretty good idea where prices will be in the next year or two. However, if inflation is 10 percent, we are less certain about prices because they are more volatile. Will price increases remain at 10 percent, jump to 13 or 14 percent, or drop back down to 6 or 7 percent? The wider range makes it more difficult for the market to pinpoint borrowing rates. Lenders are also less certain about what to charge on loans, particularly longer-term loans, because they extend further into an uncertain future. The uncertainty leads to higher risk and thus higher rates so that borrowers and investors might pay 2 to 3 percent higher rates in real terms just because inflation is high.

The basic formula for market interest rate illustrates:

$$i = i_{rf} + i_{rp}$$

Where i is the market interest rate, i_{rf} is the risk-free rate of return, which would be the interest rate on things like government treasury bills with a zero risk of default, and i_{rp} is the risk premium, which takes into account different risks, including the uncertainty about prices.

There is no magic inflation rate at which to be concerned, but it seems that when inflation reaches the 5 percent level, policymakers understand that the economy is just one step away from inflation becoming a problem. At that point, they, especially the Federal Reserve (the Fed), which plays the main policy role in managing inflation and interest rates, may begin to employ anti-inflationary policies. These policies include slowing the growth of the money supply, increasing interest rates under the Fed's control, and reducing the national debt, all of which tend to dampen GDP growth.

Thus, inflation is bad and counts negatively on a president's record. In addition to the Fed, the president has some influence over inflation. The president's fiscal policy influences how the Fed manages inflation. It matters to inflation policy, for example, whether the president's policies target smaller fiscal and trade deficits. Such policies allow the Fed greater latitude to conduct anti-inflation measures while maintaining interest rates at a level that promotes optimal levels of saving and investment (see Chapter 3). If the president chooses a fiscal policy that either tightly controls spending or that keeps taxes high enough to cover all spending, then there will also be no need to print money to fund increases in the national debt (or "monetizing the debt"), an action that can lead to inflation.

Other presidential policies affect inflation management as well. Shifting energy consumption away from sources whose availability is dwindling and whose prices ratchet continually upward also helps to keep inflation low. Alternatively, policies that continue to encourage dependency on petroleum, whether from domestic or foreign sources, will inevitably lead to higher costs of transportation and production and, therefore, higher inflation.

Because inflation is considered one of the most important aspects of economic performance, it has a substantial weight in the president's overall performance score (see Chapter 10). Inflation can have a profound negative effect on indicators that are desirable, including employment, GDP growth, and investment. But these indicators do not correlate as closely with inflation as, for example, productivity correlates with GDP, so we cannot depend on the behavior of other indicators to add to its weight in the president's performance score.

The standard measure of inflation is the *annual change in the consumer price index—all urban consumers*, or CPI-U. The CPI-U is a broad index of prices of goods and services purchased by households for consumption. This index, as well as other price indices, such as the wholesale price index (WPI), is maintained by the Bureau of Labor Statistics under the U.S. Department of Labor.

Real Interest Rates

The interest rate used here is the real prime interest rate, or real interest rate. The real interest rate is the "bank prime rate" (reported by the Board of Governors of the Federal Reserve), which is the interest rate charged by the private financial sector to businesses with the best credit rating (bank prime rate) adjusted for inflation:

$$\text{Real Prime Interest Rate} = \frac{1 + \text{bank prime interest rate}}{1 + \text{inflation rate}}$$

The inflation rate used in the formula above is the same CPI-U that is covered in this chapter. The bank prime rate can also be called a nominal interest rate, which means that it has not yet been adjusted for inflation.

This chapter briefly covers the Fed's interest rate policy and relates real interest rates to economic performance. The convention is that the lower the real interest rate, the better the president's performance. The reasoning is that with lower real interest rates the private sector is signaling that there is lower risk and, therefore, does not require as high a risk-adjusted return on loaned money. It suggests that whatever policies the president might have pursued, the environment for borrowing was better, and therefore investment costs were lower.

A caveat with real interest rates is that they might be low not because the markets perceive less risk in the economy but simply because economic activity is low, as in a recession. In the 2008 economic crisis, real interest rates fluctuated then went high again. At other times, for instance 1974 through 1975 and 1979 through 1980, the recessionary downward pressure on the real interest rates was evident.

REVIEW OF ADMINISTRATIONS' INFLATION AND INTEREST RATE PERFORMANCE—TRUMAN TO OBAMA

Inflation

Figure 2.1 shows inflation for 1946 through 2010. Inflation appears to have four main periods: (1) high inflation after WWII through 1948 (Truman); (2) low inflation during 1949 through 1972 (Truman, Eisenhower, Kennedy, Johnson, and Nixon); (3) high inflation from 1973 to 1982 (Nixon, Ford, and Carter); and (4) low inflation from 1983 to the present (Reagan through Obama).

Real Prime Interest Rate

Figure 2.2 shows that real prime rates have had five distinct periods: (1) sharply negative in four of six years after the war, which occurred

Figure 2.1   Inflation (CPI), 1946–2010

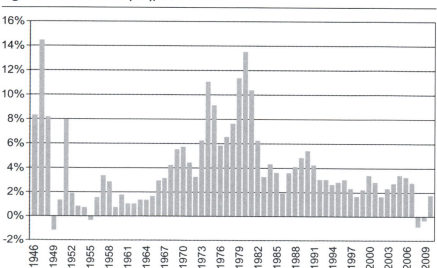

Figure 2.2   Real Prime Interest Rates, 1946–2010

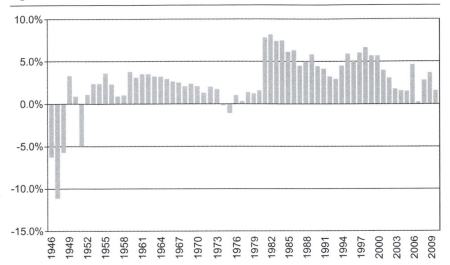

because inflation was high, while prime rates remained low because they were regulated; (2) positive but low through 1980; (3) shooting up in 1981 and remaining high, although declining through 1993; (4) a reheating of the economy in the mid-1990s that forced rates up again, and then a gradual decline through 2005; and (5) volatility when interest rates reacted to the heated economy and subprime bubble and jumped up several percentage points in 2006, fell back down when the bubble burst in 2007, and went back up in 2008 (a year of deflation), when markets became nervous as the economy edged toward crisis. Finally when the economy became depressed in 2009 (another deflationary year), rates fell again.

The presidential rankings for inflation and the real interest rate are provided in Tables 2.1 and 2.2, respectively.

Truman

Truman's most difficult challenge in the transition to peacetime, as it turned out, was not the return of high unemployment or recession but rather inflation. This fact surprised many economists who feared that after WWII the United States would return to Depression-era levels of unemployment. During the first three years after the war, the consumer price index soared, recording inflation rates of 8.3, 14.4, and 8.1 percent. The plausible explanation is that the consumer demand, which had been building since the Great Depression, was unleashed, but industry was not yet geared to consumers to produce enough goods as the United States was still moving from a wartime to a peacetime economy. Thus the early part of the Truman administration experienced high inflation. As the transition to peacetime progressed, inflation fell. Except for 1951, when inflation reached 7.9 percent (during the first year of the Korean War), inflation remained below 2 percent for the rest of Truman's administration.

Overall, Truman averaged an inflation rate of 5.2 percent during his eight-year record, ninth overall and higher than the period average of 3.8 percent. Truman also recorded a 1.5 percentage point drop in inflation (fifth best). Interest rates were kept artificially low under Truman, and, with the postwar volatility in the indicators, he had some odd results. With the relatively high inflation rates in some years, the real prime interest rate averaged −2.6 percent (the lowest and only negative rate among the 12 presidents), although that real rate increased by 3.1 percentage points, which was the second worst presidential ranking.

Eisenhower

The Eisenhower administration compiled an excellent record on inflation with an average of only 1.4 percent, with basically no increase in inflation since Truman's last year in office.

Consistent with the overall calming of the economy, Eisenhower's real interest rates were also favorable. Eisenhower's real interest rate averaged 2.5 percent, slightly below the period average of 2.6 percent, with an increase in the rate of 1.1 percentage points.

Kennedy

Kennedy had a nearly identical record on inflation to Eisenhower's: a very low average, 1.2 percent (best among all presidents), with a minimal increase. Counting the Eisenhower administration, there was extremely low inflation for the 11 years between 1953 and 1964.

The real interest rate average climbed to 3.3 percent, higher than the period average of 2.6 percent, and remained fairly steady with a 0.3 percentage point decline.

Johnson

Inflation deteriorated under Johnson. While he enjoyed reasonably low inflation rates, inflation rates crept up during his administration, from 1.3 percent in 1964 to 5.5 percent in 1969. This increase can be linked to the rapid increase in budget expenditures (see Chapter 7) for the war in

Vietnam and social programs, which laid the groundwork for the high-inflation 1970s. Johnson's average inflation rate was 3.5 percent (sixth best), but with an inflation increase of 4.2 percentage points (worst overall).

Despite the increase in inflation-related uncertainty, Johnson's real interest rate was lower than Kennedy's at 2.5 percent, and he ended his administration with a real interest rate that was 0.8 percentage point lower than when he started.

Nixon

Nixon had one of the worst records on inflation. His average inflation rate was the second highest at 6.6 percent and increased by the third highest amount, 3.6 percentage points. This record is not surprising given that inflation was already moving into the economy toward the end of the Johnson administration. The continuing expenditures for the Vietnam War and social programs, combined with lower economic growth—which meant lower tax revenues—created larger budget deficits. The Fed was also increasing the money supply at a brisk rate, with the M2[1] money supply rising 13.4 percent in 1971 and 13.0 percent in 1972. This rapid expansion of the money supply eventually found its way into the prices of goods and services, wage and price controls notwithstanding. In addition, the Arab Oil Embargo in 1973 caused a spike in petroleum prices, which also contributed to the recession a year later.

Because of some interest rate controls (such as Regulation Q),[2] and the fact that interest rates did not keep up with the increasing inflation rates because of a declining economy at the end of his administration, Nixon's average real interest rate averaged 1.0 percent with a decrease of 3.5 percentage points (the second best record for the 12 presidents).

Wage and Price Controls, August 15, 1971–April 10, 1974

Concerned about inflation and the general performance of the economy in 1971, President Nixon decided to change the course of his economic policies. In August 1971, Nixon did something that would be unthinkable today, especially for a Republican: he instituted wage and price controls. The public rather liked the controls, and the stock market (Dow Jones Industrial Average) rose 32.9 percent on the announcement, a tremendous increase. The actual wage and price "freezes" were in force for only 90 days, but the controls continued for three years. After the controls were terminated in April 1974, inflation was in double digits. Thus, the controls proved ineffective in the battle against inflation, proving that inflation can be controlled only by fundamental policies, that is, stable monetary policy and fiscal restraint.

Ford

Ford was more concerned about inflation than anything else to do with the economy. His main initiative, the Whip Inflation Now (WIN) campaign (see Chapter 1), however, was largely a voluntary approach. Inflation did fall to 5.8 percent in 1976, but the reduction was not sustained as inflation increased to 6.5 percent in 1977 and kept rising throughout Carter's presidency.

Ford's average inflation rate of 6.2 percent is well above the period average (of 3.8 percent) but was typical for the 1970s. His record is helped by the fact that the inflation rate fell 2.6 percentage points during his brief administration (third best). This decline is despite the fact that M2 growth was in double digits during 1975 through 1977.

Ford's real interest rate averaged only 0.6 percent, with an increase of 1.4 percentage points between 1975 and 1977.

Carter

Carter had the worst record on inflation by far, with an average inflation rate of 10.7 percent as well as an increase in the rate of 3.8 percentage points (second highest). One of the factors in the surge of inflation was the Fed's policy under Chairman William Miller (appointed by Carter in 1979) to target lower interest rates because of concern that high interest rates were choking off U.S. investment. This policy led the Fed to expand the money supply rapidly. As a result of this policy, the value of the dollar fell and inflation increased. Miller resigned after a little over one year (March 8, 1979, to August 6, 1979) and was replaced by Paul Volcker, who pursued a very different monetary policy (discussed under Ronald Reagan in the next section).

Carter's average real interest rate was 3.0 percent, with the largest increase at 7.5 percentage points. The lending market had finally processed the impact of inflation on risk and confidence. Real interest rates reached a peak of 7.8 percent (and nominal interest rates reached 18.9 percent) in 1981, the final year on Carter's record.

Reagan

Reagan compiled a very good record on inflation. While his average inflation rate, 4.0 percent, was slightly higher than the average for the overall period, his administration ushered in a new era of the low-inflation economy. The inflation rate fell 5.5 percentage points during his administration (best overall) from 10.3 percent in 1981 to 4.8 percent in 1989. For the next 22 years, with the exception of 1990 through 1991, inflation did not exceed 3.4 percent.

The consensus among economists is that the drop in inflation came at the price of a painful recession in 1982. The goal of Fed policy under Fed chairman Paul Volcker was to defeat chronic inflation. This goal required tight monetary policy, which, as theory predicts, led to a drop in economic activity. This is what economists believe happened in 1982, when GDP fell by 1.9 percent and unemployment exceeded 10 percent.

The Reagan administration also ushered in a new era of higher real interest rates. With still-high interest rates in the early part of his administration and falling inflation, real interest rates averaged the highest of any president, 6.3 percent. The real interest rate moderated somewhat, falling by 2.0 percentage points, the fourth largest drop overall. However, the drop was from a historically high level.

Bush 41

The senior Bush also had a respectable record on inflation. His average inflation rate of 3.9 percent was slightly above the period average of 3.8 percent. During his administration inflation fell by a further 1.8 percentage points, ending at 3.0 percent for 1993 (considering the one-year lag).

Bush 41's real interest rate averaged 3.6 percent, which was above the period average of 2.6 percent, with a 2.9 percentage point drop in the rate from Reagan's last year. The real interest rate declined but was still historically high, perhaps because the deficit level was also persistently high and because the debt was climbing. The rapid build-up of debt under these administrations increased fear and uncertainty that was reflected in the premium that borrowers would have to pay. However, the lower-inflation environment compensated to a large extent for the financial sector's fears about debt.

Clinton

The inflation environment improved even further under Clinton, with an average inflation rate over his eight years of only 2.6 percent (fifth best), plus a slight reduction in the rate from 3.0 percent to 2.8 percent (0.2 percentage point).

The real interest rate under Clinton averaged a relatively high 5.4 percent, with a 1.1 percentage point increase. This trend is perplexing if only Clinton's ability to maintain low inflation and to get control of the federal debt is considered. The other factor in real interest rates is the level of economic activity. Growth had been steady for a long time, and the economy was at or near full employment. That higher level of demand forced interest rates up significantly above the inflation rate. As in the case of Kennedy, whose real interest rate was above the period average, sometimes a higher real interest rate can be the sign of something positive in the economy.

Bush 43

Bush 43, like Clinton, also recorded a very good performance on inflation. The rate averaged 1.8 percent during his presidency, third best overall, and the rate decreased by a substantial 3.2 percentage points, second overall. Unfortunately, the decline in inflation occurred because of the deflationary impact of the collapse of the real estate and financial markets. Inflation rates were actually negative (deflationary) for 2008 and 2009, at −0.9 and −0.4 percent, respectively.

The real interest rate under Bush averaged 2.8 percent, with a 0.4 percent decline. Again, this lower interest rate was more a reflection of slower economic activity rather than of confidence in the economy.

Obama

Inflation under Obama averaged only 2.4 percent during the first two years of his record, fourth best overall. Inflation under Obama increased 3.5 percentage points above Bush's deflation rate of -0.4 percent. In terms of real interest rates, Obama recorded 0.8 percent (third best) with a 3.5 percentage point reduction (best overall), again, partly because of the weak economy, but probably also because of a general perception of lower risk in the economy.

Under Obama, the Fed has put a moderate amount of money into the economy, as measured by M2. M2 grew at 3.4 percent for both 2009 and 2010, which is actually well below the period average M2 growth rate of 6.3 percent. However, the Fed has also kept the Fed discount rate at near 0 percent, and to not much effect. It certainly does appear that, as Keynesian economists say, conducting monetary policy in a recession is "like pushing on a string."

CONCLUSION AND ISSUES FOR INFLATION AND THE REAL INTEREST RATE

With the exceptions of the Bush 43, Bush 41, and Obama administrations, low inflation correlated with a good overall economy. The growth in the money supply does appear to have a lagged effect on the inflation rate. However, the ability to access financial markets outside the United

Table 2.1   Inflation Rates by Presidential Administration

Administration	Inflation Rate	Administration	Inflation Rate Change
Kennedy	1.2%	Reagan	−5.5%
Eisenhower	1.4%	Bush 43	−3.2%
Bush 43	1.8%	Ford	−2.6%
Obama	2.4%	Bush 41	−1.8%
Clinton	2.6%	Truman	−1.5%
Johnson	3.5%	Clinton	−0.2%
Bush 41	3.9%	Eisenhower	0.2%
Reagan	4.0%	Kennedy	0.3%
Truman	5.2%	Obama	3.5%
Ford	6.2%	Nixon	3.6%
Nixon	6.6%	Carter	3.8%
Carter	10.7%	Johnson	4.2%
Period Average	**3.8%**		**N.A.**

States can also affect inflation, as we saw in the 1970s, thus weakening the link between U.S. monetary policy and the inflation rate. The 1970s inflation was also driven by war spending and increased energy costs. The impact of inflation on other indicators such as stock market growth is discussed later in the book.

Table 2.2   Real Prime Interest Rates by Presidential Administration

Administration	Real Interest Rate	Administration	Interest Rate Change
Truman	−2.6%	Obama	−3.5%
Ford	0.6%	Nixon	−3.5
Obama	0.8%	Bush 41	−2.9%
Nixon	1.0%	Reagan	−2.0%
Johnson	2.5%	Johnson	−0.8%
Eisenhower	2.5%	Bush 43	−0.4%
Bush 43	2.8%	Kennedy	−0.3%
Carter	3.0%	Clinton	1.1%
Kennedy	3.3%	Eisenhower	1.1%
Bush 41	3.6%	Ford	1.4%
Clinton	5.4%	Truman	3.1%
Reagan	6.3%	Carter	7.5%
Period Average	**2.6%**		**N.A.**

We expect that real interest rates could also be driven by the deficit and debt levels in the public sector because it would be expected that higher deficits and debt would lead to less confidence and, therefore, a higher rate of interest to pay for the added risk of lending. In addition, government borrowing competes for the same funds as the private sector and may "crowd out" private-sector borrowing. We observed that two of the presidents did have high real interest rates, but, contrary to expectations, real interest rates also fell during their administrations, even though deficits remained high (Reagan and Bush 41).

Reagan had high budget deficits and moderate GDP growth, and the real interest rate steadily declined during his administration, albeit from historically high levels at the end of the Carter administration. Carter's average real interest rate over four years was only 3.0 percent, well below that of Reagan and Bush. The high real interest rate (7.8 percent) occurred only at the end of his administration. Otherwise the real interest rate under Carter was 1.6 percent or less. It is probable that, had real interest rates not started out so high under Reagan, the combined effect of economic growth and high deficits would have significantly increased the real interest rate from the beginning to the end of his administration. Reagan's real interest rates were, indeed, well above the average real interest rate for the period for all eight years of his presidency. However, the fact that Clinton had the second highest real interest rate as well as a small increase in the rate, despite a good fiscal performance, is further evidence that a president's deficit performance is not the dominant force behind the interest rate risk premium. The level of economic activity appears to play a more dominant role in the real interest rate.

NOTES

1. M2 is defined as currency plus demand and other checkable deposits, overnight repurchase agreements, money market funds, savings, and small ($100 million or less) time deposits. In layman's terms it is cash and instruments that can be converted to cash easily and quickly.

2. Regulation Q is a U.S. Federal Reserve System rule limiting the interest rates that U.S. banks and savings-and-loan institutions can pay on deposits.

THREE

Savings and Investment: Groundwork for Growth

A penny here, and a dollar there, placed at interest, goes on accumulating, and in this way the desired result is attained. It requires some training, perhaps, to accomplish this economy, but when once used to it, you will find there is more satisfaction in rational saving than in irrational spending.

—P. T. Barnum, *The Art of Money Getting*

VALUE AND CRITIQUE OF THE INDICATORS

Savings and investment are essential ingredients to economic growth. The investor who is willing to risk his or her own, and often borrowed, capital for a potential higher return is what makes economic growth and higher living standards possible. The savers in society supply the funds that investors need to make those productive investments.

Savings and investment are influenced by at least two other indicators in our analysis, inflation and real interest rates. If interest rates are high, then people have incentives to save more (supply of funds), but businesses are discouraged by high interest rates because it costs more to borrow money to invest (demand for funds). Thus, savings and investment react in opposite ways to changes in interest rates. It is basic supply and demand, the most fundamental relationship in economics. Higher inflation also tends to have a negative effect on investment. If there is inflation, then people who save will require a higher interest rate on their savings so that their return is not eaten away by inflation.

In national accounting, savings and investment must be equal, and the interest rate is the financial price at which savings and investment are equal. However, other factors besides interest rates and inflation determine the levels of saving and investment. Investment is also determined by the expected return on the available investment opportunities in the economy and the risk of realizing that return. If the risk-adjusted expected return is higher than the interest rate, which is the investor's cost of borrowing, then the investment has met the minimum criterion for viability.

For savings, income levels are a driving factor not only of the level of savings but also of the rate. Generally, the higher a person's income is, the higher the percentage of income that is saved. Savings behavior may also be determined by an individual's expectation of lifelong income (Milton Friedman's permanent income hypothesis).[1] Investment behavior may also be driven by "animal spirits" (from John Maynard Keynes' *General Theory of Employment, Interest and Money*).[2] Whatever the forces behind savings and investment, it is generally good for the economy, and therefore for the presidents' records, to have higher levels of both.

Gross Private Investment

Gross private investment is part of GDP as we saw in the GDP equation that was presented in Chapter 1:

$$C + I + G + (X - M) = GDP$$

where C is consumption, I is investment, and X−M is exports minus imports. If investment goes up, then GDP goes up. Investment in the current year also leads to higher GDP in subsequent years. For example, if a company invests $25,000 in an employee's education in 2011, then GDP will increase by the $25,000 spent in that year. That investment in education will also help the employee to be more productive in the future, at least in theory. Conceivably, a $25,000 investment in education could lead to hundreds of thousands of dollars of extra GDP during a 40-year career.

Thus, we view investment as a good thing. Increases in levels of saving and investment are a positive achievement for a president. One benefit of incorporating these indicators into the analysis is that a president can be given credit for these indicators even if the expected growth did not materialize during his administration.

The broad components of investment as reported in the NIPA system are residential and nonresidential fixed investment and change in private inventories. The Bureau of Economic Analysis of the Department of Commerce publishes gross private domestic investment data as part of NIPA.

Personal Saving

Savings is needed to supply funds for investment. If we do not save anything from our income, then we cannot invest unless we get the funds from outside our economy. In this chapter, we use the personal saving rate rather than the gross private saving rate. The personal savings rate excludes savings by corporations and the government and typically represents less than one-third of all savings. One reason we make this choice is that the gross private saving rate and the gross private investment rate are equal for all years (though their components are different, they must, for conceptual accounting reasons, add up to the same amount). So we would not be gaining any additional performance information by using the gross private savings rate.

The personal savings rate measures, indirectly, the incentives that individuals have to save a portion of their income, presumably to ensure a better quality of life in the future and to reduce risks associated with income shortfalls. Have Americans set their priorities so they are willing to forego some consumption today for their anticipated needs tomorrow? If they have, then the president should get credit for at least presiding over an economy where such savings behavior is encouraged because these savings create greater financial security and will lead to the ability to consume more in the future.

Note that personal savings rates are calculated as a percentage of disposable income rather than GDP. This makes sense because people save from their disposable income and not from per capita GDP. The personal savings indicator used here includes the increase in financial assets (including securities and private life insurance reserves) plus the net increase in tangible assets (such as homes, factories, and inventories) minus the net increase in liabilities (such as mortgage debt on homes and other property and consumer credit). This concept follows the NIPA definition of savings,[3] which, like investment and GDP, is published by the Bureau of Economic Analysis of the Department of Commerce.

REVIEW OF SAVINGS AND INVESTMENT RATES BY ADMINISTRATION—TRUMAN TO OBAMA

The statistical evidence shows that Americans are poor savers not only at the personal level (private sector) but also in the public sector (rising government debt) and internationally, through decades of record trade deficits (mainly involving the private sector).

Savings data reveal somewhat of a paradox in that high savings rates tend to correspond to relatively weak economic performers (Nixon and Carter). One explanation is that when the economy declines, people feel less confident about spending a high percentage of their income. They opt for the security that savings offers. Clinton and Bush 43 had the lowest savings rates. In Clinton's case people seemed confident enough to spend nearly all of their income. In Bush 43's case, people went even further by tapping the equity that had been built up in their homes, albeit largely through a real estate bubble. Americans were borrowing money against home equity that would soon disappear. This "dis-saving" also suggested confidence, however unfounded, that the economy would grow indefinitely. Unfortunately that dis-saving put Americans in a weaker position to deal with the crisis that followed. In 2005 the personal savings rate was at an all-time low of 1.5 percent. When the financial crisis hit in 2008, Americans more than tripled their savings rate to 5.4. Tables 3.1 and 3.2 provide presidential rankings for gross private domestic investment and personal savings rates, respectively.

Truman

Truman recorded an average investment rate of 15.8 percent, seventh overall, close to the period average of 15.9 percent. The investment rate went up slightly, 0.9 percentage points, during his administration.

Truman's savings rate was 7.2 percent, eighth overall and near the period average of 7.1 percent. The savings rate dropped 1.4 percentage points, due in part to the fact that Americans were ready to spend when the war (and the Depression) was over. The fact that the savings rate dropped only 1.4 percentage points might imply a feeble spending response by consumers at the end of WWII. Recall from Chapter 1, however, that government spending fell by 27.1 percentage points but GDP fell by only 12.5 percentage points over two years. Thus, consumer spending was strong and prevented a far greater decline in GDP.

Eisenhower

Under Eisenhower investment rates dropped to 15.1 percent, third lowest among the presidents, including a −0.5 percent drop in the share. The personal savings rate moved up a bit to an average of 7.9 percent, but with only a 0.1 percentage point rise between the beginning and the end of the administration.

Kennedy

Kennedy averaged a 15.2 percent investment rate (fourth lowest), with a 1.0 percentage point increase in the share. Kennedy's average personal savings rate was 8.3 percent, fifth highest, with a 0.4 percentage point increase.

Johnson

Johnson averaged a 16.0 percent investment rate, with a 0.5 percentage point increase in the share. On the savings side, Johnson ranked fourth, with 8.5 percent and a 1.0 percentage point decline in the rate.

Nixon

Nixon had a 15.9 percent average investment rate, equal to the period average, with a 1.8 percentage point drop in the share. His average personal savings rate was the highest at 10.0 percent, with an increase in the rate of 2.8 percentage points, also the highest. The high personal savings rate might plausibly be explained by the fact that while there was high growth, there was also a lot of volatility and economic uncertainty during Nixon's administration. His high average savings rate may be more a reflection that consumers were nervous about the future of the economy than that they were flush with higher incomes and elected to conserve their resources.

Ford

Ford had the second highest investment rate, at 16.9 percent, combined with the largest increase in the rate, 3.7 percentage points. With respect to personal savings, his average rate was third highest at 9.1 percent, with a decline in the rate of 1.9 percentage points. Ford's numbers again can be explained by the fact that he governed during an economic rebound, with good growth but still some uncertainty.

Carter

Carter had the highest investment rate of any of the 12 presidents at 18.5 percent, with a 0.5 percentage point increase in the rate. This was one of the brightest spots in his economic record. His savings rate was second highest at 9.5 percent, with a 1.8 percentage point increase. The savings numbers are consistent with the fact that people saw the economy declining and decided to save for the rainy days ahead.

Reagan

Reagan had the third highest private investment rate, at 16.7 percent of GDP, but with the second highest drop in the rate, −2.3 percent. The savings rate under Reagan was in the middle at 8.2 percent but fell the most of any of the 12 presidents, 3.9 percentage points. This drop in the personal savings rate may indicate that people felt sufficiently confident to consume a significantly higher portion of their income as his administration progressed.

Bush 41

George H. W. Bush had the second lowest investment rate, 14.0 percent, considerably lower than the next lowest (Eisenhower's 15.1 percent). The investment rate also fell by 1.7 percentage points. His average personal savings rate was lower than the period average at 6.7 percent versus 7.1 percent, with a −0.8 percentage point drop.

Clinton

Clinton had a 16.5 percent average investment rate (compared with a 15.9 percent average for the period), fourth highest, with a 1.9 percentage point increase in the share. His savings rate was second lowest, at 4.2 percent and included a substantial drop in the rate of 3.1 percentage points, second to last place.

Bush 43

Bush 43 averaged 15.5 percent private investment share, somewhat below the period average. He recorded by far the largest drop in the investment rate, −4.9 percentage points. It appeared to many investors, apparently, that 2009 was not a good year to invest.

Bush 43 had the lowest average saving rate, at 3.4 percent, but at the same time the second highest increase in the saving rate, 2.4 percentage points. One explanation is that the overall savings rate was low because Americans were taking on debt (leverage from cashing in on equity in their homes) to buy into the real estate bubble or to increase their consumption in other ways in the early to middle part of his administration, resulting in very low savings rates. At the end of the Bush 43 administration, people lost confidence in the economy and began increasing their savings in order to build financial security in a weak economy.

Obama

Obama had the lowest investment rate for the period at 12.5 percent, well below the period average of 15.9 percent, but still 1.6 percentage points above Bush 43's last year. Again, it is a case of a weak average

Table 3.1   Investment Rates by Presidential Administration

Administration	Share of GDP	Administration	Change in Share
1. Carter	18.5%	Ford	3.7%
2. Ford	16.9%	Clinton	1.9%
3. Reagan	16.7%	Obama	1.6%
4. Clinton	16.5%	Kennedy	1.0%
5. Johnson	16.0%	Truman	0.9%
6. Nixon	15.9%	Carter	0.5%
7. Truman	15.8%	Johnson	0.5%
8. Bush 43	15.5%	Eisenhower	−0.5%
9. Kennedy	15.2%	Bush 41	−1.7%
10. Eisenhower	15.1%	Nixon	−1.8%
11. Bush 41	14.0%	Reagan	−2.3%
12. Obama	12.5%	Bush 43	−5.1%
Period Average	**15.9%**		**N.A.**

investment rate that was mainly because of the depressed and unstable economy inherited from his predecessor.

On savings, Obama's average was 4.8 percent, third lowest, with a 0.7 percentage point decrease in the share. Interest rates were low and unemployment was high, which is not a good combination to foster higher savings rates, even if people feel the need to build up their savings for a long and slow economic recovery.

Table 3.2   Personal Savings Rates by Presidential Administration

Administration	Share of Disposable Income	Administration	Trend
1. Nixon	10.0%	Nixon	2.8%
2. Carter	9.5%	Bush 43	2.4%
3. Ford	9.1%	Carter	1.8%
4. Johnson	8.5%	Kennedy	0.4%
5. Kennedy	8.3%	Eisenhower	0.1%
6. Reagan	8.2%	Obama	−0.7%
7. Eisenhower	7.9%	Bush 41	−0.8%
8. Truman	7.2%	Johnson	−1.0%
9. Bush 41	6.7%	Truman	−1.4%
10. Obama	4.8%	Ford	−1.9%
11. Clinton	4.2%	Clinton	−3.1%
12. Bush 43	3.4%	Reagan	−3.9%
Period Average	**7.1%**		**N.A.**

CONCLUSION AND ISSUES FOR SAVINGS AND INVESTMENT

Investment

Investment rates show no distinct trends over time. However, in political comparisons, it is clearly a win for the Democrats. All six Democrats increased the investment share of GDP, and the Republicans, with the exception of Ford, lowered the share. In any case, the range of investment shares of GDP was not very wide. The investment rate rankings from second to tenth place differed by less than 2 percentage points.

Even if the president gets the macroeconomic policies right and pursues responsible fiscal policy, he still has to think ahead about how the United States economy needs to develop. That means that he is concerned not only with the level but also the composition of investment. A president might have a tax cut or a spending increase that temporarily stimulates the economy. But if those stimulative policies do not promote the right mix of investments to meet the long-term needs of the nation, then the impact will indeed be temporary and ultimately costly to the federal government.

Savings

It is also difficult to establish a pattern with respect to personal savings rates. One story has been that savings rates are higher in weaker economies (Nixon and Carter) because people are afraid to consume too much and leave themselves exposed to a prolonged economic downturn. However, we also see lower savings rates in weaker economies (Bush 41, Bush 43, and the first half of the Obama administration). In the case of Bush 43, the savings rate did increase more than under any other administration (3.3 percentage points—partly because it had been so low under Clinton). There are also administrations with strong growth that recorded high savings rates (Ford, Johnson, and Kennedy) as well as low savings rates (Clinton).

Another factor in the level of savings is the increasing concentration of wealth and income in the United States. This increasing concentration would tend to lead to higher savings because rich people save more than middle-class people. Despite this influence, other factors have driven savings rates down such that the four most recent presidents have the four lowest savings rates. That would suggest that middle-class Americans have been able to save even less during the past several decades than the aggregate personal savings rates suggest.

What is important for our analysis is that the president get some credit for higher savings rates and increases in savings rates because that will (1) supply more funds to investors and (2) put individuals in a better position for the future. We are already crediting the president with GDP growth and other indicators that correlate with GDP, so it seems sensible to give credit when consumers defer consumption for a later time.

NOTES

1. This hypothesis maintains that individuals adjust their savings levels according to the income they expect over time and the level of consumption they will need or prefer. This theory implies that an individual's saving decisions are not particularly sensitive to interest rates.

2. "Animal spirits" according to Keynes referred to human urges to do things, such as to risk or not to risk resources, which could take on a collective momentum throughout the economy.

3. Another commonly used definition of savings is the flow of funds (FOF) definition, which differs from the NIPA concept in that it also includes government pension and insurance reserves, net investment in consumer durables, and net saving by farm corporations.

FOUR

Growth of the Stock Market: The Value of Private Companies

Foul cankering rust the hidden treasure frets,
But gold that's put to use more gold begets.

—William Shakespeare, *Venus and Adonis*

VALUE AND CRITIQUE OF THE INDICATOR

Stock market indexes make good presidential performance indicators. They measure the changes in values of private companies according to what individuals and institutions, that is "the market," are willing to pay for their shares of stock. This willingness to pay is based on expectations for the companies' profits, which are either distributed as dividends or invested back into the companies. Stock market indexes are therefore an indirect indicator of the effect of presidential economic policies. Although the percentage of Americans owning stock has fallen in recent years, more than half (54 percent) of Americans polled reported that they owned stock in some form.[1]

This chapter looks specifically at real growth in the Dow Jones Industrial Average (DJIA) during presidential administrations. There are many stock market indexes from which to choose, including indexes that have much broader stock market coverage, such as the S&P 500 and the Wilshire 5000. Unfortunately, we cannot use these indexes because they were established too recently to cover the analysis period. The S&P 500 began in 1957 while the Wilshire 5000 did not begin until 1974. The DJIA covers the entire analysis period, 1946 to 2011, and is probably the most reported stock market index in America.

The composition of the DJIA has changed over time as companies have started up, gone out of business, merged, and been take over. For 1946 to 2011, the DJIA is the unweighted total dollar value of the stocks of 30 leading U.S. companies divided by the number of companies in the index and adjusted for stock splits and dividends.[2] The DJIA began in 1896 and initially consisted entirely of industrial stocks. Thus, we can use the DJIA to make stock market comparisons back to the Great Depression and before.

Like all of the indicators in this book, the DJIA is lagged by one year. Some analysts might argue that the effects of the president's policy choices on the stock market might actually precede their full implementation; markets continuously try to read signals from the president and anticipate his actions. But people's expectations for companies (as reflected in stock prices) also reflect the cumulative impact of policies and the fundamentals that have taken years to build and that are attributable in part to a president's already implemented policies. In the case of the 2008 financial crisis, for instance, the market as a whole only reacted; it did not anticipate the effects of the excessive risk taking in the financial sector.[3] Thus, the DJIA indicator is appropriately lagged like all of the other indicators.

The stock market growth rate, like all growth rates presented in this book, is adjusted for inflation. The reader should also understand that the stock market growth rate is very volatile, which has implications for measuring a president's performance. From one year to the next, the growth rate can change 50 percentage points or more. During 1974 and 1975 the DJIA growth rate changed from −34.8 to +26.8 percent (a 61.6 percentage point swing in one year). As recently as 2008 and 2009 the DJIA growth rate increased in a single year from −33.2 to +19.3 percent, a swing of 52.5 percentage points.

With that kind of volatility, it is not appropriate to give too much weight to the changes in stock market growth rates from one endpoint to another of a president's administration. We do report the growth rate changes, but mainly for completeness because trend changes are provided for all other indicators in the analysis.

The DJIA, while it is an important indicator, tends to be overreported in the news. It is an easy way to fill air time, but the reporting of daily, much less by-the-minute, changes in the stock market has more entertainment value (akin to watching a geometric screen saver) than any significance in the economic well-being of the nation. Only longer-term (e.g., annual) changes in stocks have any economic significance. It is, in a way, a bad habit that people who do not trade stocks for a living glue themselves to the TV to monitor information that they will never act on and that teaches them nothing.

REVIEW OF ADMINISTRATIONS' STOCK MARKET PERFORMANCES—TRUMAN TO OBAMA

Figure 4.1 and Figure 4.2 show the end-of-year stock market levels not adjusted for inflation (Figure 4.1) and adjusted for inflation (Figure 4.2). A comparison of the two graphs underscores the importance of adjusting the DJIA for inflation. In Figure 4.1, it is almost impossible to discern relative stock market performance periods. Inflation makes growth in the years up to 1985 look negligible, but that is not the case. There was a wide range of presidential performances during 1946 through 1985. The different performances are evident only after adjusting for inflation, as shown in Figure 4.2.

Figure 4.2 shows some interesting stories in the stock market, one of which is that the four weakest records on stock market growth occurred in succession, under Johnson, Nixon, Ford, and Carter. That period covers 1965 to 1981, a 16-year period of stagnant and declining stock performance.

Figure 4.1   Dow Jones Industrial Averages, Not Adjusted for Inflation, 1946–2010

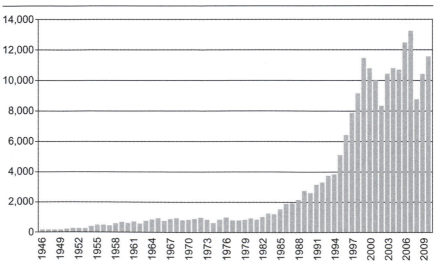

Figure 4.2   Dow Jones Industrial Averages, Adjusted for Inflation, 1946–2010

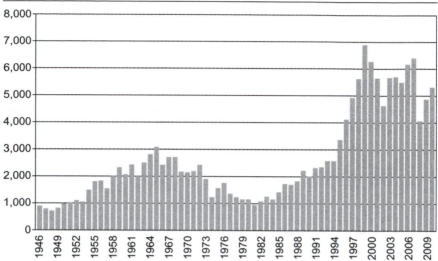

The stock market did not respond to the reasonably good to very good GDP growth during that period the way one might have expected. The boom years of the 1960s proved to be a net negative period (−0.7 percent average annual growth) for the DJIA. In addition, the years immediately after WWII did not produce a surge in the stock market despite consumers' liberation from 17 years of suppressed consumption.

The best stock market run was during the Reagan–Bush 41–Clinton years, about an 18-year period, when the stock market recovered and surpassed the real value of what it had lost in the previous 16 years. The only other really strong performance among the 12 presidents was Eisenhower's, who edged out Reagan for the highest stock market growth rate. The stock market is in another long period of stagnant but volatile behavior. Since 1999 the DJIA has depreciated in real as well as absolute terms. The year-end 2007 DJIA of 6,104.38 in real terms (13,264.82 nominal terms) was more than 11 percent below the year-end DJIA for 1999 in real terms of 6,901.02 adjusted for inflation. Except for a small percentage of dividend returns, investors would have had a similar return by putting their cash in their mattresses than they would have had investing in the Dow Jones Industrials. Table 4.1 contains the rankings for all 12 presidents.

Table 4.1   Stock Market (DJIA) Growth Rates by Presidential Administration

Administration	Growth Rate	Administration	Growth Rate Trend
Eisenhower	10.5%	Nixon	46.3%
Reagan	10.4%	Reagan	38.8%
Clinton	9.7%	Bush 43	28.9%
Obama	5.5%	Eisenhower	22.0%
Kennedy	4.7%	Carter	4.6%
Bush 41	3.9%	Truman	−4.5%
Truman	−0.2%	Kennedy	−5.1%
Bush 43	−1.9%	Bush 41	−10.7%
Johnson	−5.1%	Obama	−16.9%
Nixon	−5.3%	Clinton	−20.1%
Ford	−7.2%	Johnson	−32.1%
Carter	−8.9%	Ford	−49.1%
Period Average	**2.5%**		**N.A.**

Truman

One might have expected a higher stock market growth rate during the Truman administration, with the United States emerging as the sole industrial power and Americans hungry for consumer goods. However, Truman's average stock growth rate was flat at −0.2 percent (seventh overall), below the period average of 2.5 percent.

Eisenhower

Eisenhower had the highest DJIA growth rate, a 10.5 percent annual average for his eight-year administration. With respect to the stock market, Eisenhower may have been the beneficiary of the postwar consumption boom, as the stock market appears to have had a delayed response to U.S. companies gearing up for the consumer markets.

Kennedy

Kennedy had one of the higher DJIA growth rates at 4.7 percent (fifth overall), but only half of Eisenhower's. Again, this is somewhat of a counterintuitive result given that Kennedy's economic growth was much stronger than Eisenhower's.

Johnson

The Johnson administration marked the beginning of a long period of stock market decline. Once again, the stock market performance seemed at odds with what one would expect from good economic growth and the stimulus from the Vietnam War, which raged for most of the Johnson presidency. The market also did not seem to respond favorably to the Kennedy-Johnson tax cuts of 1964. The average annual stock market decline under Johnson was 5.1 percent, fourth worst overall.

Nixon

With the recession at the end of the Nixon administration and the debilitating Watergate scandal, it is no surprise that the stock market continued its decline. Between the end of 1972, when the Watergate scandal was just beginning, until the end of 1974 after Nixon's resignation, the DJIA dropped from 1,020.02 to a paltry 616.24 (or 2,440.24 to 1,249.98 in real terms—2005 dollars). During Nixon's full six-year record, the market dropped an average of 5.3 percent for each year (third worst overall).

Ford

Despite the recovery over which Ford presided, the stock market continued to decline an average of 7.2 percent annually during his two years in office, the second worst average among the 12 presidents.

Carter

The stock market really bottomed out during the Carter administration. In fact, the decline accelerated on a percentage basis. His 8.9 percent annual decline in the stock market was the worst among the 12 presidents. The DJIA had fallen in nominal terms to only 875.00 by 1981. In real (2005) dollars, the DJIA was only 962.60 in 1981, the lowest level for the stock market since 1949. That means that if a person invested in the DJIA in 1949 and held that investment until 1981, they would only break even, not including dividends—not exactly a high-performing investment!

Reagan

The Reagan administration marked the beginning of a new and positive trend for the stock market as it rebounded from the previous four administrations. The Reagan administration recorded the second highest growth rate among the 12 presidents, 10.4 percent per year for the eight-year administration. Although the growth rate was from a low base (again, the DJIA was only 875.00 in Carter's last year), it was still a solid achievement for the stock market to turn around so strongly for a sustained period of time.

Despite the high stock market growth, there was a disturbing event in the stock market that took place on October 19, 1987, "Black Monday." The DJIA dropped 508 points, which was 22.6 percent of the total market value, the largest one-day loss ever. Investors had become increasingly nervous over the weekend after the stock market had fallen a total of 261 points during the four previous trading sessions. Explanations for the total 769-point drop include (1) investors' unease with the large budget deficits and the S&L crisis; (2) The fact that the United States had become a "debtor nation"[4] along with indications that holders of U.S. debt were becoming uneasy with financing U.S. deficits; and the more immediate causes: (3) the announcement by Reagan's treasury secretary, James Baker, that the United States would not continue to prop up the dollar, and (4) technical causes such as "think-alike MBAs" engaged in programmed trading. The market did recover partially in the following days but did not reach its pre-crash level until mid-July 1990, more than two and a half years later. Black Monday was an unsettling event because it came four years into the Reagan recovery, when markets had been growing for a substantial amount of time and thoughts of a downturn were not prominent in people's minds. Despite this event, the stock market growth during the Reagan administration was second best overall.

Bush 41

Bush was sandwiched between two high-growth presidents but still recorded a 3.9 percent DJIA growth rate (sixth overall), well above the average level for the period of 2.8 percent.

Clinton

Under Clinton the rapid growth rate of the stock market continued. He achieved a 9.7 percent average growth rate, the third overall. It was, in a way, more challenging for Clinton to achieve a high growth rate because the market had already been growing for 12 years. As with the Reagan administration, however, the Clinton administration also witnessed a significant negative shock to the stock market. In Clinton's case, it was the bursting of the dot.com bubble.

Driven by low interest rates, an abundance of venture capital, and an investor boom mentality, the NASDAQ, the stock exchange that carried most Internet stocks, peaked at 5,048.62 points on March 10, 2000.[5] However, a shake-out of dot.coms began almost immediately after the peak. The market had been flooded with dot.coms, many of which were attempting to seize similar markets. At the same time, the venture capital on which they depended was running out. Perhaps the most famous dot.com flameout was that of WorldCom, which was also guilty of illegal accounting practices. The company filed one of the largest bankruptcies in history. Another factor cited in the collapse is that the Fed had decided that interest rates needed to be higher and had raised interest rates six times leading up to the bursting of the dot.com bubble.

Bush 43

Under George W. Bush the stock market began to decline again for the first time since Carter, 20 years earlier. The average annual stock market decline under Bush was 1.9 percent annually for his eight-year term, eighth overall.

Two main events damaged the stock market under Bush 43: the terrorist attacks on September 11, 2011, and the economic crisis of 2008. The stock market was panicked by the attacks of 9/11, which, after all, were aimed at the financial center of the United States. By August 2002, the DJIA had bottomed out at 7,591.93, the lowest level in more than 10 years. After the 2008 crisis, the DJIA hit an even lower bottom at 7,062.93 in February 2009, less than one month after Bush 43 left office. Obviously, Bush 43 could not be blamed for the 9/11 attacks, only for his response. As the stock market data indicate, the market, at least initially, did not find his response too comforting. With respect to the 2008 financial crisis, his administration's responsibility is clear. Not only were his people in key regulatory positions leading up to the collapse, but his economic philosophy of deregulation and "free" markets dictated policy that allowed unsustainable risk to build up in the financial sector.

Obama

Stock market growth under Obama averaged 5.5 percent. This rate ranks fourth out of 12 presidents.

CONCLUSIONS AND ISSUES FOR THE STOCK MARKET

Era of Stock Market Growth (1982–1999)

There are a number of explanations for the 18-year-long rise of the stock market that began in 1982. One of the factors that may have fueled this stock market surge was an increase in foreign demand for U.S. assets because the U.S. dollar had fallen in value vis-à-vis other major currencies, such as the Japanese yen. Another factor was the increasing supply of dollars in foreign hands because of record U.S. trade deficits (Chapter 6). A third factor was Reagan's lowering of the maximum capital gains rate to 20 percent (from 39 percent) in his 1981 tax bill. By 1986 Reagan felt that capital gains should be taxed at the same rate as ordinary income and raised the capital gains rate to 28 percent in his Tax Reform Act of 1986. Stock market declines were usually associated with an economic slowdown such as the 1991 recession, the 2001 recession, and the 2008 financial crisis. The stock market might have increased even faster during the 18-year growth period, but the real estate market was also absorbing the higher disposable (after-tax) incomes and the foreign-held dollars.

Effects of Inflation and Risk

One thing is clear from the DJIA trends: the stock market does not like inflation. Higher inflation is the indicator most closely correlated with the large real decline of the stock market during 1965 through 1981. The stock market also does not like the accumulation of excessive risk, at least when the day of reckoning comes. Eventually, as we saw in the S&L crisis, the dot.com bubble, and the subprime mortgage crisis, excessive and unregulated risk leads to a plummeting stock market.

Effects of Income Tax Cuts and Increases

Income tax cuts (distinguished from capital gains tax cuts) appear to be no different from tax increases in their effects on the stock market. Tax cuts may have had a positive effect on the stock market after 1981, after Reagan achieved a major tax cut and a long period of growth for the DJIA began, but Reagan had also lowered the capital gains tax. The Kennedy-Johnson tax cuts of 1964 actually marked the beginning of a long period of stock market *decline*.

The tax *increases* under Bush 41 and Clinton did not seem to damage the stock market. On the contrary, DJIA growth continued briskly through 1999. Clinton raised taxes, but inflation remained low and the stock market continued to boom. This again shows that the context of the tax cut is the main factor in determining whether it succeeds or fails. The context for Reagan's 1981 through 1983 tax cuts was that top rate before the tax cut was 70 percent, which was lowered to 50 percent. That is very different from Bush 43 squeezing out 4 or 5 percentage points more for the top income bracket, which was already taxed at less than 40 percent. Certainly the wealthy are more likely to buy stock. But the Bush 43 tax cuts in 2001 did not seem to have any lasting positive effect on the stock market. In fact, the Bush 43 administration marked the end of the long positive run of the stock market.

Obama's first-year growth rate of 9.2 percent can be viewed as a rebound growth rate from the precipitous 33.2 percent drop in the year-end DJIA for 2008. The stock market growth may also have reflected relief that the freefall of the financial markets had been halted. In summary, there is really only one example and three counterexamples out of four where stock market growth is positively correlated with tax cuts.

Comparison of the Dot.com Bubble and the 2008 Financial Crisis

Both the bursting of the dot.com bubble and the 2008 financial crisis seriously damaged the stock market. However, there are some fundamental differences between these two events. First, the dot.com collapse was far less costly than the 2008 crisis, and massive unemployment did not follow. However, as stated earlier, the stock market as a whole at the end of 2011 was more than 11 percent below its 1999 value in real terms. Second, the dot.com investors themselves, rather than the U.S. taxpayer, suffered the losses when the bubble burst.

In any case, neither Bush 43, nor Clinton, nor Reagan, sounded an alarm or heeded an alarm from regulators under their authority about trouble in the financial markets. It would be refreshing if future presidents and their economic teams were more alert and proactive in dealing with excessive market risk before it gets to the crisis stage rather than looking the other way simply because some people are making a lot of money.

NOTES

1. From Gallup poll, April 2011, http://www.gallup.com/poll/147206/stock-market-investments-lowest-1999.aspx.

2. For a good primer on the DJIA and its contents, go to http://www.stocks-for-beginners.com/dow-jones-index.html.

3. There were exceptions; a few significant investors did read the signs that the subprime market was going to collapse and made hefty bets against the market. For an excellent read on this topic see Michael Lewis, *The Big Short* (New York: W.W. Norton & Co., 2011).

4. In other words, foreigners owned more of the United States' assets than Americans owned of theirs.

5. Note that the NASDAQ is different from the DJIA. The NASDAQ is an entire stock exchange and is comprised of a higher percentage of "tech" stocks, including dot.coms, while the DJIA is comprised of stocks of large, "blue chip" companies. Therefore, the DJIA was not nearly as negatively affected by the bursting of the dot.com bubble as the NASDAQ. Still, the dot.com collapse did have a depressing effect on the DJIA, which has not appreciated in real or even nominal terms since 2000 (through the end of 2011).

FIVE

Employment and the Poverty Line: The "Other" Bottom Lines of Economic Policy

Labor is prior to, and independent of, capital. Capital is only the fruit of labor, and could never have existed if labor had not first existed. Labor is the superior of capital, and deserves much the higher consideration.

—Abraham Lincoln

VALUE AND CRITIQUE OF THE INDICATORS

If GDP were the bottom line of economic performance, then we would not need to analyze unemployment and poverty indicators. However, job creation and poverty reduction are, by themselves, ultimate economic objectives. The goal of economic policy can be seen as achieving the greatest good for the greatest number of people. If workers are idle and getting poorer while other people intensify their wealth, then our economic objectives are not being met, no matter how high growth is. As a nation we insist that the economy employ as many people as possible and reduce poverty; therefore, these indicators weigh heavily in a president's economic performance.

The lower the unemployment and poverty rates and the higher the employment growth, the greater is the equity in our economic system and the higher the economic efficiency because there is less idle labor. Policymakers are also aware that unemployment has a doubly negative impact on the federal budget deficit: the unemployed do not pay taxes, but they do often receive unemployment compensation.

The analysis here does not target income distribution, per se, as a measure of economic performance. Employment and poverty indicators are not pure distributional indicators like the Gini coefficient or income per quintile in the population.[1] However, employment and poverty indicators capture income distribution indirectly. For example, if the economy has full employment and declining rates of poverty, then we know that the growth that was achieved is broad based. That is very positive for a president's score.

Employment Growth and the Unemployment Rate

For employment performance, we look at both the unemployment rate and the actual growth rate of the number of employed people. The reason that we use both indicators is that the percentage of the total population over 16 that is part of the labor force (employed and looking for employment), called the "participation rate,"[2] fluctuates. If the participation rate goes down, then it is easier for the president to keep the unemployment rate low because fewer people are seeking employment. However, if a higher percentage of the population wants to work and the unemployment rate remains low, the president needs to be given extra credit. We can capture this achievement only if we measure the actual growth in employment (the rate of increase in number of persons employed). That is why we use both indicators. The participation rate has generally gone up during the 1946 to 2011 period (from 57.3 to 64.7 percent, with a peak of 67.1 percent during 1997 through 2000).

Employment statistics are published by the Bureau of Labor Statistics of the U.S. Department of Labor on monthly, quarterly, and annual bases.

Percent of the Population below the Poverty Line

The poverty line indicator is the Census Bureau's "percent of the population below the poverty line." This indicator has been measured since 1959. It is the only indicator we use that does not include all of the presidents because it omits all of the Truman administration and most of the Eisenhower administration. Also, annual poverty data are released later in the year than the data for the other indicators (September as opposed to January or February).

The percent of the population below the poverty line indicates how much of the growth is trickling down, or is otherwise being redistributed, to the poorest segment of society. In this analysis, it is counted as positive for a president's performance if the rate of poverty declined on his watch.

Note that the employment and poverty data that we use to compile the president's economic performance are aggregate. They do not show the imbalances that exist between specific groups of Americans. For example, while the 2010 poverty rate was 15.1 percent of the population for all groups of Americans combined, the poverty rate for African Americans is 27.4 percent. For Hispanic Americans the poverty rate is 26.6 percent and for non-Hispanic white Americans it is 9.9 percent. Thus there are additional socioethnic issues embedded in the aggregate numbers. Despite this additional dimension to poverty, we use only the aggregate poverty rate to measure a president's performance.

REVIEW OF ADMINISTRATIONS' EMPLOYMENT AND POVERTY PERFORMANCE—TRUMAN TO OBAMA

Figure 5.1 illustrates the fluctuations of the unemployment rate and shows several distinct cycles, ranging from seven to 16 years. These cycles also align with changes in administrations as the rankings below reflect. Unemployment was kept at 6.0 percent or less in all but two years during 1946 through 1975. Thereafter, of the next 36 years, annual unemployment rates exceeded 6.0 percent 19 times. Thus, more recent decades have seen systematically higher unemployment.

Figure 5.1   Unemployment Rate, 1946–2010

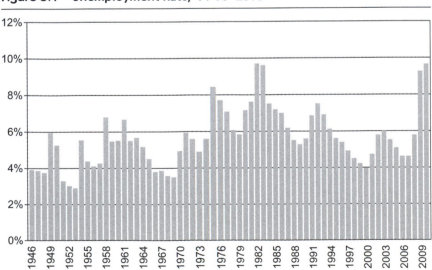

Fiugre 5.2   Percent of the Population below the Poverty Line, 1959–2010

Figure 5.2 shows that the behavior of the percentage of the population below the poverty line indicator tracks the unemployment rate fairly closely, except during the 1970s. When the unemployment rate falls, so does poverty. However, poverty remained low in the mid to late 1970s despite periods of substantial unemployment in 1970 and 1974 through 1975. Rankings for unemployment are in Table 5.1, unemployment rankings are in Table 5.2, and population below the poverty line rankings are in Table 5.3.

Truman

Labor unions were relatively powerful during the Truman era compared with today. During the war, the president had the power to seize businesses that were "war-essential" if they were experiencing labor strikes. In the transition to a peacetime economy, a number of major unions wanted to flex their muscles and waged strikes. Truman generally supported union workers, and labor unions made gains in wages and benefits during his administration. However, Truman sought to limit union power after the war, and at times he found himself at odds with unions.

Truman's Use of the Taft-Hartley Act

To check the power of unions, Truman invoked provisions of the Taft-Hartley Act, such as the 80-day cooling-off period and limitation of union

Table 5.1 Employment Growth Rates by Presidential Administration

Administration	Growth Rate	Administration	Growth Rate Trend
Ford	3.5%	Ford	4.8%
Johnson	2.3%	Obama	4.3%
Carter	2.2%	Kennedy	2.3%
Truman	2.0%	Reagan	1.0%
Reagan	1.9%	Johnson	0.3%
Kennedy	1.8%	Bush 41	−0.6%
Clinton	1.6%	Clinton	−1.5%
Nixon	1.6%	Eisenhower	−1.6%
Eisenhower	0.9%	Carter	−2.6%
Bush 41	0.6%	Truman	−3.1%
Bush 43	0.3%	Nixon	−3.7%
Obama	0.0%	Bush 43	−3.8%
Period Average	**1.4%**		**N.A.**

participation in politics.[3] His use of the Taft-Hartley Act was somewhat ironic because he had actually vetoed the bill (his veto was overridden). The act also meant that the executive branch of the federal government could obtain legal strikebreaking injunctions if an impending or current strike "imperiled the national health or safety." Under this provision,

Table 5.2 Unemployment Rates by Presidential Administration

Administration	Unemployment Rate	Administration	Unemployment Trend
Johnson	3.8%	Reagan	−2.3%
Truman	4.0%	Clinton	−2.2%
Clinton	4.9%	Johnson	−1.7%
Eisenhower	5.4%	Kennedy	−1.5%
Kennedy	5.5%	Ford	−1.4%
Bush 43	5.8%	Obama	−0.3%
Nixon	5.9%	Carter	0.6%
Carter	6.7%	Truman	1.0%
Bush 41	6.7%	Bush 41	1.6%
Reagan	7.2%	Eisenhower	3.8%
Ford	7.4%	Bush 43	4.5%
Obama	9.3%	Nixon	4.9%
Period Average	**5.7%**		**N.A.**

Table 5.3   Percent of the Population below the Poverty Line by Presidential Administration

Administration	Population below the Poverty Line	Administration	Poverty Line Trend
Ford	11.7%	Johnson	−6.9%
Nixon	11.9%	Clinton	−3.5%
Carter	12.5%	Kennedy	−2.9%
Bush 43	12.8%	Reagan	−1.2%
Clinton	12.9%	Ford	−0.7%
Reagan	13.9%	Eisenhower	−0.5%
Johnson	14.2%	Nixon	0.2%
Bush 41	14.4%	Obama	0.8%
Obama	15.1%	Bush 41	2.3%
Kennedy	19.8%	Carter	2.5%
Eisenhower	22.1%	Bush 43	2.6%
Period Average	**14.1%**		**N.A.**

Note: No poverty-line data were available for Truman.

Truman took the United Mine Workers to court and threatened to draft striking railroad workers. In 1952, Truman had the federal government seize the steel mills. The Supreme Court later overturned this seizure. A 53-day strike followed, which culminated in a new contract for the steel union.

Employment Act of 1946

After the war, Congress passed the Employment Act of 1946. The fear at the time was that the economy would slip back to the high unemployment that plagued the United States prior to the war. Early versions of the bill, which was originally called the Full Employment Act, mandated that the federal government use all of its economic powers to achieve full employment. Conservatives in Congress viewed this mandate as socialistic and an overreach of the federal government's economic power. In the final version, this mandate was reduced to a suggestion that federal government should "promote maximum employment, production, and purchasing power." The bill was renamed the Employment Act of 1946, which Congress passed and Truman signed. The act created the Council of Economic Advisors to ensure that the president had top economic expertise in-house, so to speak, to advise him on economic policy. The Employment Act also required that the president publish an annual

Economic Report of the President, which all presidents are still obliged to do.

Immediately after WWII there was an increase in unemployment from a very low level of 1.9 percent in 1945 to 3.9 percent in 1946. Also in 1946, the employment growth rate was 4.6 percent, which means that a lot of employment was created immediately after the war but that there were even more people looking for jobs, having left the armed services.

Truman's administration recorded the second lowest average unemployment rate at 4.0 percent, though unemployment did rise by 1.0 percentage point (to 2.9 percent) during his administration. Employment grew at an average annual rate of 2.0 percent, fourth best. This employment growth rate seems low because one would expect that a lot of employment would have to be created to absorb Americans who had demobilized. However, the labor force participation rate did not change much from 1945 (58.8 percent) to 1949 (59.2 percent).[4] The participation rate really did not start increasing steadily until the 1970s. The participation rate actually fell to 57.3 percent in 1946, which suggests that many demobilized people did not seek civilian jobs.

There is no poverty line data for Truman because the U.S. government had not yet begun to collect this statistic. However, Truman's growth and employment numbers suggest that the poverty rate would almost certainly have declined significantly during his administration.

Eisenhower

Eisenhower's overall employment record could be characterized as "low average." He had a modest average employment growth rate of 0.9 percent, compared with the average for the period of 1.5 percent. Although his average unemployment rate was a fourth-best 5.4 percent, the unemployment rate increased 3.8 percentage points during his administration (third worst).

Eisenhower was the first president for whom the poverty line data exist, but only for the last three of the eight years of his presidency, 1959 to 1961. When the poverty line indicator began in 1959, 22.4 percent of the American population fell below the poverty line (39.5 million people out of a total population of 176.6 million). The average poverty rate under Eisenhower was a period-high 22.1 percent, with a 0.5 percentage point drop in the rate. The decrease in the rate would have been more substantial, but Eisenhower's administration concluded with a mild recession, which kept the poverty rate high.

Kennedy

Kennedy's employment record could be described as "high average." Under Kennedy, employment grew at 1.8 percent, above the period average of 1.4 percent and sixth best overall. His unemployment rate averaged 5.5 percent (fifth best), with a decline in the unemployment rate of −1.5 percentage points (fourth best). With respect to poverty, the average rate was 19.8 percent, with −2.9 percentage point decrease. The drop in the poverty rate was an excellent accomplishment for such a brief administration.

Johnson

Johnson had an excellent employment record with a 2.3 percent employment growth rate (second best) and a 3.8 percent average unemployment rate (best overall), with a −1.7 percentage point decline in unemployment.

Johnson also had the best record on poverty, averaging a rate of 14.2 percent but, more importantly, showing a decrease in the rate of poverty of 6.9 percentage points (in only five years as president), by far the greatest progress in poverty reduction of any president. Between the beginning and end of his presidency, the number of Americans in poverty had fallen by 11.9 million. One can trace a direct connection of this poverty reduction to the overall good economic performance during his administration; the low unemployment; Johnson's "War on Poverty," which elevated poor people's living standard through a variety of programs (Chapter 7); and, perhaps, even the war in Vietnam.

Nixon

Nixon had a generally weak record on employment, although his employment growth rate average of 1.6 percent was slightly higher than the period average of 1.4 percent. His unemployment rate was 5.9 percent (seventh out of 12), but the unemployment rate increased by 4.9 percentage points, the largest increase of the 12 presidents. The reason for the large increase in unemployment was that Nixon's record ends with the recession of 1974 and 1975.

On poverty, Nixon's record was respectable. While poverty fell only 0.2 percentage points, it averaged 11.9 percent, well below the period average of 14.0 percent and the second lowest average for all presidents.

Ford

Ford had the highest employment growth rate, 3.5 percent, and, almost paradoxically, the highest unemployment rate, at 7.4 percent, but with a reduction in unemployment of 1.4 percentage points. Both the high employment growth and the reduction of unemployment reflect the fact that his two-year record coincided with the economy emerging from a recession.

Ford averaged the lowest rate of poverty, 11.7 percent, with a slight decrease in the rate of 0.7 percentage points.

Carter

Carter had a mixed employment record, with a good level of employment growth, at 2.2 percent (third overall and a higher rate than either Reagan or Clinton!). His average unemployment rate was 6.7 percent, ranking eighth out of the 12 presidents, and with a small increase in the unemployment rate of 0.6 percentage point.

It might seem contradictory that Carter's employment growth was good but his unemployment rate was not. Two factors explain this contradiction. First, his increase in unemployment was small, partly because he inherited a still-high unemployment rate from Ford. Second, the participation rate during Carter's administration increased from 62.3 to 63.9 percent. This meant that the economy not only had the burden of having to employ a growing population but also an additional 1.6 percent share of that population. So, while employment growth was good, it was harder to keep unemployment down because the number of people who were looking for work increased even faster.

Carter's average poverty rate was relatively low at 12.5 percent but with an increase of 2.5 percentage points (second most) owing to generally weak economic conditions at the end of his administration.

Reagan

Overall, Reagan's employment record could be characterized as "above average to good." Reagan had the fourth best employment growth rate at 1.9 percent, compared to the period average of 1.4 percent. Reagan's average unemployment rate of 7.2 percent was second highest, but the unemployment rate declined the most during Reagan's administration of any of the 12 administrations—2.3 percentage points.

Again, it may seem contradictory that, although employment increased faster under Carter than under Reagan (2.2 percent vs. 1.9 percent), Reagan nevertheless had a much better record in reducing the unemployment rate than did Carter. The explanation for this apparent contradiction is that (1) Reagan was in office for eight years, twice as long as Carter, which meant that his growth rate of 1.9 percent was applied to eight years, while

Carter's 2.2 percent employment growth rate was applied to only four years; and, much more importantly (2) the total labor force grew faster under Carter (2.3 percent annually) than under Reagan (1.6 percent). Thus, it was a far greater challenge for Carter to keep unemployment down than it was for Reagan.

On poverty, Reagan averaged 13.9 percent, sixth overall and higher than Carter or Clinton. He recorded a 1.2 percentage point reduction in the poverty rate (from 14.0 percent to 12.8 percent). In absolute terms, the number of people in poverty remained essentially the same (31.8 million when he came into office and 31.5 million when he left office). This reduction in the poverty rate is a disappointing outcome given the reasonably good average GDP growth rate and the employment creation during his presidency.

Bush 41

Bush 41 had a weak record on employment, with the third lowest employment growth rate of the 12 presidents, 0.6 percent. He had the fourth highest unemployment rate, 6.7 percent, with a 1.6 percentage point increase in the rate. With respect to poverty, Bush's average was 14.4 percent (eighth overall), with the third highest increase in the rate, 2.3 percentage points.

Clinton

Like Reagan's, Clinton's employment performance was "above average to good." Though 16.7 million net jobs were created during the Clinton administration, his average employment growth rate was 1.6 percent, slightly above the period average of 1.4 percent. Yet it was a strong performance given that Clinton was able to continue growth in employment after Reagan had recorded a 16.9 million net jobs gain. As a result Clinton was able to lower the unemployment rate by a further 2.2 percentage points, the second largest drop of any president since WWII. He also recorded the third lowest unemployment rate, 4.9 percent. The reduction in the unemployment rate was also aided by the fact that the labor force grew at a fairly modest rate of 1.3 percent during his administration (compared with employment growth of 1.6 percent). The slower-growing labor force meant that it was easier to reduce unemployment and keep it low.

Clinton's poverty record was very good. The poverty rate fell substantially under Clinton (3.5 percentage points, second only to Johnson). His average poverty rate was 12.8 percent, fifth overall.

Bush 43

Bush 43 had the worst overall record on employment. First, he had the second lowest growth rate of any president, 0.3 percent. Although his average unemployment rate was a respectable 5.8 percent, only a little above the period average of 5.7 percent, it was only because he inherited an extraordinarily low unemployment rate from Clinton of 4.7 percent. By the end of his administration, the unemployment rate had risen to 9.3 percent, an increase of 4.5 percentage points, the second most of any president.

Bush's average poverty rate was 12.8 percent, but the rate increased by 2.6 percentage points, the most of any president.

Obama

Obama's brief record on employment is weak, although it does not compare to the deterioration that took place under George W. Bush. Obama's two-year record had flat employment growth of 0 percent. Even that flat growth rate represented an improvement over Bush's last year by 4.3 percentage points in the growth rate. Obama also had the highest unemployment rate, at 9.3 percent, with a 0.3 percent decrease in the rate. This record reflects a continuation of the difficulties in extracting the economy from the crisis that hit in full force in 2008 and which proved much deeper and much more expensive than previous recessions. There was good economic news in early 2012 with the unemployment rate continuing to fall to 8.3 percent.

On poverty, because poverty data are reported later in the year than other data (September, instead of February for the other indicators), there is only one year of data for the Obama administration for this analysis. As expected given the weak economy, poverty increased to 15.1 percent, 1 percentage point above the period average and 0.8 percentage points higher than Bush's last year.

CONCLUSIONS AND ISSUES FOR EMPLOYMENT AND POVERTY

Employment

The data show that employment growth during the 66-year period has tended to be steady and not very high, averaging 1.4 percent. The employment successes of Reagan and Clinton are the result of moderate and steady employment growth over sustained periods. These findings should help Americans formulate more realistic and modest expectations for future job creation. Another factor that people need to bear in mind is variations in the growth of the labor force. A factor in Clinton's and Reagan's success is that the labor force grew more slowly after 1981 than it did in the earlier part of the period. This means that the more recent presidents did not have to create jobs as fast in order to keep unemployment low.

There are also a number of factors that have affected a president's ability to create jobs. One is globalization, which has shifted a substantial amount of American manufacturing employment to countries with much lower labor costs. U.S. presidents, Republican and Democrat, have done little or nothing to moderate this outflow of mostly manufacturing jobs. Globalization has proceeded without impediment from the Reagan administration through the Bush 43 administration. As a result, American consumers can buy cheaper imported products, but a larger share of Americans are working at jobs that pay less than the manufacturing jobs that were shifted overseas. Between 1980 and 2010 the percentage of Americans employed in manufacturing dropped by more than half, from 21 percent to 10 percent. There is certainly a technological component to the reduction of manufacturing employment, but it is more the case that products formerly made in the United States are now made overseas.

Another factor making it more difficult to employ Americans is the influx of immigrant labor. Employers, which are often individual American households, enjoy the advantage of immigrant laborers in that they work for less money. But many Americans have to compete with immigrant workers, who are accustomed to earning far less than even poorly paid Americans. The long-run effects of both globalization and loose immigration enforcement have been cheaper goods and services, but also a shift to a smaller middle-class and a larger underclass. In addition, although globalization has led to greater exports from the United States, the United States' $8 trillion in trade deficits has meant that our trading partners have been creating a lot more employment from American consumption than the United States has from foreign consumption. Again, despite rhetoric from presidents of both major parties, little has been done to improve American labor's international competitiveness.

Poverty

With all of the economic growth since the early 1970s, it is surprising that the poverty rate in the United States has never been lower than it was in 1973, 11.1 percent. Despite the growth since that time, along with expanded social programs, no president has been able to get the poverty rate lower than 11.3 percent, which occurred in 2000 under Clinton.

Under most recent presidents, the poverty rates actually went up. Bush 41, Bush 43, and Carter had weak records on poverty. In those cases, weak to bad economies were the main factor. In the case of Reagan, while the poverty rate did fall, it seems that it should have fallen much more. Reagan inherited a rather high poverty rate from Carter at 14.0 percent and, after eight years in office and averaging a GDP growth rate of 3.4 percent, he had reduced the poverty rate only 1.2 percentage points to 12.8 percent. Thus, growth alone does not necessarily reduce the poverty rate significantly, especially if taxation and social policies are not geared to poverty reduction.

Clinton, by contrast, had a much better record on reducing poverty during his administration than did Reagan, with essentially the same GDP growth rate. Clinton inherited a poverty rate of 15.1 percent from Bush 41 and left a rate of 11.7 percent, almost three times the poverty reduction of Reagan. Clinton's successor, Bush 43, managed to hike the poverty rate back up to 14.3 percent. With the economy still in the doldrums, poverty went up further to 15.1 percent during Obama's first year of record.

The stubbornness of the poverty line to remain above 11 percent of the population is related to the impacts on employment of globalization and immigration. These impacts, along with less progressive tax policy, have led not only to higher poverty rates but to a more lopsided income distribution overall.[5] Reducing poverty below the period low of 11.1 percent, which was achieved almost 40 years ago, will require not only sustained economic growth but also a commitment to effective antipoverty programs and a sufficiently progressive tax regime.

NOTES

1. The Gini coefficient and income by quintile are two commonly used indicators of income distribution. The value of the Gini coefficient is 0 for perfectly evenly distributed income and 1 where a single person receives all of the income in a population. Thus, as the Gini coefficient rises towards 1, income is becoming more concentrated in the hands of the wealthy. The Gini coefficient increased under Reagan, Bush 41, and Bush 43 (greater income inequality) and was level during the Clinton administration. Income per quintile of the population simply measures the percentage of income that each fifth of the population earns. Currently, the top 20 percent of the population receives about 50 percent of the total income in the United States. Wealth is much more concentrated, with the top 1 percent owning about 40 percent of all national wealth and the top 20 percent owning about 80 percent of the nation's wealth.

2. The participation rate is the percentage of the noninstitutional population that is part of the labor force. It has risen from 59 percent in the 1960s to over 66 percent in the 2000s. This increase poses a challenge to the economy, and for presidents who come later in the period, to supply jobs for the population.

3. For more information on the Taft-Hartley Act, go to http://www.u-s-history.com/pages/h1667.html.

4. Remember that the participation rate does not include military personnel (the "noninstitutional" population).

5. The top 10 percent of America's most wealthy individuals own 71.5 percent of the nation's wealth, while the bottom 40 percent of Americans have only 12.8 percent of the wealth; Federal Reserve Bulletin 2009, *Changes in U.S. Family Finances from 2004 to-2007: Evidence from the Survey of Consumer Finances.*

SIX

U.S. Exports and International Trade Balance: America's Global Competitiveness

This is the moment when we must build on the wealth that open markets have created, and share its benefits more equitably. Trade has been a cornerstone of our growth and global development. But we will not be able to sustain this growth if it favors the few, and not the many.

—Barack Obama

VALUE AND CRITIQUE OF THE INDICATOR

The trade of goods and services has been a growing part of both the U.S. and world economy since WWII. Trade affects the quality of life of a nation because of its impact on employment, financial sustainability, the environment, and technology transfer. How we conduct our trade policy will therefore influence each of these critical areas. In this chapter, we focus on the purely economic aspects and analyze exports and trade balance as percentages of GDP as indicators of presidential performance. The indicators are published by the U.S. Department of Commerce as part of the NIPA.

Recall the GDP equation from Chapter 1:

$$C + I + G + (X - M) = GDP$$

where X is exports, M is imports, and $(X - M)$ is the trade balance. The premise in our assessment of performance is that it is a good thing to have higher exports because this means more income for U.S. producers and more jobs for American workers. It is also a premise that *it is not a good thing to have a trade deficit* because it means that Americans are consuming more of imports than they are producing of exports and are, therefore, accumulating trade debt. While trade deficits may indicate that Americans are able to consume more products than if trade were balanced, it also means that people in other countries are getting more work and income compared with American workers. We use both indicators because the president should be rewarded for higher exports, but penalized if imports are still higher than exports.

Could Trade Deficits Actually Be a Good Thing?

Economists do not necessarily agree on the "goodness" or "badness" of trade deficits. Some economists view a trade deficit as a positive indication about the U.S. economy because it demonstrates that other countries are willing to accept our dollars and give us real goods in exchange. The willingness to accept our currency shows that they view the United States as a place where they could profitably invest and/or buy U.S. goods in the future. Having other countries hold large amounts of our currency and assets makes us and our trading partners more interdependent because other countries have a stake in the United States' well-being. On the other hand, while accumulating trade debt may make us more interdependent, it does not make us wealthier. It makes other countries wealthier. That is why we count a negative trade balance as a negative for presidential performance.

Distinction between the Trade Deficit and the Federal Budget Deficit

It is also important to understand that the trade deficit differs from the federal deficit in that the trade deficit is a deficit primarily of the U.S. private sector vis-à-vis the private sectors of other countries. However, it is still a debt. The U.S. economy will have to redeem a portion of the debt whenever the foreigner who holds U.S. dollars decides to spend them, so the debt does create a liability for our nation and reduces our flexibility in economic policy.

Composition of Trade and Environmental and Labor Issues

We do not consider the composition of exports and imports in this performance assessment, as that would greatly complicate the analysis and require significant value judgments. Yet the composition of exports and imports is where environmental, labor, and equity issues emerge. For example, if the United States exports raw logs from important biodiversity areas (e.g., "old growth" forests), is that a good thing for America? Probably not, because we lose an irreplaceable environmental asset. We also do not maximize employment because the logs are not processed in the United States. If we drill for oil in sensitive land or sea zones and export it to the world market, are we gaining energy security? Again, probably not, and there is the added cost of damaging the environment. In order to keep the analysis focused on quantitative indicators, we do not consider these aspects, but they are important to the well-being of our nation.

Because the trend indicators for exports and trade balance fluctuate quite a bit, they are not as important in capturing economic performance as are the average export and trade balance shares.

A REVIEW OF ADMINISTRATIONS' INTERNATIONAL TRADE PERFORMANCE—TRUMAN TO OBAMA

The trade data during 1946 through 2011 show at least two major trends:

1. Exports have steadily increased as a percentage of the U.S. economy over time.
2. The trade balance has worsened over time.

These findings show another reason for using both indicators. That is, presidents in the latter part of the period are at a systematic advantage with respect to exports as a share of GDP but are at a systematic disadvantage with respect to the trade balance. So the time biases balance out when both indicators are used.

Nine of the 12 presidents had positive trends in export shares of GDP. In other words, their terminal-year export share of GDP was higher than that of their initial year. The rankings for the two indicators are found in Tables 6.1 and 6.2. Figure 6.1 depicts the U.S. trade balance as a percent of GDP for 1946–2010.

The trade balance was positive from 1946 to 1975 with the exception of small deficits in four of the 30 years. In 1976, the trade balance turned negative and has not been positive since. The higher-percentage deficits eased in the 1990s to below 2 percent of GDP, shot up during 1999 through 2008, and eased a bit at the end of the period.

Truman

Truman recorded an increase in the export share of GDP, of 1.0 percentage points. This increase seems small given that the United States was the

Figure 6.1   U.S. Trade Balance as a Percentage of GDP, 1946–2010

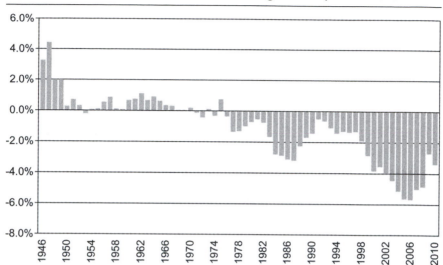

lone standing industrial power at the end of WWII. Although Truman was the first in the time period, he did not have the lowest export share. He recorded a 5.4 percent share, while Eisenhower and Kennedy had lower shares.

Truman had the best overall trade balance, a positive 1.6 percent of GDP, with a negligible improvement of 0.1 percentage point. Again, one might have expected that the United States, emerging strong from WWII, would have achieved a greater improvement in the trade balance. One explanation could be that the nation's trading partners were not yet able to afford U.S. exports and that the United States still needed to help these countries through a rebuilding period after the war.

Beyond these results, Truman had three signature initiatives that had large impacts on foreign trade: the signing of the Bretton Woods Agreement, the establishment of the General Agreement on Tariffs and Trade, and the Marshall Plan.

Bretton Woods System of International Exchange (1945)

At the end of WWII, policymakers created a new structure for the countries of the world in which to trade and invest. The Bretton Woods Agreement was signed on December 27, 1945, in Washington, DC, to create this new structure. The agreement sought to establish a stable international environment through fixed exchange rates,[1] currency convertibility,[2] a gold standard that maintained a gold price of $35 per ounce, and a provision for orderly exchange-rate adjustment in the event of "fundamental disequilibrium"[3] between major currencies. These changes represented a major step forward in stability in international exchange.

General Agreement on Tariffs and Trade (GATT, 1947)

Another major feature of the world trade structure set up after the war was GATT, which established trading rules. GATT consolidated bilateral trade agreements and created a liberalized trade regime based on the principle of nondiscrimination (a privilege extended to one signatory was extended to all); the "most-favored nation clause"; industry protection through tariffs (which were more efficient than quotas); and a mechanism to resolve trade disputes between signatories. A rapid expansion of trade followed, which was a factor in European and Japanese recovery after WWII as well as in sustained growth in the U.S. economy. The Truman administration supported this new free-trade agreement, and since it was signed, the United States has seen a gradually rising volume (exports and imports) of trade.

The Marshall Plan (1948–1952)

The Marshall Plan for European Reconstruction was an innovative and successful effort to rebuild the economies of both allies and enemies from WWII. It was named for President Truman's secretary of state and five-star general from WWII, George C. Marshall. It was the largest foreign aid program ever carried out. The plan cost $13.2 billion during the four-year period. The United Kingdom ($3.2 billion), France ($2.7 billion), West Germany ($1.4 billion), and Holland ($1.1 billion) were the largest recipients. Although much of the infrastructure of these countries was badly damaged, the resources of the Marshall Plan could be used effectively because the "human capital," or education and skill levels, of the populations was high and intact. It was considered a highly successful program and demonstrated that the Truman administration had learned from history: it is better to rebuild your former enemy than to drive it back into the control of an extreme ideology, as had previously happened to Germany after World War I. The Truman administration used its resources to strengthen political alliances, which was essential to projecting the West's power as it competed with Communist Bloc countries.

Eisenhower

Eisenhower had the lowest export share of GDP, 4.7 percent. The share increased modestly, 1.0 percent, during his administration, so his record is considered below average in this instance, even though it was typical of the time to have a low exports share of GDP.

In terms of the trade balance, Eisenhower had a very good record, this time benefiting from being president in the early part of the period. His overall trade balance was the third best of all the presidents at 0.4 percent and a 1.0 percentage point improvement in the balance.

Kennedy

Kennedy's export share was 5.1 percent of GDP, second lowest, with the share increasing only slightly, 0.2 percentage point. He had the second highest positive trade balance, 0.8 percent of GDP, with a slight improvement recorded during his three years.

Trade Expansion Act

Despite his low export share, Kennedy signed an important trade bill, the Trade Expansion Act of 1962. This act gave authority for the United States to participate in the Kennedy Round of Multilateral Trade Negotiations. It also gave the president the authority to negotiate reciprocal tariff reductions of up to 50 percent. This authority expired June 30, 1967. The act also required the Tariff Commission to inform the president of the possible economic effects of reduced tariffs. This Trade Expansion Act replaced the Trade Agreements Act of 1934, as amended.

Johnson

Johnson's average export share was at 5.2 percent of GDP, with no change in the share during his five-year administration. Johnson also averaged a positive trade balance 0.4 percent, but with a deterioration in the balance of 0.9 percentage points.

Nixon

Nixon continued the trend of rising export shares of GDP, averaging 6.8 percent—eighth overall—including the largest increase in the share, 3.2 percentage points. He averaged a slightly positive trade balance, 0.2 percent, for his six-year record, though still with an improvement of 0.8 percentage points.

Ford

Ford's average export share was 8.0 percent despite a trend drop of −0.6 percent. His average trade balance was −0.6 percent, with a significant deterioration of 2.1 percentage points. The results seem somewhat odd given the generally positive economic circumstances during his administration. The Ford administration marked the beginning of negative trade balances, which accelerated under Reagan and have continued to the present day.

Carter

During Carter's administration exports shot up to 9.2 percent of GDP, fifth overall, with an increase in the share of 1.9 percentage points. Carter averaged a negative trade balance close to that of his predecessor of −0.7 percent. It makes sense that the deterioration in the average trade balance was only modest because when economic times are bad in the United States, the nation imports less, which improves the trade balance. Sometimes the dollar is also weaker, which makes our exports cheaper and more attractive to other countries, while imports become more expensive to us. Thus, a weak dollar often improves the U.S. trade balance.

Reagan

Reagan was out of step with the export trend because exports as a percent of GDP actually fell back to 8.0 percent (from Carter's 9.2 percent) and his export share declined by 0.6 percentage point. In terms of the trade balance, Reagan had the third worst trade balance at −2.2 percent, with the third highest worsening of the trade balance, 1.2 percentage points. This result is due to the drop in export share combined with a significant increase in imports. The likely cause of the worsening balance was a strong dollar, driven in part by the high-interest-rate policy at the Fed under Volcker, combined with a lengthy economic recovery that improved Americans' purchasing power with respect to imports, particularly in the first half of the 1980s. An interesting sidelight to the Reagan administration is that, in 1987, the United States became a "debtor nation," meaning that for the first time foreigners owned more U.S. assets than Americans owned of foreign assets. Since that time, America's net debtor status has only deepened from decades of trade deficits as well as budget deficits, an increasing percentage of which is financed by foreigners. Approximately half of the publicly traded U.S. national debt is currently owned by foreigners (see Chapter 8).

Bush 41

The trade indicators for Bush 41 behaved as expected for a slow-growing economy. The slow growth produced lower incomes, and a weaker dollar discouraged import purchases. Exports increased to an annual average of 9.8 percent of GDP for his four-year administration. The trade balance improved compared with that of Reagan but was still negative at −0.8 percent of GDP.

Clinton

Under Clinton, exports surged and averaged 10.8 percent of GDP. At the same time, the trade balance continued in the red, at −2.1 percent on average.

NAFTA

One of the most important policies in accelerating globalization of the U.S. economy was the 1994 ratification of the North American Free Trade Agreement (NAFTA) between the United States, Canada, and Mexico. Since the ratification of that treaty, trade volume has expanded rapidly between the three countries, with the United States experiencing large trade deficits with respect to Canada and Mexico. The U.S. trade deficit with Mexico expanded from +$1.3 billion in 1994 −$64.7 billion in 2008. The U.S. trade deficit with Canada expanded from −$14.0 billion to −$78.3 billion during the same period.

Bush 43

As the economy deteriorated and the dollar continued to weaken, exports as a percent of GDP continued upward and reached the second highest average for a president, 10.8 percent, with a 1.4 percent increase in the share trend.

However, trade deficits reached a new plateau under Bush 43. In the middle of his administration, 2003 to 2008, the trade deficits were 4.5, 5.2, 5.7, 5.8, 5.1 and 5.0 percent of GDP (the six highest trade deficits). The next highest trade deficit for any president in any year was 4.4 percent under Truman for 1947. The next highest after that was 3.8 percent under Clinton in 2000. The average trade balance for Bush 43's eight-year presidency was −4.8 percent of GDP, the worst average of all 12 presidents. The trade balance trend improved by 0.8 percentage point, but that was because the U.S. economy declined rapidly in 2009, and imports fell relative to exports.

Table 6.1   Exports Share of GDP by Presidential Administration

Administration	Share of GDP	Administration	Share Trend
Obama	13.3%	Nixon	3.2%
Bush 43	10.8%	Obama	2.5%
Clinton	10.8%	Carter	1.9%
Bush 41	9.8%	Bush 43	1.4%
Carter	9.2%	Truman	1.0%
Ford	8.0%	Eisenhower	1.0%
Reagan	8.0%	Bush 41	0.7%
Nixon	6.8%	Kennedy	0.2%
Truman	5.4%	Clinton	0.2%
Johnson	5.2%	Johnson	0.0%
Kennedy	5.1%	Reagan	−0.6%
Eisenhower	4.7%	Ford	−0.6%
Period Average (%)	**7.9%**		**N.A.**

Obama

Exports were by far the highest under Obama at 13.3 percent of the GDP, with a 2.5 percentage point increase. The trade balance under Obama was −3.7 percent of GDP, second to last place among presidents, with a 1 percentage point deterioration in the trade balance.

Table 6.2   Trade Balance Share of GDP by Presidential Administration

Administration	Share of GDP	Administration	Share Trend
Truman	1.6%	Eisenhower	1.1%
Kennedy	0.8%	Nixon	0.8%
Eisenhower	0.4%	Bush 43	0.8%
Johnson	0.4%	Carter	0.7%
Nixon	0.2%	Bush 41	0.7%
Ford	−0.6%	Kennedy	0.1%
Carter	−0.7%	Truman	0.1%
Bush 41	−0.8%	Johnson	−0.9%
Clinton	−2.1%	Obama	−1.0%
Reagan	−2.2%	Reagan	−1.2%
Obama	−3.7%	Ford	−2.1%
Bush 43	−4.8%	Clinton	−2.6%
Period Average	**−1.0%**		**N.A.**

CONCLUSIONS AND ISSUES FOR TRADE

What does it say that the more recent presidents have seen an increase in exports as a percentage of GDP but also a persistent and substantial trade deficit? It says that the United States has become more open and is able to export more, but it also suggests that the United States ability to consume foreign products has far exceeded its ability to sell its products abroad. America's growing dependency on imports of petroleum alone accounts for nearly 20 percent of imports.

Trade Deficits and the Dilution of U.S. Ownership

The dollar's status as an international currency has been a tremendous economic advantage for the United States. This value is evidenced by the amount of trade deficits that the outside world is willing to finance. The nonstop trade deficits since 1976 have totaled $8.6 trillion (not adjusted for inflation). Of the $8.6 trillion borrowed since then, $6.0 trillion has been borrowed just since 2002 (eight years of G. W. Bush and two years of Obama). As stated earlier, some economists take the position that it is a good thing that we have these deficits because it shows that other countries view our currency as desirable. But it also means that other countries have accumulated claims on our country. These countries earn U.S. dollars from American consumers to buy American land and own American assets. It may be good that other countries like what U.S. currency can buy, but it is not good that Americans own less of their own country.

Incurring debt as a government, whether it is federal debt or trade debt, is not the same as an individual taking on debt. Certainly, individuals may have the capacity to incur long-term debt as they do when they borrow for a mortgage on their home. But the United States has not taken just a one-time loan; it has borrowed each and every year since 1976, and the debt has continued to climb. Even the United States' creditworthiness has to have a limit, just as other countries have a limit to their capacity to finance U.S. trade deficits. It is not clear how much more capacity the world has for financing the United States' excess consumption of imports, but we do know that $8.6 trillion of that capacity has been used up. That would not appear to be either a sustainable or an economically healthy position for the United States. While globalization and free-trade agreements have benefited U.S. consumers and some exporters, they have also left the nation with high trade debt, lower manufacturing employment and stagnating wages.

Causes of the Trade Deficits

The acceleration of the trade deficits in the early 1980s coincided with several other major economic trends. The surge of the stock market, the increase in the real interest rate, the disappearance of significant inflation, and the increase in budget deficits have all happened since the early 1980s.[4] All of these trends began early in the Reagan administration.

The cause of the trade deficits can be linked to the key policies at that time, including the Fed's anti-inflation policies, Reagan's tax cuts, and deregulation. The Fed policy was to raise interest rates in an effort to defeat inflation, which did work. On the other side, with the mounting trade deficits, a lot of cash flowed into foreign hands. Both the stock market and the real estate market could absorb this foreign cash. In addition, Reagan's tax cuts put more cash in Americans' hands, which could also flow into the real estate and stock markets. Foreign-owned dollars also bought large amounts of U.S. debt securities, which were more plentiful because of the massive federal budget deficits. We have seen a surge in foreign ownership of U.S. debt not only in absolute terms but also as a share of total U.S. debt. It is clear that running trade deficits dilutes American ownership.

NOTES

1. Fixed exchange rates mean that the exchange rate between two currencies does not fluctuate continuously; it changes only if one of the countries decides to change the value, presumably because supply and demand dictate a change in the price.

2. Currency convertibility means simply that one currency, e.g., British pounds, could buy another currency, e.g., U.S. dollars. Developing countries, for example, could not use their own national currency to buy currencies of industrial countries. Hence, their currencies were not convertible.

3. If the fixed exchange rate is not changed in response to changes in supply and demand, then disequilibrium occurs that requires a change in the fixed exchange rate.

4. The large trade deficits began in the 1980s, though small ones had begun in 1976.

PART II

Fiscal Economy: The President's Influence on the Public Sector

Part II is about economic events, policies, and results in the public sector. Public-sector economic activities focus on the types of things that the private sector is not able to do but that are necessary for a modern country, such as providing the national currency, national defense, social safety nets, environmental protection, regulating commerce, and making and enforcing laws. The president has considerable influence over raising revenue to pay for these and other activities. Because he prepares the federal budget, he also has influence on the allocation of revenue to specific programs. Chapter 7 leads off Part II with a discussion of the size and growth of the federal budget. In Chapter 8 we look at how well the president balances what he spends with the amount of revenue he is able to raise for the federal budget. Part II concludes with Chapter 9 on the levels of taxation for each administration, taking the position that lower taxes are better than higher taxes.

We also look at the composition of expenditures and taxes in order to provide context to presidential performance. However, we do not incorporate a president's choices in the composition of expenditures and taxes into his quantitative record.

SEVEN

Federal Budget Growth and Share of the Economy: Maintaining a Public/Private Balance

My problem lies in reconciling my gross habits with my net income.

—Errol Flynn

VALUE AND CRITIQUE OF THE INDICATOR

"All things being equal," as economists often say, it is better to have a smaller budget because it suggests greater efficiency of the government. This chapter assesses presidential administrations in terms of their budget growth and budget share of GDP, including how much a president raised or lowered the rates and shares. We assume that a president has done a better job if he has kept the budget growth rate and share lower, even if there might be good reasons for a rapid increase in government expenditures. In other words, this chapter assesses how well a president performed by requiring fewer resources for the public sector. While the effectiveness of the programs that the president chose to implement or the wars he chose to wage are part of the narrative of presidential performance, these are not considerations in his quantitative performance score.

The federal budget growth and federal budget share of the economy actually tell two different parts of the budget story. If the budget grew fast, that is counted as a negative for the president. A budget does not have to grow fast unless there is, for example, a recession, in which case economic history tells us government spending is the right prescription. An increase in the federal budget as a share of GDP is also considered a negative because it is better if the budget is a smaller share of the economy.

The reasoning is not that the government is bad but that it should do as much as possible with a limited amount of resources.

Before going further with the discussion of the federal budget, we need to address a couple of terminology issues that are important when discussing the funding of Social Security later on. Federal budget items are divided into on- and off-budget categories.[1] The Department of Defense (DOD) budget, the Health and Human Services (HHS) budget, discretionary spending—essentially all of the departments are "on budget." Social Security, for example, is "off" budget. This distinction is important because these two programs have their own separate funding source, which is the payroll taxes that the employee and employer pay. The budget we refer to in this chapter includes the *combined on- and off-budget categories*. That is typically what the news media refers to as "the budget." When we discuss the debt and the deficits, we will also be discussing the combined on- and off-budget deficits. The same is true for taxation; we include all taxes that fund both on- and off-budget items.

The official data are from the Office of Management and Budget (OMB), which falls under the Office of the President.

REVIEW OF ADMINISTRATIONS' PERFORMANCES ON THE FEDERAL BUDGET—TRUMAN TO OBAMA

The first four presidents in the period (Truman, Eisenhower, Kennedy, and Johnson, 1946–1969) had successively higher budget shares of GDP, increasing from 16.9 to 18.9 percent of GDP. Clinton breaks the string and has the next lowest share at 19.4 percent. The trend of successively higher budget shares resumes briefly with Nixon. Obama, coming at the end of the period, has the highest federal expenditure share at 24.1 percent of GDP. Between Nixon and Obama, the presidents' shares more or less also increase: the more recent the president, the higher the share, with the exception of Bush 43, who had a lower average budget share. It makes sense that the earlier presidents would have lower shares of GDP because fewer demands were placed on government. Later in the period, the aging of Americans meant that Social Security and Medicare would drive up federal expenditures and become larger parts of the budget over time.

As discussed under Truman below, the transition from a wartime to a peacetime budget caused high volatility for the federal budget. The federal budget did not fully adjust to the demobilization from WWII until 1947, though it was still a rapid adjustment. In this book we often use the indicator average for the entire 1946 to 2011 period as a benchmark for

Figure 7.1 Federal Budget as a Percentage of GDP, 1946–2011

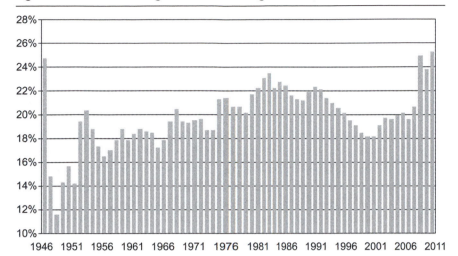

individual presidential performances. In the case of the federal budget growth rate, the choice of the initial year makes a bigger difference to the period average than for any other indicator.

Using the year of 1946 as the initial year to measure budget growth over the period, rather than the more "normal" year of 1947, reduces the average federal budget growth rate by one full percentage point over the 1946 to 2011 period to 2.5 percent, compared with 3.5 percent if 1947 The reason is that the federal budget in 1946 was still coming down from the astronomical WWII highs. In 1946, the federal budget was 24.8 percent of GDP; by 1947, it settled at 14.8 percent of GDP.

During 1991 through 2001, the federal budget outlays declined each and every year from 22.3 percent of GDP in 1991 to 18.2 percent in 2001. The economy was also good at generating revenue in the latter part of that period so that the budget achieved surpluses during 1998 through 2001 under Clinton. By 2002 the economy entered another period of increasing and high deficits. Tables 7.1 and 7.2 rank presidential administrations according to their average budget shares of GDP and growth rates, respectively. Figure 7.1 depicts federal budget outlays as a percent of GDP.

Truman

Truman's case is unusual because of the extreme decrease in the budget share of GDP during the early years of his administration. The demobilization from WWII had a profound effect on the government budget. In 1945, the wartime federal budget was 41.9 percent of GDP, but the next year it fell to 24.8 percent, a drop of 17.1 percentage points! The next year, 1947, the budget share fell a further 10.0 percentage points to a more representative peacetime level of 14.8 percent.

Because of this volatility related to wartime expenditures, Truman's budget performance story is a bit tricky to tell. If we include the year 1946, before the government had fully demobilized, Truman's budget share is 16.9 percent (the lowest and, therefore, best of the 12 presidents), with a 21.5 percentage point *reduction* in the share (by far the lowest and also the best record). If we measure his record beginning in 1947, Truman would have an even lower budget-to-GDP ratio at 15.8 percent but with a large *increase* in the share of 5.6 percentage points (second highest among the presidents). The 15.8 percent share of GDP is really more representative of the very low shares he recorded during his administration (four years of which were below 15 percent of GDP). However, we need to be consistent with our private-sector indicators such as GDP. If Truman's record is punished when GDP falls because of the sudden and massive drop in government spending, then he should receive credit for the reduction in government spending. Thus, we measure his record beginning in 1946.

Therefore, his average budget share was 16.9 percent, with a 21.5 percent reduction in the share. Truman's federal budget growth rate was −5.2 percent, which was the lowest of the 12 presidents and the best record.

Despite his relatively low budget share and growth rate, Truman's administration had a surge in spending in 1952 and 1953 because of expenditures related to the Korean War. Expenditures increased to 19.4 percent and 20.4 percent of GDP, respectively. In 1952, the budget growth rate was 49.6 percent, by far the highest single-year budget growth rate during the period. The next highest budget growth rate was 17.4 percent (in 2009).

Eisenhower

Eisenhower was not a big spender. He had the second lowest budget share of GDP at 17.8 percent, with a −2.0 percentage point reduction in the share. His federal budget growth rate was −0.5 percent, second lowest. Note that Eisenhower took power just as the Korean War was ending at a budget spending peak (20.4 percent of GDP, a rate not exceeded until 1968). Thus, he was in a good position to reduce federal spending.

Kennedy

Kennedy, in keeping with the trend, had the third lowest budget share of GDP, 18.6 percent, with a negligible 0.1 percentage point increase in the share. His budget growth rate was substantial, at 4.5 percent, which was third highest, compared to a period average of 2.5 percent. Despite this high budget growth rate, the budget share did not increase very much because GDP was also growing rapidly.

Johnson

Johnson's budget share edged up to an average of 18.9 percent, with a 0.9 percent increase in the share. Johnson's budget growth rate was the highest among presidents, averaging 5.5 percent in real terms for his five-year presidency, more than double the average budget growth for the period. Like the case of Kennedy, his budget share did not increase much because the GDP growth rate during his presidency was high (4.6 percent). The rapid spending increase was mainly because of Vietnam War expenditures but also because of the new Medicare and Medicaid programs. Medicare expenditures went from 0 percent of the budget in 1966 to 3.2 percent in 1970. In 2011, Medicare alone accounted for 12.9 percent of the federal budget.

Nixon

With Vietnam War expenditures continuing and Medicare and Medicaid expenditures doubling in absolute terms, Nixon's budget share moved up further to 19.5 percent (sixth highest) with a more substantial increase in the budget share of 1.9 percentage points (second highest). Nixon's budget growth rate was 2.7 percent (in a three-way tie for sixth).

Ford

Ford's average budget share crept yet higher, reaching 21.1 percent, even with a 0.6 percentage point reduction from Nixon's last year (which was a relatively high 21.4 percent of GDP). Ford's budget growth rate was the same as Nixon's at 2.7 percent.

Carter

Carter's average budget share was very slightly higher than Ford's at 21.1 percent (carried to more decimal places) but with a 1.5 percentage point increase in the share. Carter had a rather high average budget growth rate at 3.9 percent (fourth highest).

Reagan

Somewhat surprisingly, Ronald Reagan had the second highest federal budget share of GDP, 22.4 percent, with a modest reduction in the budget share, from endpoint to endpoint, of 1.0 percentage point. There does not seem to be any real justification for such a high budget share; there was no war, and the recession was only during the first year of his record (1982). There was however a substantial amount of spending on the military, which increased from 22.7 percent of the budget in 1980 to 28.1 percent in 1987 before settling back to 26.5 percent of the budget in 1989. Under Reagan, the budget grew 2.5 percent annually, equal to the average growth rate for the period and ranking roughly in the middle of the 12 presidents (sixth lowest).

A lot was going on with the budget during the Reagan administration. In addition to major changes in income taxes, there were reforms to Social Security. These reforms had been recommended in 1983 by a blue-ribbon commission chaired by future Federal Reserve chairman Alan Greenspan.[2] At the time, and for a long time thereafter, policymakers seemed convinced that these reforms had saved the megaprogram in both the short and the long run. As the reform is examined more closely, and with more than 25 years of results, however, it is clear that changes to the programs did more to misallocate tax revenues than to put the program on a sound footing. The effect of the Social Security reforms on Reagan's budget performance, however, was a positive one. The Social Security surpluses were lumped in with the other government revenues so that Reagan's deficits seemed smaller than they actually were (Chapter 8).[3]

Bush 41

Bush 41's budget share averaged a little lower than Reagan's at 21.9 percent, with a small increase in the share of 0.2 percentage points. Bush's average budget growth rate was fifth lowest at 1.7 percent. Part of the explanation for the lower budget growth was the Gramm-Rudman-Hollings[4] debt legislation, which forced budget cuts to meet deficit targets.

Clinton

Clinton had the fifth lowest budget share, 19.4 percent, and he lowered the budget expenditure share of GDP the second most among the 12 presidents, by 3.2 percentage points. Clinton's average budget growth rate was 1.5 percent, the third lowest. Between his tax increases, economic growth, and moderate spending habits, it easy to understand why there was such a large positive fiscal turnaround during his administration.

Bush 43

Bush 43's budget growth rate was 5.3 percent, second highest only to Johnson, and without Johnson's economic growth to pay for the higher budgets. Yet Bush 43's average budget share over his eight years in office was only 20.5 percent of GDP, about the middle of the rankings. The reason why Bush had a high budget growth rate but a moderate share is because he inherited from Clinton a low budget share of 18.2 percent of GDP in 2001 and left Obama the highest budget share of the period, 25.2 percent of GDP, in 2009.

Remember that the federal budget goes by a fiscal year (October 1 to September 30), so that, even without any lag, Bush 43's fiscal year 2009 budget, including TARP expenditures, were underway nearly four months before Obama took office.

Obama

Despite weak indicators in key areas, Obama does not fare as badly with the budget indicators as one might think. Compared with Bush 43's last year, the budget share dropped 1.1 percentage points by 2011. As expected in this severe economic downturn, Obama had the highest budget share overall at 24.1 percent. With respect to budget growth, Obama averaged -0.3 percent, third lowest overall. The public sector spending level was essentially maintained, although one might question why public-sector spending should not increase at a faster rate given that the unemployment rate was stuck at 9 percent of the workforce for much of 2011. The year 2009 was a historically bad year for the economy (Bush 43's last year of record), which sometimes creates odd results, at least early on in Obama's record.

CONCLUSIONS AND ISSUES FOR FEDERAL BUDGET SHARE AND GROWTH

Composition of Federal Budget Expenditures

We have examined the amount of what the presidents have spent. Now we take a brief look at how the presidents have spent the federal revenues (and borrowings). While we do not include the composition of expenditures

Table 7.1   Federal Budget Shares of GDP by Presidential Administration

Administration	Budget Share of GDP	Administration	Change in Share
Truman	16.9%	Truman	−21.5%
Eisenhower	17.8%	Clinton	−3.2%
Kennedy	18.6%	Eisenhower	−2.0%
Johnson	18.9%	Obama	−1.1%
Clinton	19.4%	Reagan	−1.0%
Nixon	19.5%	Ford	−0.6%
Bush 43	20.5%	Kennedy	0.1%
Ford	21.1%	Bush 41	0.2%
Carter	21.1%	Johnson	0.9%
Bush 41	21.9%	Carter	1.5%
Reagan	22.4%	Nixon	1.9%
Obama	24.1%	Bush 43	7.0%
Period Average (1946–2010)	**19.8%**		**N.A.**

in the performance assessment, it is interesting to see how the president (and Congress) expressed their priorities and how they reacted to the circumstances they faced through their actual spending.

Table 7.2   Federal Budget Growth Rates by Presidential Administration

Administration	Federal Budget Growth Rate	Administration	Trend
Truman	−5.2%	Obama	−14.5%
Eisenhower	−0.5%	Ford	−10.2%
Obama	−0.3%	Johnson	−8.4%
Clinton	1.5%	Bush 41	−4.3%
Bush 41	1.7%	Truman	−2.3%
Reagan	2.5%	Eisenhower	−1.0%
Ford	2.7%	Reagan	0.1%
Nixon	2.7%	Carter	1.7%
Carter	3.8%	Kennedy	2.0%
Kennedy	4.5%	Clinton	2.2%
Bush 43	5.3%	Nixon	15.2%
Johnson	5.5%	Bush 43	15.8%
Period Average	**2.5%**		**N.A.**

The OMB has six main categories of budget expenditure. These categories and their subcategories are:

- **Defense:** no subcategories
- **Human resources:** Social Security, Medicare, income security, health, education, training, employment and social services, and veterans' benefits and services
- **Physical resources:** transportation, commerce and housing credits, natural resources and the environment, community and regional development, and energy
- **Net interest on the debt (on- and off-budget):** no subcategories
- **Other functions:** agriculture, international affairs (including foreign aid), general science, space and technology, administration of justice, and general government
- **Undistributed offsetting receipts:** receipts collected by the government that are not attributed to any functional category (e.g., receipts from employee retirement contributions, royalties from oil leases, and proceeds from the sale of federal assets.

The total of all categories is 100 percent of the federal budget.

The Fluctuation of Defense Shares and the Shift to Human Resources

Figure 7.2 covers the entire 1946 to 2011 time period and shows some interesting shifts in expenditure. The largest shift we see is from defense spending to human resources. Defense expenditures as a share of the budget quickly subsided after WWII, dropping from 89.5 percent of the budget in 1945 to 30.6 percent of the budget by 1948. By 1952, the defense share was back up to 68.1 percent of the budget because of the Korean War. Spending on defense declined steadily to 42.8 percent of the budget until the Vietnam War. The defense share of the budget reached a Vietnam War maximum of 46.0 percent in 1968 at the peak of the war. In 2011 defense spending was 20.1 percent of the budget, a relatively high rate compared with the 1990s. Expenditures on human resources followed a much steadier trend and increased their share of the budget from 28.4 percent in 1960 to 65.7 percent in 2011.

Interest on the National Debt

The interest on the national debt is important because of its potential to gobble up budget share and displace valuable programs. This category

Figure 7.2   Composition of Federal Outlays, 1946–2011

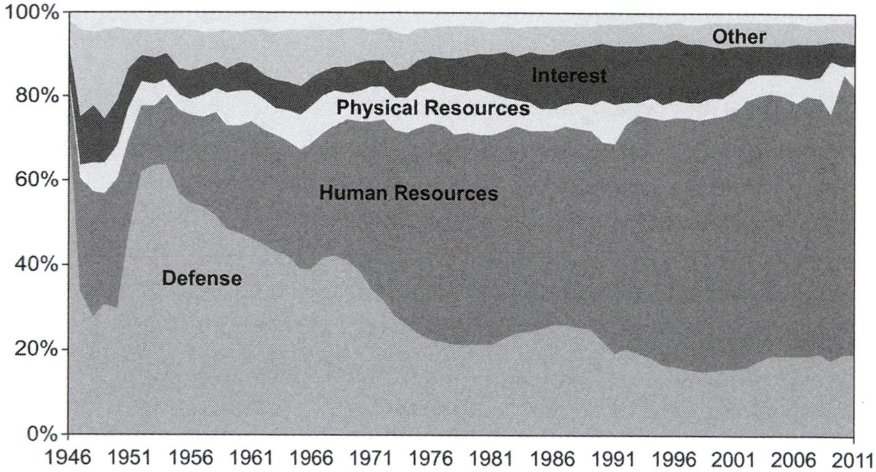

does not behave quite the way one might expect, as it has generally reduced its share in recent years. However, interest on the debt will likely be a much more significant category in the coming years. The reason is not only the mounting national debt but also the risk that interest rates will not stay at the near-zero level for the long term. If interest rates do spike, then the government will need a lot more resources to service its debt (see Chapter 8 for further discussion). The risk of higher interest payments was increased under Bush 43 because his administration shortened the term structure of the national debt, which means that the national debt needs to be refinanced, or "turned over," more frequently. It was good that the shorter-term structure took advantage of very low short-term interest rates, but it was also a short-sighted policy that exposes the government to higher debt servicing costs in the future.

The 2008 Financial Crisis: Effects on Budget Composition

Table 7.3 focuses on the 2008 crisis. Three of the categories of expenditure were fairly steady through the pre- and postcrisis periods: national defense, other functions, and undistributed offsetting receipts. Net interest on the debt actually declined, and that might seem unusual given the mounting debt. However, low interest rates, combined with the shorter-term structure, have driven down the cost of servicing (paying the interest on) the national debt. The yield on treasury securities that are of three-year maturity is barely half of 1 percent.

Table 7.3 Federal Budget Shifts Pre- and Post—2008 Financial Crisis

	National Defense	Human Resources	Physical Resources	Net Interest	Other Functions	Undistributed Offsetting Receipts	Total Federal Outlays
2005	20.0	64.2	5.3	7.4	5.7	−2.6	100
2006	19.7	63.0	6.2	8.5	5.2	−2.6	100
2007	20.2	64.4	4.9	8.7	4.8	−3.0	100
2008	20.7	63.6	5.4	8.5	4.8	−2.9	100
2009	18.8	61.3	12.6	5.3	4.6	−2.6	100
2010	20.1	69.0	2.6	5.7	5.0	−2.4	100
2011	19.6	67.0	4.5	6.4	4.9	−2.4	100

The two categories that fluctuated the most were human resources and physical resources. Human resources actually went down in 2009, which is unusual given the level of need for unemployment compensation and because of the lack of jobs during and after the crisis caused more people to take Social Security benefits earlier in life. In 2010, however, the human resources share increased to 69.0 percent, the highest level ever, before settling to 67.0 percent in 2011. On the physical resources side, the percentage for physical resources jumped to 12.6 percent (the period high) in 2009 but then fell to 2.6 percent of the budget (the period low) by 2010 before moderating to 4.5 percent.

How High Should the Federal Government Share of GDP Be?

What sort of guidelines and lessons can we gain from historical budget trends? For example, what would a healthy budget growth rate be, and what would an appropriate budget share of GDP be given the realistic demands on the federal government?

In terms of share of the economy, we have to take into account the inevitable, continually increasing demands on the budget for health care and Social Security because of the aging of the population. We need to do a better job of protecting the environment and invest in a transition out of resource-intensive economic growth. We are underinvested in infrastructure and in transforming the energy sector. The responsibility of the federal government is not necessarily to incur all of these costs, but it must at least set an incentive structure for the private sector to pursue these national priorities.

It is unlikely that expenditures could or should fall below pre-2008 crisis levels, and they will likely have to increase as a share of GDP. At the precrisis level, the budget share of GDP was a little over 20 percent. Clinton averaged 19.4 percent. Once the economic crisis is fully resolved and the bad loans and derivatives are bled out of the system, the expectation for a budget share of GDP should probably be between 20 and 21 percent with an additional 1 to 2 percentage points because of investment priorities mentioned above, for a total of 21 to 23 percent. This range again depends on the great simplifying assumption "all other things being equal," that is, no further socioeconomic disruptions, wars, or other such events. With the high level of discord in the U.S. political system, that assumption may be more unrealistic than ever.

As far as budget growth rates go, it depends a great deal on how the broader economy is growing. Fast economic growth accommodates additional budget expenditures without increasing the budget share of GDP.

But there has to be some longer-term, "conservative"[5] restraint in launching new federal expenditures. These expenditures can become long-term commitments that will increase the debt when the GDP growth rate falls in the short and the medium term. We will then be left with an increase in the deficit and the debt. When increasing government spending, we need to consider whether the increase represents a temporary or long-term commitment. Although strong GDP growth covered President Johnson's free spending, his spending commitments proceeded into perpetuity. The programs he initiated may well have been worth it, but policymakers must have the ability to understand that such programs require regularly adjusting funding plans to reflect financial and demographic realities and the political will to implement those adjustments.

NOTES

1. The OMB in its *Analytical Perspectives 2011* explains "off-budget" as follows: "Off-budget refers to transactions of the Federal Government that Congress [has] designated . . . by statute as 'off-budget.' Currently, transactions of the Social Security trust fund and the Postal Service fund are the only sets of transactions that are so designated. The term is sometimes used more broadly to refer to the transactions of private enterprises that were established and sponsored by the Government, most especially 'Government sponsored enterprises' such as the Federal Home Loan Banks. (Cf. budget totals)." The on-budget and off-budget amounts are added together to derive the totals for the federal government. These are sometimes referred to as the "unified" or "consolidated" budget totals. For more information, go to http://www.whitehouse.gov/sites/default/files/omb/budget/fy2012/assets/concepts.pdf.

2. Report of the National Commission on Social Security Reform, January 1983. The report is available at http://www.ssa.gov/history/reports/gspan2.html.

3. The Social Security program accounted for $748 billion of expenditures in 2011, or 19.6 percent of the total federal budget. In 1946, Social Security was only $358 million, or 0.84 percent of the budget. While Social Security has delivered immense benefits to older Americans, it has also become an immense challenge for more recent presidents to fund. Today the program is in financial trouble.

During Carter's administration in 1977, the program encountered cash flow problems, and temporary remedies were implemented to keep payments flowing to beneficiaries. By 1982, cash flow problems resurfaced and it was time to take longer-term measures. President Reagan pointed

Alan Greenspan to chair the National Commission on Social Security Reform to recommend measures to restore the solvency of the Social Security program. The commission recommended payroll tax increases and benefits cuts (e.g., a gradual increase in the retirement age), but no provision was made to protect the surpluses of the program that emerged in 1984 and continued through 2008. And so, by law, these surpluses were spent every year along with other federal revenues. During the 25 years of surpluses, a trust fund of $2.6 trillion (end of 2010), on paper, was accumulated. If the Trust Fund had been protected and could have been drawn, then Social Security would have had a 20- to 25-year cushion as greater numbers of baby-boomers retired.

For Social Security recipients to tap money from the Trust Fund, the U.S. Treasury must now generate new funds to pay its I.O.U.s to the Trust Fund by increasing taxes, borrowing or printing money. Therefore, the Trust Fund does not provide a cushion at all. And because the Social Security program went into deficit in 2009, the program is already in serious trouble without a further payroll tax increase and benefit cuts.

The Democrats, for their part, have systematically understated the financial problems of Social Security (and Medicare). In the recent past and currently, some Democrats will still claim that Social Security is solvent until 2035 (or whatever year the actuaries of Social Security currently estimate). The basis for this claim is the belief that the several-trillion-dollar balance in the Social Security Trust Fund is intact.

In the end the real effect of the 1983 Greenspan Commission reforms was to tax wage earners too much while failing to protect the program on which these same wage earners would later depend. The real beneficiaries of the policy to generate Social Security surpluses were the high-income individuals. Why? Because the increased budget revenue from Social Security taxes meant that there was less pressure to increase taxes on wealthier people. Thus, the Social Security reforms by the Greenspan Commission temporarily solved Social Security's cash flow problem but created an illusion of security in the out-years (2017–2035) while effectively transferring several trillion dollars of wealth from the poor and the middle class to the wealthy.

4. Senators Ernest Hollings, Warren Rudman, and Phil Gramm sponsored the Balanced Budget and Emergency Deficit Control Act of 1985, which was signed by President Reagan. This legislation was in response to the historically high budget deficits under Reagan. The Act required deficits to fall within certain limits or automatic spending cuts would be triggered.

5. "Conservative," here, is in the sense of good conservative risk management, not in the political sense.

EIGHT

Federal Budget Deficits and the National Debt: A President's Fiscal Responsibility

> I am not worried about the deficit. It is big enough to take care of itself.
> —President Ronald W. Reagan

VALUE AND CRITIQUE OF THE INDICATORS

The president does have a fair degree of control over federal budget deficits and the national debt, indirectly through his impact on the economy and more directly through decisions about taxing and spending. In the absence of war, recession, and other urgent spending needs, deficits and the national debt should be as low as possible. This chapter rates presidents according to the deficits and debts that they averaged and by how much they raised or lowered the deficits and debts.

When the government needs resources for a war for the survival of the country, or when there is a recession and the public sector has to compensate for the downturn in the private sector, deficits *should increase*. So, as we asked in the previous chapter, why penalize a president for increasing the deficit at all times and in all cases? *What about the context?*

We already capture recession and recovery through a number of other indicators. The way it plays out in the president's record is that if the economy is growing but deficits are still high and debt is increasing, then the president is properly penalized because spending is too high or taxes are too low. However, when there is a recession, the president, if he is a good Keynesian who has learned the lessons from the Great Depression in the 1930s (Annex 2), will increase the deficit to stimulate the economy with public resources. During that time, the president gets a double penalty, one on the general economy side (the recession) and one on the public-sector side (budget deficits). This double penalty is probably fair because if the economy has not recovered but deficits continue to be high, then the United States is slipping into a weaker economic position. The capacity of the federal government to take on more debt to fight the recession is diminishing. So the president is compelled to do whatever he can to get the economy growing as soon as possible and to lower the unemployment rate and, subsequently, the deficits.

The specific indicators used here are (1) federal budget deficits as a percentage of the total federal budget and (2) the total national debt (both public and privately held) as a percentage of GDP. The deficit as a percentage of the total budget indicates to what degree revenues are out of line with expenditures. The average deficit for the 1946 to 2011 period was a fairly significant 9.1 percent of the total budget. This means that, in any given year, the government spent 9.1 percent more than it took in revenue.

The national debt indicator includes all U.S. government debt owed to private individuals and private institutions, both domestic and foreign, and intragovernmental debt, which is debt owed to government trust funds, such as Social Security and Medicare. This intragovernmental debt is an important component of the debt because most of it is a liability (approximately $2.6 trillion at the end of 2011) to future Social Security beneficiaries that was incurred from spending the Social Security Trust Fund.

The national debt is measured as a percentage of GDP rather than in absolute terms. The debt as a percentage of GDP is a better measure of the debt because it captures better the overall economy's ability to "carry" that level of debt. For example, the debt of $271.0 billion in 1946 was very burdensome to the U.S. economy in that year because the GDP was only $222.2 billion, and thus the debt was 121.7 percent of GDP. In today's economy, with a GDP of $15.1 trillion, that $271.0 billion debt would be only 1.7 percent of GDP. The official debt and the deficit indicators are from the U.S. Office of Management and Budget.

REVIEW OF ADMINISTRATIONS' PERFORMANCES ON FEDERAL DEFICITS AND DEBT—TRUMAN TO OBAMA

Deficits

Deficits are a constant concern of presidents. Presidents know that they may be held accountable if too many budgets run deficits. Current

Figure 8.1   Federal Budget Deficits as a Percentage of Total Budget, 1946–2011

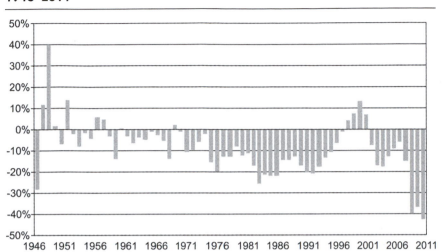

deficits are the highest they have been as a share of the budget since WWII, as Figure 8.1 shows. These deficits are a direct result of the costs of two wars and prolonged military occupations, tax cuts initiated in 2001, and of having to repair the damage to the financial sector from the collapse of the real estate and derivatives bubbles in 2008. The real accountability for the economy occurs when the debt accumulates and the cost of servicing the debt, which depends on both interest rates and the level of debt, causes a drag on the budget and constricts spending choices. At that point, cherished government programs are cut or eliminated altogether. The United States is going to be feeling this pain in the coming years when interest rates rise and debt levels remain high. Tables 8.1 and 8.2 provide the presidential rankings for deficits and debts, respectively.

After WWII, deficits tended to be small, and there were even some surpluses under Truman and Eisenhower. Deficits really did not take off until the Reagan administration and continued through Bush 41, a 12-year period of high deficits. Under Clinton, deficits diminished and surpluses emerged in the last four years of his record for the unified (on- and off-) budget. Under Bush 43 deficits reached record levels again. When the economy went into severe recession in 2008 under Bush 43, the deficits exploded and continued into the Obama administration.

Figure 8.2   National Debt as a Percentage of GDP, 1946–2011

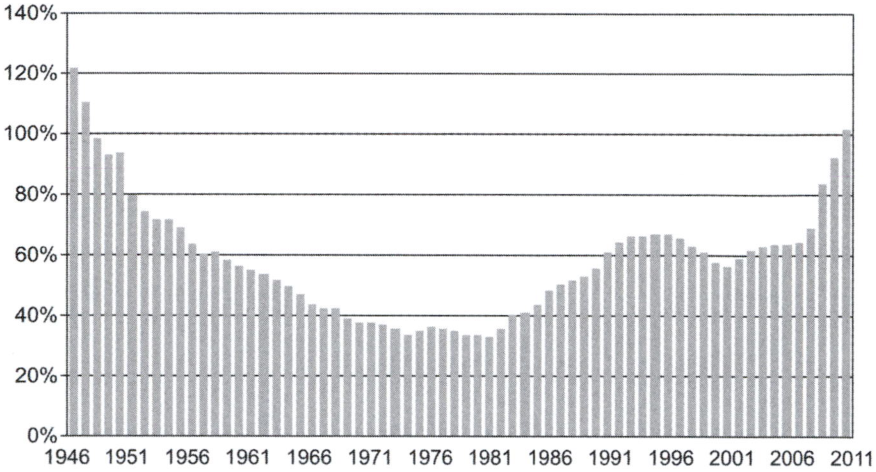

Debt

Figure 8.2 shows the trend in the U.S. national debt for 1946 through 2011. The reduction of the debt as a percentage of GDP during 1946 through 1981, Truman through Carter, was a great accomplishment. This debt reduction was achieved despite deficits occurring in most years. There was really no extraordinary policy measure; the key was to keep deficits small and achieve occasional surpluses while the economy continued to grow. For example, Kennedy ran deficits for all three years of his record, but the national debt as a percent of GDP fell from 55.2 percent to 49.3 percent.

The result of this steady fiscal responsibility was to pay down the debt from 121.7 percent of GDP in 1946 to only 32.5 percent by 1981. Clearly, with today's massive deficits, there will be the need once again for another long-term pay-down. As the United States potentially faces a bleak fiscal future, there is at least some reassurance that Americans have faced enormous debt in the past and conquered it. The negative side is that we are not in as good a position as we were in the 1940s, 1950s, and 1960s to pay down the debt because it will be more difficult to sustain growth and keep deficits low.

Truman

Truman's record begins in 1946, which is a demobilization year for WWII. That means that the deficit and debt were extremely high, so both of these indicators count against Truman. It is fair that the high deficit should be counted on Truman's record because the U.S. economy was still being stimulated by this deficit.[1] However, Truman's record is well rewarded for the drop in both the deficit and the debt that occurred during his administration.

On the deficit, Truman had the best record of the 12 presidents and was the only president who averaged a surplus on the budget, 2.4 percent of the total federal budget. He improved the deficit share of the budget by 42.8 percentage points, by far the most among the 12 presidents.

Truman also had the best record with respect to the national debt. While he had the second highest average debt as a percentage of GDP, 92.9 percent, the reduction was a massive 46.1 percentage points from 117.5 percent in 1945 to 71.4 percent in 1953. Basically, the economy grew relative to the debt, and the WWII debt level was brought nearly under control within a single presidential administration. This performance was remarkable, particularly considering that his administration incurred the costs of the Korean War (1951–1953). In contrast, the wars in Afghanistan (2001–present) and Iraq (2003–2011) coincided with a rapid increase in the national debt, from 56.4 percent of GDP in 2001 to 85.2 percent of GDP in 2009.

Eisenhower

Eisenhower had the third best record on the deficit, with a deficit averaging −2.0 percent of the budget and a 5.1 percentage point reduction in the deficit share of the budget. On the national debt, Eisenhower also had a strong record and continued the task of paying off WWII costs, averaging a debt level of 62.0 percent of GDP. More importantly, he lowered the debt share by 16.2 percentage points, which was second only to Truman's debt reduction.

Kennedy

Kennedy's average deficit was −5.3 percent, compared with a period average deficit of -9.0 percent, with a 1.6 percentage point deterioration in the deficit share of the budget. Still, Kennedy continued the trend of shrinking the debt relative to GDP, with an average of 51.5 percent of GDP and a 5.9 percentage point reduction (fifth overall).

Johnson

Johnson's average deficit was −4.4 percent of the budget, with a 6.8 percentage point improvement in the deficit share of the budget. He had the fourth best overall record with respect to the deficit.

The national debt continued to decline as a percentage of GDP. Johnson's average debt-to-GDP ratio was 42.7 percent and included a 10.7 percentage point drop (third best) in the debt share during his administration. This is a substantial feat when considering the rapid growth of the budget from the costs of the Vietnam War. However, revenues kept up with the costs, and the economy grew faster than the debt, so debt as a share of GDP fell significantly.

Nixon

Nixon's deficit was −7.8 percent of the budget, still below the period average of −9.0 percent but the highest of the postwar presidents until then. There was also a large increase in the deficit's share of the budget, 17.8 percentage points, second highest. This increased deficit share was large partly because Johnson ended his administration with a surplus (positive 1.8 percent) and Nixon ended in a recession (with a sizeable −16.0 percent deficit).

Despite the weak deficit record, the national debt as a percentage of the GDP continued to decline. Nixon's average debt was only 36.1 percent of GDP, representing a further 3.9 percentage point drop in the share.

Ford

Ford's average deficit was quite large at −16.5 percent (fourth highest) but with a 2.9 percentage point improvement in the trend. Ford had the second lowest average debt share of GDP, 36.0 percent, but was the first in the series of postwar presidential administrations in which the debt share of GDP actually increased (1.1 percentage points).

Carter

Carter averaged a deficit that was −11.3 percent of the budget (sixth highest), with a decrease in the deficit share of 1.5 percentage points.

Despite the relatively high deficits, Carter had a good record with respect to the national debt, achieving the lowest average postwar national debt as a percentage of the economy, 33.5 percent, including a further 3.3 percent reduction in the debt share of GDP.

Reagan

The Reagan administration was a major turning point in America's fiscal position. Reagan's average deficit was −19.0 percent of the budget (third highest), with a 1.7 percent increase in the share (fourth highest).

On the debt side, Reagan reversed the downward trend in the debt as a percentage of GDP, and it averaged 45.4 percent of GDP for his eight-year term. He also raised the debt level by 20.6 percentage points of GDP, second most and a staggering amount when considering that the nation was at peace and the economy was growing.

Bush 41

Bush 41 was forced to deal with serious deficit problems left by Reagan. However, Reagan also left Bush 41 with the opportunity to cash in the "peace dividend" from the end of the Cold War. With the breakup of the United States' archrival, the Soviet Union, it was not justifiable to sustain high levels of defense expenditures. During the Bush 41 administration, defense as a percentage of the federal budget fell from 26.5 percent (1989) to 20.7 percent (1993). This reduction translated into budget savings at the time of roughly $80 billion annually.

To deal with the large budget deficits, Congress was considering a bill (the Omnibus Budget Reconciliation Act—OBRA, 1990), which could force automatic spending cuts if budget deficit targets were not met. Because the economy had been slowing down, there was a great deal of pressure on Bush 41 to reach a compromise with Congress that would reduce the deficit on both the expenditure and the revenue sides. The Democrats were reluctant to propose revenue increases because they feared being portrayed as "tax-and-spenders." On the other hand, Bush 41 knew that signing on to a tax increase would violate his campaign pledge of "no new taxes."

The final version of the OBRA included an increase in the tax rate of the high income tax bracket, the elimination of some deductions, no capital-gains tax cut, a smaller increase in gas taxes, and smaller cuts in Medicare (Chapter 9 has additional details). OBRA passed on October 28, 1990. Although Bush broke his pledge not to raise taxes, the OBRA was a first step in putting America back on a sustainable fiscal footing and was expected to reduce budget deficits by $490 billion over five years. The legislation was more commonly known as the Budget Enforcement Act (BEA).

The BEA also had specific provisions that required Congress and the president to deal with the deficit. For example, the administration had to reveal whether any legislation increased or decreased the deficit. If BEA targets were exceeded, then across-the-board spending cuts would be triggered. This approach is similar to that of the "Super Committee" that was created by the Budget Control Act of 2011, whereby if sufficient cuts could not be agreed upon by the 12-member committee (six Democrats and six Republicans), then automatic cuts would be instituted.

Despite the requirements of the BEA, the high-deficit, higher-debt regime from the Reagan years continued. Bush 41's average deficit was higher than Reagan's at −19.3 percent of the budget (compared with the period average of −9.0 percent and second highest overall). During the course of Bush 41's administration, deficits as a share of the budget worsened (increased) by 4.8 percentage points.

Bush's average debt reached 61.7 percent, with a 13.0 percentage point increase above Reagan's last year of record.

Clinton

Clinton managed to turn around the disadvantageous fiscal position created by Reagan. He had the second best record on the deficit, with an average of only −0.2 percent of the budget (nearly averaging a balanced budget) and an improvement in the deficit share of the budget of 25.0 percentage points, the second best of all postwar presidents.

Although he averaged a relatively high national debt of 63.0 percent of GDP, he lowered the debt by 9.7 percentage points (fourth best), thus reversing the trend under Reagan and Bush 41.

A big part of the positive fiscal turnaround under Clinton was the 1993 Omnibus Budget Reconciliation Act (1993), a follow-up series of tax and expenditure measures to bring about fiscal sustainability. The major provisions of the 1993 act were:

- Creation of (higher) 36 percent and 39.6 percent tax brackets for top income earners
- A 35 percent income tax rate for corporations
- Removal of the income cap on Medicare payroll tax
- An increase in the amount of Social Security benefits subject to taxation from 50 to 85 percent
- An increase in the gas tax of 4.3 cents per gallon
- A phase-out of the personal exemption and a limit on itemized deductions was made permanent[2]

Bush 43

Bush 43 managed to quickly reverse Clinton's fiscal improvements and then some. His overall deficit was −15.9 percent of the budget. What is most stunning is the change in the deficit as a percentage of the budget. Bush 43 inherited a 6.9 percent surplus and left with 40.2 percent deficit, a −47.0 percentage point worsening in the deficit share of the budget!

This record represented the worst deterioration of the budget deficit of any president.

His average debt was 66.3 percent of GDP (third highest), with an increase of 28.8 percentage points (more than any other president).

Obama

Obama has had to cope with a miserable deficit situation, and the standings reflect it. In the first year of his record, the federal budget deficit was −37.4 percent of the budget and the next year it was −36.1 percent, for an overall average of −36.7 percent, the worst average among the presidents. There was a 4.1 percentage point decrease in the deficit share of the budget (fifth best).

Obama had the highest debt-to-GDP ratio (96.5 percent), which was even higher than that of Truman, who inherited the debt from WWII. In addition, the debt-to-GDP ratio increased 13.5 percentage points. This debt increase was the third highest among presidents. However, this debt increase took place in just two years. It took Bush 43 eight years to raise the debt 28.8 percentage points.

Obama faced major opposition in dealing with the debt crisis from Republicans whose policies had contributed to the 2008 economic collapse. The refusal of House Republicans to raise the ceiling on the national debt in the summer of 2011 was an example of the bitterness of that opposition. It was a highly unusual move for a political party to create doubt and uncertainty in the financial markets that the debt ceiling would be raised. Part of the motivation for the budgetary brinksmanship appeared to be the desire to eliminate specific programs with which Republicans disagreed.

The number one economic problem was not the deficit (as important as that has become) but that the economy was still sluggish and threatening a second recessionary dip. In such a situation, lessons from economic history strongly indicate that it is much more important to stimulate economic growth than it is to cut the deficit. Excessive or indiscriminate cuts in spending could cause the economy to contract and plunge into a second-dip recession, which would be far more costly than the money saved from spending cuts.

Obama challenged the wisdom of the Tea Party–dominated Republican Party in trying to reduce the debt. Obama asserted that the Tea Party was advocating the same tax cut and deregulate economic philosophy that had driven the economy to crisis and the debt to nearly 100 percent of GDP. To be fair, Obama had his own contribution to the deficit. He tacked on a payroll tax reduction so that lower-income individuals would have a

Table 8.1   Deficits as a Share of the Federal Budget by Presidential Administration

Administration	Deficit Share of Budget	Administration	Change in Share
Truman	2.4%	Truman	42.8%
Clinton	−0.2%	Clinton	25.0%
Eisenhower	−2.0%	Johnson	6.8%
Johnson	−4.4%	Eisenhower	5.1%
Kennedy	−5.3%	Obama	4.1%
Nixon	−7.8%	Ford	2.9%
Carter	−11.3%	Carter	1.5%
Bush 43	−15.9%	Kennedy	−1.6%
Ford	−16.5%	Reagan	−1.7%
Reagan	−19.0%	Bush 41	−4.8%
Bush 41	−19.3%	Nixon	−17.8%
Obama	−36.7%	Bush 43	−47.0%
Period Average	**−9.0%**		**N.A.**

break on their taxes. It is true that lower-income earners pay very little federal income tax, but they do pay substantial payroll taxes. While this payroll tax cut helps improve distribution of income, it also places greater stress on Social Security and Medicare because their funding through the payroll tax is reduced.

Table 8.2   National Debt as a Share of GDP by Presidential Administration

Administration	Debt Share of GDP	Administration	Change in Share
Carter	33.5%	Truman	−46.1%
Ford	36.0%	Eisenhower	−16.2%
Nixon	36.1%	Johnson	−10.7%
Johnson	42.7%	Clinton	−9.7%
Reagan	45.4%	Kennedy	−5.9%
Kennedy	51.5%	Nixon	−3.9%
Bush 41	61.7%	Carter	−3.3%
Eisenhower	62.0%	Ford	1.1%
Clinton	63.0%	Bush 41	13.0%
Bush 43	66.3%	Obama	13.5%
Truman	92.9%	Reagan	20.6%
Obama	96.5%	Bush 43	28.8%
Period Average	**58.6%**		**N.A.**

CONCLUSIONS AND ISSUES FOR DEBT AND DEFICITS

Probably the main lesson learned from presidential management of debt since 1946 is that when there is a chance to shrink the debt as a share of the economy, the president should do it. A president should not incur budget deficits and the national debt for overgenerous tax cuts as Reagan and Bush 43 did. Running up debt when there is no compelling reason, such as a war for survival or a serious economic downturn, leaves the nation fiscally vulnerable and ill positioned to deal with expensive priorities in the future.

Given the potential for increases in interest rates on the U.S. debt at any time, it is probably a good idea to aim for a debt level that is less than half of GDP. That way, interest payments on the debt will not threaten to crowd out many of the other priorities of the federal budget.

Social Security Funding and Impact on the Deficit and the Debt

The subject of Social Security funding was discussed in Chapter 7, but how the changes in the Social Security funding under Reagan specifically affected the debt and the deficits merits additional explanation. Beginning in 1984, Social Security surpluses began to emerge and would grow for the next 25 years before they evaporated in the financial crisis of 2008. These surpluses, which were off-budget surpluses, were combined with the overall budget revenues (from individual and corporate taxes). The effect was to camouflage the size of the deficit with money meant for the future beneficiaries of the Social Security Trust Fund, in other words, retiring baby-boomers. The deficits appeared smaller, but the overall national debt, which includes the government's debt to the Social Security Trust Fund, was mounting faster than the reported deficits would indicate. Cumulatively, in the past quarter century, about $2.6 trillion, the size of the Social Security Trust Fund, has been added to the national debt through the practice of spending the Trust Fund.

Financial Crisis Impact on the Deficits and Debt: Lost Revenue versus Increased Spending as the Cause of the Debt Surge

A portion of the public, which includes the Tea Partiers, is under the impression that the reason the deficits are so high is that Barack Obama decided to take the federal checkbook and spend huge amounts of money, because—that is what liberal democrats do. There does not seem to be any connection made between the fall in federal revenue from the 2008 financial and real estate meltdown on one hand and the surge in budget deficits

Table 8.3   Trend in Federal Revenue and Deficits with the Financial Crisis ($ billion)

Year	Revenue	Outlays	Deficit	Deficit % of Budget
2006	2,406.9	2,655.1	−248.2	−9.3
2007	2,568.0	2,728.7	−160.7	−5.9
2008	2,524.0	2,982.5	−458.6	−15.4
2009	2,105.0	3,517.7	−1,412.7	−40.2
2010	2,162.7	3,456.2	−1,293.5	−37.4

on the other. Nor is there any acknowledgement of conventional economic policy that dictates that policymakers should compensate for declines in the private sector through public-sector spending—the same policy that has kept recessions from becoming depressions for the past 70 years.

The surge in debt and deficits is clearly a direct result of the economic crisis that hit the United States in 2008. The crisis has had a doubly negative impact on the debt: (1) a massive decline in federal tax revenue, and (2) a massive increase in spending and tax cuts aimed at stimulating economic activity and compensating for lost income. Table 8.3 shows that federal tax revenues fell by $44 billion in 2008 and another $419 billion in 2009. The deficit increased almost $300 billion to $458 billion in 2008 and increased another $954 billion to $1.4 trillion in 2009.

So when House Budget Committee chairman Paul Ryan asserted, for example, that the U.S. government does not have a revenue problem, he belongs to a group of people who do not understand the impact of an economic crisis on the government budget balance.[3]

Table 8.4 illustrates what deficits would be in the "without crisis" scenario. Take 2006 as a normal, precrisis year for government revenue and outlays when there was a budget deficit of $248.2 billion. Next, we apply the standard 2.3 percent growth rate for revenues and 2.5 percent growth rate for outlays (the average growth rates for 1946 through 2011).

If we subtract actual revenues from estimated "normal" trend revenues, and actual outlays from "normal" trend outlays, it is clear that almost as much of the deficit comes from a drop in revenue as comes from an increase in outlays. There was a $472 billion revenue shortfall in 2009 ($2,576.8 billion minus $2,105.0 billion) and a $473 billion revenue shortfall in 2010 ($2,636.1 billion minus $2,162.7 billion).

Table 8.4   Trend in Federal Budget Revenue and Deficits without the Financial Crisis ($ billion)

Year	Revenue	Outlays	Deficit	Deficit % of Budget
2006	2,406.9	2,655.1	−248.2	−9.3
2007	2,462.2	2,724.1	−261.9	−9.6
2008	2,518.9	2,794.9	−276.0	−9.9
2009	2,576.8	2,867.6	−290.8	−10.1
2010	2,636.1	2,942.1	−306.1	−10.4

Source: Derived from OMB Data available at http://www.whitehouse.gov/omb/budget/Historicals/.

If spending had also stayed on its long-term trend, and there's no reason why it would not have without the crisis, then outlays would have been $650 billion less in 2009 and $514 billion less in 2010. With the crisis, the deficit reached $1.293 trillion in 2010, and without the crisis the deficit would have been $306 billion, a difference of nearly $1 trillion.

Forty-seven percent of this excess deficit was because of revenue shortfall and 53 percent because of increased outlays. The increased outlays were mainly because the federal government was compelled to compensate for the contraction in the private sector as well as to pay the increased demand for social safety net programs for the poor and unemployed, which soared during the crisis. These costs are in addition to the ongoing military expenditures in Iraq and Afghanistan and the loss in revenue from the Bush 43 tax cuts.

Given these facts, it is disingenuous to blame the president who inherited a full-scale financial crisis as responsible for the resulting massive deficits. The political question is how much time should a president be given to fix the problems he inherited? It is not clear that three or four years is enough. There is some encouraging news on the deficit front, namely that the budget deficit for 2011, while still very high, was $345 billion less than had been estimated in the budget ($1.299 trillion actual vs. $1.645 trillion estimated).

NOTES

1. Recall that the Great Depression had not been overcome until the government spent huge sums of money to mobilize to fight WWII.

2. "An Economic Analysis of the Revenue Provisions of OBRA-93," Congressional Budget Office, January 1994.

3. If fiscal policy is allowed to starve a program of resources while demand for the program's services continues to rise, then there is, by definition, a serious revenue problem. By not addressing the revenue side of the fiscal ledger, one is automatically led to a policy of spending cuts, which is aim of "small government" Republicans. But that is not how effective fiscal policy works.

NINE

Federal Taxation: Raising Revenue Effectively for the Public

An economy hampered by restrictive tax rates will never produce enough revenue to balance our budget, just as it will never produce enough jobs or enough profits.

—John Fitzgerald Kennedy

I just think that—when a country needs more income and we do, we're only taking in 15 percent of GDP, I mean, that when a country needs more income, they should get it from the people that have it.
—Warren Buffett

VALUE AND CRITIQUE OF THE INDICATOR

The basic question of tax policy is how much money do we need to pay for the government that we insist on having? This basic question can be complicated because we have to decide collectively as a nation what the government should and should not do. Whether we opt for elective wars, corporate subsidies, farm subsidies, or subsidies for the poor, they all will have an impact on how much money the government needs to raise.

In a properly functioning government, once the federal budget is approved, tax revenues should come pretty close to meeting the cost, with exceptions for economic downturns or wars for survival.

Tax policy is also the main tool, other than targeted legislation, that policymakers use to promote or discourage a wide range of specific behaviors. Promoting investment, protecting the environment, and hiring

American workers are all important goals that can be furthered through tax policy. Unfortunately, with this flexibility also comes vulnerability to lobbying for "loopholes" that often provide no benefit to the United States but that drain resources from the Treasury and create larger budget deficits.

When policymakers use tax policy to promote economic, social, and environmental behaviors that are good for the country, they also have to take care not to inhibit economic production through over-taxation. Policymakers must always be aware that it is economic production in the private sector from which tax revenues are generated to fund their programs.

As with other public-sector indicators, there is a dilemma with federal tax revenue as a share of GDP as a performance indicator. While we measure a lower share of taxes as a better performance, that lower tax share can also indicate a weak economy. In addition, a president might find himself in a war where additional taxes are necessary to pay for the war. If the war is a necessary war of self-defense, then the president's economic record should not be penalized for the higher taxes.[1]

In this chapter, we use federal tax revenues as a percentage of GDP as the indicator. Federal tax revenues include federal income tax paid by individuals, federal payroll tax paid by individuals and employers (which funds Social Security and Medicare), and corporate, or business, tax. The source of the data is the U.S. Office of Management and Budget (OMB), which is the source of official U.S. federal budget data.

REVIEW OF ADMINISTRATIONS' PERFORMANCE ON TAXATION—TRUMAN TO OBAMA

Despite the tax cuts, increases, and reforms over the years, total federal taxes as a percent of GDP remained remarkably level for most of the 1946 to 2011 period. Between 1951 and 2008 taxes ranged between 16.1 and 20.6 percent of GDP. Of those 58 years, 45 had tax shares between 17.0 and 19.0 percent of GDP. The years 2009 through 2011 were exceptional as tax shares of GDP fell to 15.1 percent for 2009 and 2010, the lowest rate since 1950 when federal tax revenues were only 14.4 percent of GDP. In 2011, the tax share of GDP was only 15.4 percent, the second lowest share since 1950. Despite these exceptions, there is a modest time bias in that earlier presidents tended to have lower tax revenue shares of GDP than did more recent presidents, which favors the performance records of the earlier presidents.

Figure 9.1   Federal Taxes as a Percentage of GDP, 1946–2011

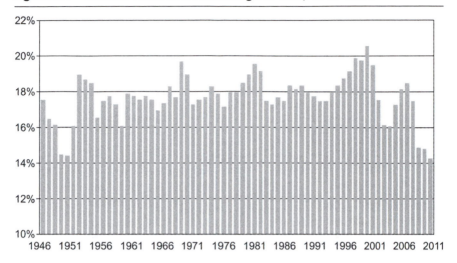

Later in this chapter we examine the composition of tax receipts over time, which provides historical context for resolving tax policy issues in the current debate. The rankings of the individual presidents are presented in Table 9.3.

Truman

Truman had the second lowest tax-revenue-to-GDP ratio at 16.6 percent, with a 1.7 percentage point decrease in the share. Despite quite high marginal rates on the highest income levels (90 percent for the top rate) during the Truman administration, these rates rarely kicked in, and effective rates were low overall.

Eisenhower

Eisenhower's tax share was fourth lowest at 17.4 percent, with a 0.9 percentage point reduction in the tax share of GDP.

Kennedy

Kennedy's tax share of GDP was 17.7 percent (the same as the average for the period), or fifth lowest out of all 12 presidents. He also recorded a 0.2 percentage point decline in the share of taxes. This record extends through 1964, the year in which the "Kennedy tax cut" was actually passed, while Johnson was president. Again, though tax rates were high, these rates were not widely applied so the overall tax take by the federal government was relatively low.

Kennedy-Johnson Tax Cut (1964)

This tax cut was signed by President Johnson in February 1964. The tax cut called for across-the-board reductions of individual tax rates, with the top rate reduced from 91 to 77 percent in 1964 and further to 70 percent in 1965. These rates, before and even after the tax cuts, are astronomical by today's standards. The tax cut also reduced corporate taxes to 22 percent on the first $25,000 of taxable income, and the corporate tax rates on the remainder went from 52 to 50 percent in 1964 and to 48 percent in 1965. Tax deductions for capital depreciation were also enhanced.

Conservatives often claim this tax cut as an early vindication of supply-side economics. Indeed, resources were shifted from the government to the private sector. The tax cut also was a conscious decision to favor temporary increases in budget deficits in order to promote fuller use of resources (higher employment) and more rapid economic growth rates rather than the pattern of slower growth rates and small deficits of previous years. The tax cuts did seem to work pretty well as GDP growth was high throughout the latter part of the 1960s and much of the 1970s.

In a way, these levels of tax rates and associated GDP growth rates must be perplexing for the antitax lobby. Even after the Kennedy-Johnson tax cut was implemented, the top tax rate on individuals was 35 percentage points higher than it was after the Bush 43 tax cuts. The corporate tax rate was 13 percentage points higher. Somehow it was possible to have a historically high GDP growth rate even with tax rates that would be considered exorbitant by today's standards. It makes the fierce opposition to returning to Clinton-era tax rates (of 39.6 percent top rate on income) to restore some fiscal balance seem almost absurd in a historical context.

Johnson

Johnson had the fourth highest tax share of GDP, at 18.0 percent, and the highest increase in the share, at 2.1 percentage points, despite the 1964 tax cut. This increase is in part because of the need to raise funds to pay for the Vietnam War, which included the levying of a 10 percent surcharge on individual income in 1968. This surcharge offset much of the 1964 tax cut and is why the federal tax take under the Johnson administration was relatively high.

Nixon

Nixon is in a three-way tie at 18.0 percent tax share of GDP, along with a 1.8 percentage point decline the tax share, which was the second largest tax share reduction.

Ford

Ford's tax share of GDP was 17.6 percent, fifth best overall, with a negligible increase in the share, of 0.1 percentage point.

Carter

Carter had the second highest tax share of GDP, at 18.8 percent. At the same time, he had the third highest increase in the share, at 1.6 percentage points.

During Carter and before, taxpayers had been pushed into higher tax brackets because of inflation. Although a person's income may not have increased in real terms, his or her tax rate did. For example, in 1967 a person earning $200,000 would just reach the top marginal tax rate of 70 percent.[2] By 1978, the tax brackets had not changed (because they were not indexed to inflation), so a person making $200,000 in 1978 would still be taxed at a marginal rate of 70 percent. However, in that 11-year period, inflation amounted to 66.9 percent. After adjusting for this inflation, the person's income was now only $119,840 in real terms, but the income earner was still paying the top rate. Thus, with this "bracket creep," people were paying higher taxes, even though there was neither a vote in Congress to raise taxes nor a real increase in their income.

Reagan

Reagan had one of the higher federal tax revenue shares of GDP, 18.0 percent (part of the three-way tie), but with a 1.2 percentage point reduction (third overall).

Tax policy took center stage in the Reagan presidency; because he was convinced that higher rates had been a drag on the economy, he made lowering them a top priority of his first administration. Thirty years later, the Reagan tax record is cited by both Democrats and Republicans to promote their separate points of view, and so we discuss in some detail the factual record of his tax policies and their results.

The Reagan Tax Cut (1981)

Perhaps the most heralded economic policy measure in the conservative world since WWII was the Reagan tax cut that was passed in 1981 and implemented in three tax rate reductions (10 percent, 10 percent, and 5 percent) during 1981 through 1983. Considered the cornerstone of supply-side economics, the tax plan had been circulating in Congress for a number of years in the form of the Kemp-Roth" tax cut proposal, which had called for three successive 10 percent reductions in tax rates (Chapter 1). Ever since the Reagan tax cut and the economic growth response in the 1980s, conservative Republican economic policy has been dominated by a one-directional tax policy—tax cuts anywhere, everywhere, and always, even though Reagan's record tax policy was anything but one-directional.

President Reagan's tax policies have been vigorously debated for decades, not only as to their effects on the economy but even regarding what they entailed. Conservatives build their very identity around their perceptions of Reagan's policies, proudly proclaiming the benefits of those policies. But today's conservatives are being rather selective in their recollection of President Reagan's tax policies. Democrats, in countering

Table 9.1   Legislated Tax Changes by Ronald Reagan as of 1988 ($ billions)

Tax Cuts	
Economic Recovery Tax Act of 1981	−264.4
Interest and Dividends Tax Compliance Act of 1983	−1.8
Federal Employees' Retirement System Act of 1986	−0.2
Tax Reform Act of 1986	−8.9
Total cumulative tax cuts	**−275.3**
Tax Increases	
Tax Equity and Fiscal Responsibility Act of 1982	+57.3
Highway Revenue Act of 1982	+4.9
Social Security Amendments of 1983	+24.6
Railroad Retirement Revenue Act of 1983	+1.2
Deficit Reduction Act of 1984	+25.4
Consolidated Omnibus Budget Reconciliation Act of 1985	+2.9
Omnibus Budget Reconciliation Act of 1985	+2.4
Superfund Amendments and Reauthorization Act of 1986	+0.6
Continuing Resolution for 1987	+2.8
Omnibus Budget Reconciliation Act of 1987	+8.6
Continuing Resolution for 1988	+2.0
Total cumulative tax increases	**+132.7**

Source: Office of Management and Budget, *Budget of the United States Government, Fiscal Year 1990* (Washington: U.S. Government Printing Office, 1989), p. 4–4.

the doctrinaire antitax stance, point out that Reagan also *raised* taxes significantly a number of times during his administration. The two political sides also disagree about whether the Reagan tax policies raised or lowered federal tax revenues. Given how loose the news media typically allows such discussions to be, it is worth taking a more rigorous tally of just what were the tax cuts and increases during the Reagan administration (Table 9.1) [3] and reviewing how federal tax revenues responded (Table 9.2).

The OMB estimates in Table 9.2 are based on the value of tax changes to the federal budget. It is clear that Reagan followed a much more pragmatic and less doctrinaire approach to tax policy than do his admirers today. To be sure, the net effect of his tax policies was tax reduction. However, there were more tax increases (11) than tax cuts (4).

Tax Reform of 1986

The tax reform of 1986 signed by President Reagan was implemented over two years and was perhaps a more significant piece of legislation than the 1981–1983 ERTA. One of the main features of the reform was to reduce the number of tax brackets in order to "flatten out" the tax structure. Prior to 1987, there were 15 tax brackets for single taxpayers and 14 for married taxpayers. The maximum tax rates were 50 percent in both categories. This system was replaced by a five-bracket system in 1987 (a transitional year), and a two-bracket system thereafter. Married and single individuals were taxed at 15 percent up to a certain level of income and 28 percent thereafter. At higher levels of income, the benefits associated with the 15 percent rate were phased out. Among the reduced or eliminated tax deductions were interest on consumer loans, medical expenses,

Table 9.2   Federal Revenue and Outlays under Reagan ($ billions)

Year	Revenue	Outlays	Deficit	Deficit % of Outlays
1981	599.3	678.2	−79.0	−11.6%
1982	617.8	745.7	−128.0	−17.2%
1983	600.6	808.4	−207.8	−25.7%
1984	666.4	851.8	−185.4	−21.8%
1985	734.0	946.3	−212.3	−22.4%
1986	769.2	990.4	−221.2	−22.3%
1987	854.3	1,004.0	−149.7	−14.9%
1988	909.2	1,064.4	−155.2	−14.6%
1989	991.1	1,143.7	−152.6	−13.3%

sales tax, political and charitable contributions, and unreimbursed business expenses.

The tax reform also curtailed tax shelters: the investment tax credit was repealed, the generous depreciation schedules of the 1981 ERTA were scaled back, and losses from tax shelters were no longer deductible against other taxable income. Businesses did receive a reduction of the top corporate tax rates.

Revenue and Deficit Effects of Reagan's Tax Policies

Table 9.2 provides a record of what happened to federal tax revenue, outlays, and deficits under Reagan. The net effect of Reagan's federal tax increases and tax cuts was sizeable deficits for every year of his administration. Overall, revenues were about $1.4 trillion less than expenditures. Despite strong GDP growth during 1984 through 1989, deficits remained high. One fact that might be difficult for some conservatives to accept is that Reagan's predecessor, Jimmy Carter, despite finishing with a weak economy, recorded double the rate of revenue growth compared with that of Reagan, 4.3 versus 2.2 percent in real terms per year.

The Reagan tax story is of tax cuts that were partially counteracted by tax increases in other areas and in other times in his presidency, and growth that raised income levels on which taxes were assessed. The Democrats have to accept that growth and employment creation, post tax cuts (and tax increases), were good after the 1982 recession. The conservatives have to accept that the tax policies ushered in a new era of high deficits and that the claims that cutting taxes would raise revenues, as suggested by the Laffer curve,[4] were not valid.

Bush 41

The elder Bush had a tax revenue share of 17.7 percent, equal to the period average and slightly lower than Kennedy (carried to more decimal places) for seventh place. He also recorded a reduction in the share of tax revenue of 0.9 percent. The potential revenues from his tax increase as part of the Omnibus Budget Reconciliation Act of November 5, 1990 (OBRA 1990) were more than offset by the recession in 1991. The main features of OBRA 1990 were as follows:

- A new 31 percent tax bracket was created from the previous top bracket of 28 percent.

- Personal exemptions were temporarily phased out.
- Itemized deductions were limited through 1995.
- The Medicare income cap was raised from $53,400 to $125,000.
- The gasoline tax was increased and extended through 1995.

Conservatives blame Bush's failure to win a second term on his violation of his "No new taxes" pledge. Even though Reagan himself had raised taxes in a number of different ways throughout his administration, Bush 41 was never forgiven. The reality was that Bush 41 was essentially forced to raise taxes because of the Gramm-Rudman-Hollings deficit control requirements.[5]

Clinton

Clinton had the highest revenue share of GDP at 19.3 percent, in other words, last place among the 12 presidents. Federal tax revenue also increased a full 2 percentage points as a share of GDP under his administration, second to last place. The components of the tax increase were:

- Creation of 36 percent and 39.6 percent (applied to incomes of $250,000) tax brackets for top wage earners
- 35 percent income tax rate for corporations
- Removal of the income cap on Medicare payroll tax
- Increase in the amount of Social Security benefits subject to taxation from 50 to 85 percent
- Increase in the gas tax of 4.3 cents per gallon
- Phase-out of the personal exemption and limit on itemized deductions were made permanent.[6]

The removal of the income cap for Medicare payroll tax meant that all of one's income, not just the first $125,000 (as was the case under Bush 41), was subject to the 2.9 percent Medicare tax rate. The Social Security payroll tax remained capped (adjusted upward for inflation each year).

While Clinton's higher tax share counts against his record, it is actually an indication of healthy economic performance. The tax increases that Clinton instituted raised revenue rapidly, and by the end of his administration, the Reagan-Bush 41 budget deficits had disappeared. The national debt was falling not just as a percentage of GDP but in absolute terms.

Bush 43

Bush 43 had the third lowest average tax share as a percentage of GDP, 17.1 percent. He also had the greatest reduction in taxes as a share of GDP, −4.4 percentage points. When Bush came into office, there was a mild recession (assessed against Clinton's record). Bush 43 reacted by signing a tax cut in 2001, formally known as the Economic Growth and Tax Relief Reconciliation Act (EGTRRA) of 2001, which contributed to the lower share. Taxes as a share of GDP declined for four straight years from 20.6 percent of GDP in 2000 to 16.1 percent in 2004. Tax shares climbed up to 18.5 percent in 2007. As the economy declined, unemployment soared at the end of his administration, and the tax share dropped to 15.1 percent by 2009. The main provisions of Bush 43's tax cuts (EGTRRA) included:

- Lowering tax brackets from 15 percent to a new 10 percent bracket, as well as four other bracket reductions by 2006—28 to 25 percent, 31 to 28 percent, 36 to 33 percent, and 39.6 to 35 percent.
- Large increases in exemption from estate tax with complete phase-out of estate tax by 2010
- Tax rebates—$300 to individuals, $500 to single parents, and $600 to married couples.

The EGTRRA also had a "sunset provision" which meant that, unless extended, the tax changes would revert to their pre-EGTRRA status on January 1, 2011. By including this provision, the act was able to avoid a Senate rule (the Byrd rule) that would allow senators to block a bill that would increase the deficit beyond a 10-year period.

At the end of his administration it was evident that the tax cut that Bush 43 signed proved both too large and too economically unproductive for its fiscal cost. He recorded the lowest average GDP growth and the highest increase in the national debt of any of the 12 postwar presidents. Despite the ineffectiveness of the Bush tax cuts, antitax fervor intensified, stoked by antitax lobbyists like Grover Norquist,[7] who placed further pressure on politicians never to raise taxes, which included signing a pledge to that effect.

Obama

Obama had the lowest average percentage of federal tax revenue as a share of GDP, at 15.3 percent. He gets credit for a number-one ranking on taxes, but it was not necessarily a good sign for the economy. Obama's closest contemporary who managed a reasonably well-performing economy, Bill Clinton, had an average federal-tax-to-GDP ratio of 19.3 percent. If Obama had such a tax-to-GDP ratio, the overall federal deficit would be about $500 billion (compared with more than $1.3 trillion in 2011). This low rate of tax revenue further discredits the claim by some Republicans that "we do not have a revenue problem, we have a spending problem."

Extension of Bush Tax Cuts and Other Measures

Obama appeared ready to let the Bush 43 tax cuts expire at the end of 2010, at least for the top 2 percent of income earners. However, he faced withering opposition from the Republicans, nearly all of whom had signed the Grover Norquist no-tax-increase pledge. Those who signed the pledge were effectively saying that lower taxes were an end in themselves, no matter what the prevailing economic circumstances. These policymakers were signing away one of the most important tools of economic policy. Having to dealing with a substantial block of politicians who adhered to this ideological position has greatly complicated Obama's efforts to maintain fiscal sustainability and accelerate economic growth. In the end, Obama relented and extended the Bush tax cuts for all income groups for an additional two years.

To inject a measure of equity and a more effective stimulus into the tax package, Obama added a payroll tax cut to the 2010 year-end economic package. The vast majority of Americans pay more in payroll taxes (which fund Social Security and Medicare) than they do in federal income taxes. By cutting payroll taxes, Obama could benefit the average person and his or her employer. Like any tax cut, there are fiscal costs, in this case to programs already in financial difficulty (Social Security and Medicare). However, the payroll tax cut is likely to be more stimulative than the Bush 43 income tax cut because those who pay a higher share of their income in payroll taxes also spend a higher share of their disposable (after-tax) income. The payroll tax cut also partially rectifies the abuse by both Republicans and Democrats of spending the Social Security Trust Fund. It was mostly middle-income tax payers who funded the Social Security surpluses, but all Americans, including the wealthy, benefited by spending

Table 9.3   Tax Revenue as a Share of GDP by Presidential Administration

Administration	Share of GDP	Administration	Change in Share
Obama	15.3%	Bush 43	−4.%
Truman	16.6%	Nixon	−1.8%
Bush 43	17.1%	Reagan	−1.2%
Eisenhower	17.4%	Eisenhower	−0.9%
Ford	17.6%	Bush 41	−0.9%
Kennedy	17.7%	Kennedy	−0.2%
Bush 41	17.7%	Ford	0.1%
Nixon	18.0%	Obama	0.3%
Johnson	18.0%	Truman	1.1%
Reagan	18.0%	Carter	1.6%
Carter	18.8%	Clinton	2.0%
Clinton	19.3%	Johnson	2.1%
Period Average	**17.7%**		**N.A.**

them. So Obama will gain some stimulus advantages but will have yet another worsening problem to deal with in the near future, the funding of Social Security and Medicare. In the meantime, at least, lower- and middle-income Americans do get some degree of tax relief.

CONCLUSIONS AND ISSUES FOR FEDERAL TAXATION

The Conflict between Ideology and Economic Policy

If the record on results from tax policy says anything, it says that ideology and economics do not mix. Ideological prescriptions for tax policy that require taxes always to go up or to go down simply do not stand up to the test of history. The economic context must support the policy for tax cuts or tax increases, and those cuts or increases need to be appropriately sized. As we have seen, there were a number of instances where that was not the case. A summary of the tax cuts and increases from the historical data review underscores the importance of tax policy that fits the economic circumstances:

1. **Kennedy/Johnson tax cut (1964–1965):** good growth, stable fiscal balance, implemented in a regime of high marginal tax rates (the highest was 90 percent) and in an economy that had experienced a number of recent recessions

2. **Reagan tax cut (1981–1983):** good growth, but with high structural deficits with national debt rapidly increasing as a percentage of GDP

(Recall that there were also a number of tax increases as well under Reagan—the 1983 payroll tax and the 1986 tax reform which closed loopholes and eliminated some deductions.)

3. **Bush 41 tax increase (OBRA 1990):** lower deficits than otherwise, but recession and slow recovery caused persistent deficits; The tax increase was triggered by legislated deficit controls

4. **Clinton follow-up tax increase (OBRA 1993):** sustained growth and strong fiscal improvement, elimination of deficits

5. **Bush 43 tax cut (2001):** moderate growth changing to severe recession, historically high deficits, implemented in a regime of already relatively low tax rates

6. **Obama tax cut extensions (2010):** weak effect in stimulating demand and increasing employment[8]

The Context for the Reagan Tax Cut

In Reagan's case, the context was appropriate for a tax cut. Taxes had been creeping upward during the 1970s because the tax rate thresholds were not indexed to inflation.[9] In addition, in the 11 years prior to his administration, there had been three recessions, in 1970, 1974, and 1980. Taxes share of GDP had indeed reached a 12-year high of 19.6 percent of GDP in 1981. There was also a very low debt-to-GDP ratio so the country could afford some short-term deficits. Finally, the marginal tax rates were high, with the top marginal rate at 70 percent. This favorable context was in sharp contrast to the economic context of the Bush 43 tax cuts.

Shortly after the Reagan tax cuts were fully implemented in 1983, the economy responded with an above-average level of growth and was out of recession for the next six years. The problem with the tax cuts was that they were not correctly calibrated. They were too large, such that even when the economy was growing well the deficits remained high. And, when GDP growth rates fell under Bush 41, the deficits became even larger.

Applying the Reagan Tax Principles 30 Years Later

There are powerful antitax groups who invoke the success (albeit qualified) of the Reagan tax cuts as a continuous justification for tax cuts. There are two major caveats to those who would use the 1981 Reagan tax cut as a blueprint for current tax policy:

1. The conditions that supported a significant tax cut then have not been replicated since.

2. The Reagan tax cut was too generous because it produced high deficits even as unemployment fell and the economy grew.

Regarding the first caveat, if tax rates are relatively low (e.g., below 40 percent for the top rate) and the economy is not in serious distress, then further tax cuts may not be a net benefit to the economy. To the second caveat, while the Reagan tax cut appeared to spur the economy, the tax cut should have been smaller. America could have had the same growth but without the severe increase in debt. Reagan's record is also complicated by a number of other tax initiatives (including the 1983 Social Security tax increase and the 1986 tax reform), which were a mix of tax increases and cuts. The tax increases were not nearly as much as the 10–10–5, three-year cut during 1981 through 1983, and so the net effect of Reagan's policies was a significant tax reduction.

The relatively unproductive Bush 43 tax cuts are one historical counter to the claim that tax cuts are always good. Another is the Clinton tax policy. Clinton's tax increases not only did not deter growth as Republicans had warned, but his tax increases also helped make enormous progress in improving the nation's fiscal balance. The context for Clinton's OBRA 1993 was a regime left by Reagan and Bush 41 of relatively lower taxes, high deficits, and a somewhat sluggish recovery. Antitax zealots have not been able to explain why the economy responded so favorably to Clinton's tax increase.

Composition of Federal Tax Receipts

The composition of taxes is an important component of developing tax policy. Understanding the context of where tax revenues come from and in what proportion helps policymakers develop tax policies that are more sensible and fair. Figure 9.2 shows the composition of federal tax receipts. Tax receipts fall into five categories: (1) individual income tax; (2) corporate income tax; (3) social insurance taxes (mainly Social Security and Medicare payroll taxes); (4) excise taxes; and (5) other tax receipts.

There has been a striking shift in the tax burden over time: the increase in social taxes (mainly Social Security and Medicare) and the decline in corporate taxes. The corporate tax share fell from 32.1 percent in 1952 to 10.2 percent of total tax receipts in 2010. At the same time, social insurance taxes increased from 9.7 percent (1952) to 30.5 percent (1981) and to 40 percent in 2010. Given this long-term trend, the case for lowering the

Figure 9.2   Composition of Federal Taxes, 1946–2011

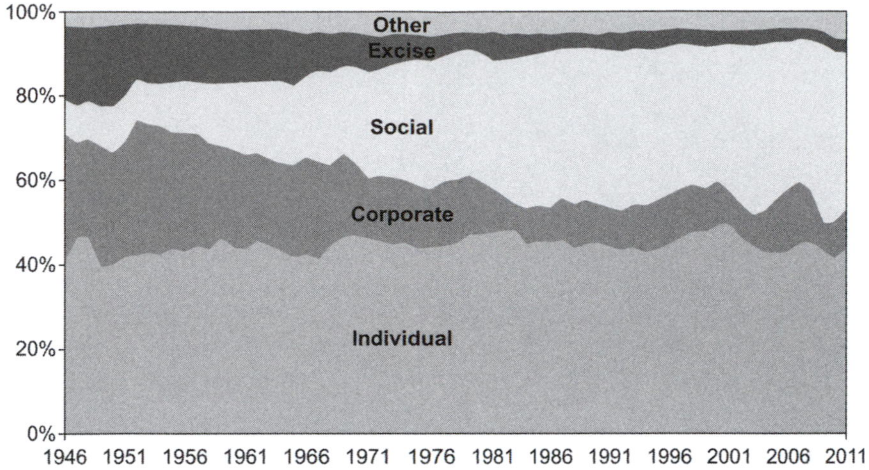

corporate tax share is difficult to make. Under Kennedy, corporate tax rates were 48 percent, and his administration recorded the highest GDP growth. Still, one could envision lower rates perhaps than the 35 percent statutory rate that many corporations do not actually pay, but not without closing tax loopholes that would at least fully compensate the U.S. Treasury for the rate reduction.

Distributional Aspects of the U.S. Tax System

At the extremes of the American economic spectrum, there are people who are fabulously wealthy while there are others who cannot afford decent food, clothing, or shelter. In general, the incomes of the poor and middle class have stagnated during the past several decades. Progressive tax policy is often used to moderate the more extreme effects of the market economy. However, some politicians view these realities as fair results of the market system, and to tamper with them could thwart incentives to work hard and be productive.

Figures 9.3 and 9.4 illustrate how much the tax system "corrects" for income inequalities by comparing pretax and after-tax income shares. If the lower-income quintiles have a higher share of total income after tax than they do before tax, then the tax system has redistributed income from the rich to the poor. Figures 9.3 and 9.4 show that the taxation of income achieved only a small redistributive effect, with the share of

Figure 9.3   Pretax Share of Family Income

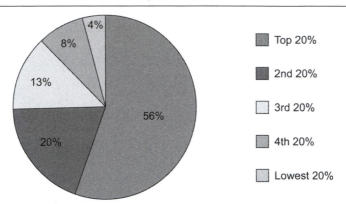

income of the top 20 percent dropping from 56 percent to 52 percent, and with lower-income people increasing their income share only 1 or 2 percentage points.

These results suggest that while the wealthy do pay a lot of taxes, the tax burden has not significantly affected their share of total income in the economy. The policy conclusion from this is that there is significant scope to increase taxes on the wealthy. This is particularly true of the top 1 percent income bracket. During the past decade, the share of total income of the top 1 percent increased from 10.3 percent to 16.3 percent from 1995 through 2006. This represents almost a 60 percent income share increase for the richest Americans.

Figure 9.4   After-Tax Share of Family Income

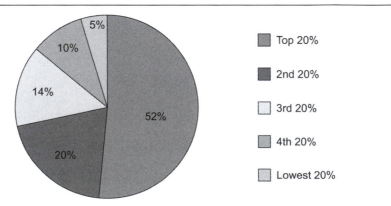

A Flat Tax Solution?

One form of tax reform that deserves mention, more for its perennial appearance in the tax debate than for its merit or feasibility, is the flat tax. Flat tax proposals have floated around Congress for decades in one form or another. The U.S. tax code came pretty close to a single flat tax after Reagan's 1986 tax reform, when there were only two tax brackets, 15 percent and 28 percent. This tax regime did not last very long.

Politicians are unlikely to agree to one level of tax rates for all, particularly given the weak effects even the current progressive tax system has on income distribution. Savvy policymakers are even more unlikely to give up a tool that allows them the ability to influence certain types of behavior for the public good, whether it is discouraging the pollution of the environment, hiring American workers, or researching medical breakthroughs or other innovations. A flat tax might be appealingly simple and bring down the costs of complying with the tax code,[10] but it detracts from the public's power to promote those activities essential to preserving and improving society.

NOTES

1. One could reasonably argue that none of the wars since 1946—the Korean War, the Vietnam War, the Gulf War, the Afghanistan War, and the Iraq War—have been wars for survival.

2. National Taxpayer's Union website, History of Federal Individual Income Bottom and Top Bracket Rates, http://ntu.org/tax-basics/history-of-federal-individual-1.html.

3. A 1988 OMB report summarized Reagan's tax cuts and tax increases during his administration and their estimated budget impacts.

4. The Laffer curve was conceived by supply-side economist Arthur Laffer. The Laffer curve was a graph that depicted government revenues rising with tax cuts and falling with tax increases.

5. Gramm-Rudman-Hollings Balanced Budget and Emergency Deficit Control Act of 1985, December 12, 1985, and Budget and Emergency Deficit Control Reaffirmation Act of 1987.

6. "An Economic Analysis of the Revenue Provisions of OBRA-93," Congressional Budget Office, January 1994.

7. Grover Norquist is the head of an antitax lobbying organization called Americans for Tax Reform (founded in 1985).

8. Keynes observed that hoarding of cash tends to take place in a recession. Therefore, increasing the money supply and cutting taxes are likely to

be ineffective. In a deep recession, Keynes recommended government spending, which would ensure that money was spent and not hoarded.

9. Taxpayers kept moving into higher tax brackets not because their real income was going up but because the thresholds for each tax rate were not adjusted for inflation.

10. Estimates of the total national cost of compliance with the tax code are wide ranging. Pro–flat tax groups sometimes quote exaggerated estimates of up to $500 billion. More reliable estimates place the cost at round $50 billion annually.

PART III

Combining Public and Private Indicators: Overall Presidential Performance Rankings

TEN

Economic Performance Rankings from Harry Truman to Barack Obama

We have always known that heedless self-interest was bad morals; we now know that it is bad economics.

—Franklin D. Roosevelt

OVERVIEW

The presidents have been scored on *individual* performance indicators, and in this chapter these indicators are brought together for an *overall*, composite measure of performance. This overall measure is the Presidential Performance Index (PPI).

Two things are needed in order to make this index. First, all of the individual indicators must be in the same units so we are not mixing apples with oranges. Second, we need to reflect the fact that the indicators are of different importance to economic performance.

We recognized at the outset that any ranking of presidents risks being labeled as biased by anyone who does not like the results. To strengthen confidence in the rankings, we present the composite ranking in several ways, based on different assumptions. We create three different indexes: a base case, which is the best representation of economic performance, and two additional indexes, each with its own strengths and weaknesses. If the results from the different approaches are similar, then the results are stronger and we can be reasonably confident that the presidents' economic performances have been ranked accurately.

Three Methods to Rank the Presidents

The previous nine chapters presented rankings for the averages and trends for 17 different economic indicators and therefore a total of 34 indicators. These are the results of more than 2,200 data points (66 years and 34 indicators to cover the 12 presidents), so there is already a good indication of who did well and who did not. Whatever method is used to combine these 17 indicators, the resulting overall presidential rankings should be generally consistent with individual indicator rankings as well as the storyline of the presidents' policies.

Two of the methods require the use of statistical techniques that make it possible to combine the indicators into a common unit. The third method is simpler but perhaps not as accurate in capturing the presidents' relative performances. Annex 1 explains all three methods in greater detail. The three methods are:

1. Standard deviations method (base case)

2. Min-max method

3. Simple average of all presidential rankings for each indicator

For methods 1 and 2, the first task is to convert the indicators for each president into the same unit. For method 1 we take the average value for each of the indicators and then calculate the number of standard deviations from the mean for each president. That is the common unit that we use—the number of standard deviations from the mean. The standard deviation takes into account how much variation there is in the indicator and precisely how far apart the presidents' performances are, which gives a more accurate measure of performance than just tallying up all the presidential rankings. For example, GDP growth ranged from 5.3 percent for Kennedy down to 1.6 percent for Bush 43. The mean, or average, GDP growth rate for a president is 3.1 percent, and the standard deviation is 1.2 percent. A president gets credit for the number of standard deviations above the mean and deduction for the number of standard deviations below the mean. In this example, Kennedy is 1.83 standard deviations *above* the mean, and Bush 43 is 1.23 standard deviations *below* the mean.

Method 2, or min-max, requires that the indicators be expressed as percentage of the difference between the maximum and the minimum values for each indicator. This method also captures the magnitude of the difference between presidential performances. Method 3 is simply to add up all the rankings for each president for each indicator and divide by the number of indicators.

Weighting Schemes

The second step is to select the weights for each indicator, that is, to specify the relative importance of each indicator in explaining a president's economic performance. We could use equal weights across the board, which is simple and easy. However, that weighting scheme would give too little weight to indicators like inflation, the stock market, and the poverty line, which are not as closely related to the other indicators. It also would ignore the fact that the importance of the trend indicators depends on whether the indicator is a growth rate or a share. As pointed out earlier, differences in the administrations' beginning and end points with respect to growth rates are generally not very important to evaluating performance because they fluctuate too widely. With equal weights we would attribute too much performance significance to a brief fluctuation of an indicator that has little economic meaning. The only advantage of equal weights is that it involves fewer subjective judgments and may be easier to defend, but only in that respect.

There is no way of determining with certainty how much more important one indicator is with respect to another. There is always a significant subjective element in the selection of weights. In the base case and min-max methods, the relative importance of the indicator is represented by assigning each indicator a category of importance: Most Important, Important, Less Important, and Least Important. Most important is four times as important as least important. For the 17 indicators, the category weights work out as follows:

Most important	4.9%
Important	3.7%
Less important	2.5%
Least important	1.2%

Table 10.1 shows how each indicator is weighted in the base case. When the weights are totaled for the private-sector indicators and for the public-sector indicators, there is about a three-quarters priority for the private sector and one-quarter for the public sector. This private-public balance of weights is reasonable in measuring presidential performance in that, while the president has more control over the public sector indicators, he is mainly trying to affect indicators in the private sector, like growth, employment, and poverty reduction.

Table 10.1   Category Weights for Presidential Performance Indicators

Private-Sector Indicator	Average	Trend	Public-Sector Indicator	Average	Trend
1. GDP Growth	Most	Less	13. Federal Budget as a Percent of GDP	Less	Less
2. Unemployment Rate	More	More	14. Federal Budget Growth Rate	More	Least
3. Employment Growth Rate	More	Least	15. Federal Deficit as a Percent of Federal Budget	Less	Less
4. All Business Sector Productivity Growth	Less	Least	16. Total Federal Debt as a Percent of GDP	Less	More
5. Inflation Rate	Most	More	17. Federal Taxation as a Percent of GDP	More	Less
6. Real Interest Rate	Less	More			
7. Personal Savings Rate	Less	Least			
8. Gross Private Investment Rate	Less	Less			
9. Dow Jones Growth Rate	More	Least			
10. Percent Below the Poverty Line	More	Most			
11. Exports as a Percent of GDP	Less	More			
12. Trade Balance as a Percent of GDP	Less	More			
Total Weight	**39.5%**	**33.3%**	**Total Weight**	**14.8%**	**12.3%**
Total Private Sector	**72.8%**		**Total Public Sector**	**27.2%**	

WHAT THE PRESIDENTIAL PERFORMANCE INDEX (PPI) MEANS

The PPI is an overall measure of how the U.S. economy performed during each presidential administration and is the basis for the overall ranking of presidential economic performance. PPI captures not only the ultimate goals of economic policy, which are growth (increase in GDP), equity (increase in employment and reduction of poverty), and fiscal sustainability (reduction of debt and deficits), but also the intermediate goals of economic policy (higher savings and investment, lower inflation and interest rates), which will lead to desired outcomes in the future. It also captures the trends in all of these aspects of economic performance. The PPI for the simple average method uses a different scale. In addition, in Truman's case there are only 16 indicators because there is no poverty-line indicator for Truman. For the other 11 presidents, there are averages and trends for 17 indicators.

Given all of the indicators and their relative importance and lagged effects, how did the 12 post-WWII presidents rank overall? Tables 10.2, 10.3, and 10.4 provide the answer to that question.

Ranking the Indicators, Method 1: Base Case, Standard Deviations

The base case for presidential economic performance is shown in Table 10.2 and graphically in Figure 10.1. From Table 10.2, the presidential rankings appear to fall into six distinct levels of performance:

Later we review whether these rankings are consistent with rankings for individual indicators and are plausible based on what we have learned about economic history since WWII. Before summarizing the performance of each presidential administration, the two other methods for calculating rankings are examined in order to test the resilience of the base case finding of presidential performance. Each president's performance score and narrative is discussed in greater detail later in the chapter.

Table 10.2   Overall Rankings Based on Standard Deviations

Administration	Composite Score
Truman	176.0
Kennedy	100.0
Johnson	51.5
Eisenhower	40.7
Ford	39.5
Clinton	14.5
Nixon	2.8
Reagan	−23.2
Obama	−68.9
Bush 41	−73.1
Carter	−111.4
Bush 43	−148.4

1. Excellent	Truman, Kennedy
2. Good	Johnson, Eisenhower, Ford, Clinton
3. Fair	Nixon, Reagan
4. Weak	Obama, Bush 41
5. Poor	Carter
6. Very Poor	Bush 43

Ranking the Indicators, Method 2: Min-Max

The min-max method is another established statistical method to bring dissimilar units into a common unit. The min-max method, rather than using the mean, subtracts the value for the president with the lowest average for the indicator (Y_{min}) from the each president's average for the indicator (Y) and then divides it by the value for the president with the highest average for the indicator (Y_{max}) minus the minimum presidential average:

$$\frac{Y - Y_{min}}{Y_{max} - Y_{min}}$$

Figure 10.1   Depiction of Presidential Performance Index: Base Case

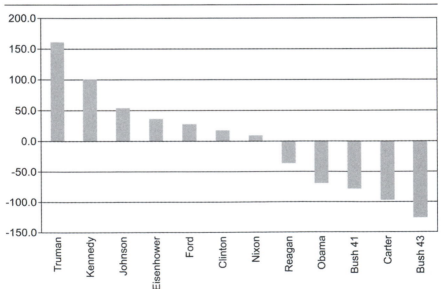

Table 10.3   Overall Rankings Based on Min-Max Method

Administration	Composite Score: Category Weights
Truman	189.5
Kennedy	100.0
Johnson	37.6
Ford	34.7
Eisenhower	25.2
Clinton	19.3
Nixon	−6.5
Reagan	−7.8
Obama	−58.6
Bush 41	−64.0
Carter	−120.8
Bush 43	−142.5

What is measured is each president's performance relative to the best-performing president for that indicator. If a president had the maximum average for the indicator, then his value is 1. If he had the minimum average, then the value is 0. The other presidents fall somewhere in between. The same weighting scheme is used for the min-max method in Table 10.3 as was used for the base case. This method helps to reduce the influence of extreme values.

The min-max method produces results that are only slightly different from the standard deviation method. Both the order of the rankings and the margins between the presidents are very close. Only Ford and Eisenhower, who were next to each other anyway, switch places. Truman and Kennedy are still at the top. Johnson, Eisenhower, Ford, and Clinton are in the next, "good" tier. Nixon, and Reagan are in the "fair" tier. Obama and Bush 41 are in the "weak" tier, and Carter and Bush 43 are at the bottom, just as with the standard-deviation base case method.

Ranking the Indicators, Method 3: Simple Average of All Indicator Rankings

Method 3 is the simplest approach. It simply averages the rankings for each president for every indicator average and trend. Recall that the poverty-line indicator was not calculated as far back as the Truman administration (and only for part of the Eisenhower administration).

Table 10.4   Overall Rankings Based on Average Indicator Rankings, Not Weighted

Administration	Average Rank, Unweighted
Truman	5.1
Eisenhower	5.6
Kennedy	5.7
Ford	5.9
Clinton	6.2
Johnson	6.3
Nixon	6.5
Obama	6.7
Reagan	6.9
Carter	7.1
Bush 41	7.5
Bush 43	7.9

While method 3 has the advantage of being straightforward, it does not capture the magnitude of gaps between presidents' performances for each indicator. For example, Truman reduced the national debt by 46.1 percentage points. The next best performance was Eisenhower's, but he was a very distant second at 16.1 percentage points. The simple average of rankings method would count the performance differential as only as one place out of 12 of a difference, when in fact the difference in debt reduction performance was large. Table 10.4 shows this method only with equal weights.

Note that the simple average ranking method uses a different scale from the other two methods. What Table 10.4 shows is the average rank each president achieved across all of the indicators. The lower the number, the better the ranking. Truman's score is 5.1, which means that his average ranking was a little above fifth place for each indicator. This score is good enough for first place. The last-place finishers, Bush 41 and Bush 43, ranked between seventh and eighth—7.5 and 7.9 respectively, for all the indicators.

This very basic method of ranking produces results that are also similar to the base case. Truman, Eisenhower, and Kennedy are at the top. Next are Ford, Clinton, and Johnson. Nixon, Obama, Reagan and Carter are next, with Bush 41 and Bush 43 at the bottom. Carter and Obama are a little overrated in this method, and Reagan and Johnson are a little underrated. These are consequences of giving important indicators the same weight as much less important indicators. But, in general, even this very different method produces results that are not radically different from the base case.

OVERALL RANKINGS AND STORIES OF INDIVIDUAL PRESIDENTIAL ECONOMIC PERFORMANCES

Throughout this book, indicator performance has been traced to policies, and now we can relate the overall narrative of each president's performance with his overall score. We can also reinforce policy lessons from comparisons of the economic performance of presidents—in particular, which policies work best and under which circumstances.

1. Harry S. Truman (1945–1953)

Truman ranks first. Consistent with his top ranking, Truman had many strong indicators, with only a few negatives on his record. A big part of the story of Truman's score is the massive improvement in the fiscal stance of the United States. The positive components include, foremost, reduction of the national debt, lowering the budget growth and share of the GDP, and reduction of the tax share of GDP. On the private-sector side, he averaged the highest positive trade balance. His unemployment rate was also low. On the negative side, GDP growth was low (with much volatility), and the debt share was high. As expected because of the exorbitant costs of WWII, Truman's average debt share was second highest among the 12 presidents. However, his reduction of the debt share far outweighed the negative impact of the average debt share.

In addition to his strong score, Truman had some "big-ticket" economic accomplishments. Truman could be said to be one of the most significant presidents since WWII. When the wartime economy transitioned to a peacetime economy, Truman successfully avoided economic disorder, and the economic adjustment went reasonably well even as 12 million decommissioned personnel were absorbed into the economy. The huge war debt of 127 percent of GDP was paid down at a rapid pace. The main threat turned out to be inflation (rather than unemployment), but that proved only transitory. His administration helped develop the postwar trade framework (supported by the Bretton Woods agreement and GATT) and contributed to the rebuilding of war-torn Europe. And, despite is battles with striking workers, helped labor improve working conditions.

2. John F. Kennedy (1961–1963)

Kennedy had the second best overall economic record. Kennedy's economic record was only three years, but it was three of the best years of the entire 66-year analysis period. Kennedy's score was helped by strong

GDP growth (the highest among the 12 presidents), extremely low inflation and unemployment, a positive trade balance, and progress in reducing poverty. There were generally good indicators all around. He also had only one significant weakness, the fewest of any of the presidents, and even that was minor—exports were below average. Kennedy ranks second in the min-max analysis as well, and third in the ranking average.

Two of Kennedy's biggest initiatives, his New Frontier and the tax cuts, were actually carried through in the Johnson administration. The Trade Expansion Act aimed at moving America toward a freer trade environment and was also continued under Johnson.

3. Lyndon B. Johnson (1963–1969)

Johnson had a very good economic performance and is ranked third. The strongest points of his economic record are extraordinarily good employment indicators, excellent progress on poverty reduction, and high GDP growth. Other positive aspects include an improvement in the debt share and a positive trade balance. On the negative side, the trend in inflation was upward, the stock market declined in real terms, export shares were below average, and tax shares were above average. However, the positive indicators were of a higher magnitude than the negative indicators.

Johnson's Main Accomplishments

Johnson, like Truman, had a number of big-ticket accomplishments with payoffs long after his administration ended. These accomplishments included following through on Kennedy's tax cut and passing the Civil Rights Act of 1964. Johnson's other major accomplishments were the passage of Medicare—guaranteed health care for retired persons—and Medicaid—health care for people who could not afford health insurance. These signature programs have provided real benefits and peace of mind to the poor, the elderly, and other vulnerable citizens in America. For tens of millions of Americans Medicare and Medicaid have meant the difference between going to a doctor or not, of diagnosing and treating medical conditions or not, and of not having to choose between food and medicine.

Unfortunately, in some of the latter administrations, the presidents and Congress did not manage the financial aspects of these programs, or of Social Security, particularly well. As a result, these programs are now placing severe fiscal pressure on an already-strained U.S. fiscal position. The aspects of the financial environment for these programs include the costs of health services, the management (spending) of the trust funds, and the management of the overall debt. It is not part of Johnson's legacy that Medicare is in financial trouble, but it is a lesson that major entitlement programs need their costs and benefits and revenue sources adjusted periodically as demographics change and the structure of the U.S. economy evolves.

4. Dwight D. Eisenhower (1953–1961)

Eisenhower came in fourth place out of the 12 presidents, very slightly ahead of Ford. His strong standing might seem counterintuitive given the recessions of 1954, 1958, and 1960. However, his strong performance indicators substantially outweigh his negatives. His best performance indicators were a positive trade balance, low inflation, a growing stock market, low deficits, and a low growth rate of the federal budget. His negatives were not particularly severe and included a high average poverty rate, which was characteristic of that period in history, somewhat weak exports, a low average GDP growth performance, and a low average employment growth rate.

The comparison of Eisenhower's record with Truman's is interesting because Eisenhower's record bears three recessions, while Truman's contends with postwar volatility. In the end, Truman's fiscal improvements give a big margin to Truman over Eisenhower in the base case (as well as the other statistical methods).

Eisenhower's economic legacy is strengthened by two historically important accomplishments. During his administration, the United States continued the pay-down of the national debt and launched America's main transportation infrastructure project of the twentieth century, the national highway system. These accomplishments yielded economic benefits that strengthened the American economy in the long run.

5. Gerald R. Ford (1974–1977)

Ford ranks fifth, and his story is fairly straightforward. Ford's economic record benefited from his ascension to the presidency during a recovery. He had three strong positive indicators and three moderate negatives. The GDP growth rate was strong, along with private investment and employment growth. The main negatives for Ford were the continued decline of the stock market and weak exports and trade balance. In the area of fiscal performance, Ford's record was essentially a wash, that is, about average among the 12 presidents.

Nixon's loss was Ford's gain. Gerald Ford's good ranking can be attributed mainly to good fortune. With only a two-year record (the shortest of the 12 presidents) and an economy coming out of recession, it is understandable that his overall record would be good. Ford's trends are measured from the relatively deep 1975 recession to the relatively strong growth year of 1977.

6. William J. Clinton (1993–2001)

Bill Clinton had a good economic record, ranking sixth overall. However, he had the best record among the six presidents since the 1978 period midpoint. Clinton had three strong points and two reasonably strong ones to bolster his record. First, he reduced unemployment and kept it low. Second, he reduced the deficits' share of the federal budget. Third, his administration achieved good progress in poverty reduction. His other strong point was the growth of the stock market. He has three notable negatives on his record as well. Taxes as a share of GDP were high, the trade balance was very negative, and personal savings were very low.

Clinton versus Reagan

It is interesting to view Clinton's economy through a comparison with that of Reagan as both are widely viewed as having strong economic records. Each administration recorded similarly good employment growth, between 16 and 17 million *net* increase in persons employed during each of the eight-year administrations. Under Reagan unemployment fell from 7.6 percent to 5.3 percent. Under Clinton it fell from 6.9 percent to 4.7 percent.

Clinton and Reagan had similar employment growth and similar GDP growth. Under Reagan, inflation plummeted, and under Clinton, inflation stayed very low. The main difference is that Clinton also achieved a major improvement in the nation's finances, while Reagan severely damaged the nation's finances. Economically speaking, Clinton is Reagan without the debt. Clinton's growth also led to much greater poverty reduction than under Reagan. That is why, economically at least, Clinton ranks several places higher than Reagan.

Clinton's Legislative Record and Deregulation

Clinton had a number of positive accomplishments, including turning around the nation's finances (undone under Bush 43), passing the Family

Leave Act, NAFTA, and welfare reform, though the latter two are debatable as to their positive impacts. He was unsuccessful in his health care reform in 1994, though some elements of the original plan, such as portability of coverage (the ability to continue similar insurance coverage even after changing employers) were accomplished in smaller pieces in later years.

One aspect of Clinton's economic record, in view of the causes of the 2008 financial crisis, that may not serve his legacy well is the strong current of financial deregulation that ran through his administration. This deregulation was championed by key Clinton advisors, including his two treasury secretaries, Robert Rubin and Lawrence Summers, as well as his Fed chairman, Alan Greenspan, whom he reappointed in 1995. As we discussed, this deregulatory mentality led to two measures that contributed significantly to the financial crisis of 2008: the Commodity Futures Modernization Act (CFMA) and the repeal of Glass-Steagall. Both measures had nearly unanimous Republican support, but they would not have been possible without Clinton's support.

The Dot.com Bubble

Another blemish on the Clinton economic record was the dot.com bubble. In the 11 years since that bubble burst, the stock market actually lost value not only in real terms but even absolute terms. Granted, there has been significant economic mismanagement since the Clinton administration that contributed to depressed stock prices. However, if the Bush 43 administration is to be accountable for gross negligence in regulating the subprime mortgage "industry," then the Clinton administration should be held accountable for not being more proactive in dealing with the stock market speculation that was rampant throughout much of his administration.

The main differences between the dot.com bubble and the 2008 financial crisis are that the 2008 financial crisis was far more expensive, involved widespread regulatory failure including that of the Federal Reserve, and required hundreds of billions of dollars in bailouts. We are still suffering from the effects of the crisis that hit in 2008.

7. Richard M. Nixon (1969–1974)

Despite being in the second performance tier, seventh overall, Nixon had some bright spots in his economic record. His main positive indicators were a high savings rate, a positive trade balance with increasing exports, and a low real interest rate. His negatives are in the more core indicators, including weak GDP growth, increasing inflation, and worsening unemployment. Nixon's case is one where the president had good intermediate indicators, which paid off after he left office. Nothing really stands out, good or bad, in Nixon's performance with respect to fiscal indicators.

Nixon's Main Accomplishments

Nixon, like Johnson and Truman, had a number of historically significant achievements, including the termination of the gold standard and the Bretton Woods trading system, which no longer made sense economically. He also signed key environmental legislation, which, while it might not have stimulated the economy, certainly has led to a better quality of life for most Americans, at least those who drink water and breathe air. The opening of China through diplomacy was an initial step in China's meteoric economic and technological growth during the past three decades.

Nixon would have scored higher, moving even to the good range, had his alleged criminal actions not led to his resignation in 1974. Without Watergate, he would have finished his term in 1977, a recovery year; thus his trends would have been positive for the most part rather than negative.

8. Ronald W. Reagan (1981–1989)

The presidency of Ronald Reagan has been elevated to almost mythic status in some political circles, both as the defeater of communism and as the great tax cutter, a champion of the free market and deliverer of the U.S. economy from stagflation. With that aura, he should rank near the top, if not at the very top, in economic performance, instead of eighth overall, which is where the indicators in this analysis place him.

The components of Reagan's economic score show a mixed bag. On the positive side, his best achievement was the reduction of inflation and improvement in stock market growth. Employment indicators were only slightly above average compared with the other presidents. His negatives are mainly the trade deficit, the increase in the national debt, and the share of the federal budget deficits in the budget. Oddly, taxes as a share of GDP were not a big factor either way in Reagan's economic performance score.

Seismic Economic Shifts

In a number of ways, the Reagan presidency ushered in a new era for the U.S. economy. During his administration, major long-term shifts, some good and some bad, began in key economic indicators, including:

- Lower inflation
- Higher stock market growth
- High real interest rates
- High trade deficits
- High budget deficits and national debt

Under Reagan, the chronic inflation of the 1970s was wrung out of the economy, mainly through Federal Reserve policy under Paul Volcker (who had been appointed by Carter and reappointed by Reagan). Reagan inherited double-digit inflation, which he had dubbed "the cruelest tax of all." Since Reagan took office, inflation rose above 4.0 percent only five times and above 5.0 percent only once in the 29 years since 1982. His presidency was also the beginning of a surge in the stock market after several decades of modest growth. Stocks surged an average of more than 10 percent for each year of his eight-year presidency.

On the minus side, Reagan's presidency marked the beginning of sustained record trade deficits that have continued to this day. Though trade deficits actually began in 1976 under Ford, Reagan took them to a new level of 3.2 percent of GDP from a previous high of 1.3 percent. Reagan's economic legacy also includes an entirely new and higher level of peace-time budget deficits. While Reagan may have joked that the "deficit was big enough to take care of itself," the new trend under Reagan was not joking matter: a national debt that went from a period low of 32.5 percent to 56.5 percent of GDP by the end of his administration. The accumulation of debt and the S&L crisis during Reagan's term created a difficult challenge for his successor, Bush 41, to put America's fiscal position on a sustainable path. Real interest rates also entered a new and higher realm. Though Reagan inherited high nominal and real interest rates from Carter, the real rates never settled back down to pre-Carter levels, even though the economy appeared to be performing well after the early part of his presidency.

As mentioned, one area where Reagan did not effect a major, long-term shift was in the level of tax revenue as a percentage of GDP. Tax shares of GDP were at 19.6 percent at the beginning of his administration (1981) and fell only 1.2 percentage points to 18.4 percent in 1989 despite the substantial reforms of the tax system during the Reagan administration.

Appointment of Alan Greenspan

Another aspect of Reagan's record is the appointment of Alan Greenspan, both to reform Social Security in 1983 and to lead the Federal

Reserve in 1987. This appointment had strong affects on the next four presidents. We have already discussed the policy errors made in the Social Security program, including rejecting President Clinton's proposal to save and invest the Social Security Trust Fund. Reagan and Greenspan also shared an economic philosophy that led to deregulatory policy choices that would ultimately lead to financial disaster in 2008.

Perceptions and Reality

When Reagan's record is put all together, probably neither his fans nor his detractors are close in characterizing his economic performance. As we examined Reagan's record closely, we found that his employment growth was good at 16.9 million net jobs—an annual growth rate of 1.9 percent—and a GDP growth rate of 3.4 percent. Both were good but not as phenomenal as his fans imagine. In fact, these strong points of Reagan's economic record were pretty close to the average for all presidents (3.0 percent growth rate and a 1.5 percent employment growth rate). His fiscal performance was much worse than average for the 12 presidents as he reversed a 33-year trend of shrinking the national debt relative to GDP.

He comes out with about a low average economic performance overall, not as bad as the Bush 41, Bush 43, or Carter, but not as good as Clinton or Johnson either. He is actually one place below Nixon and one above Obama in his scored performance. The main qualifier to his average-level performance is the long-term trends that began during his administration, which tilt his record further to the negative side.

9. Barack H. Obama (2009–)

The overwhelming economic challenge in Obama's presidency has been to limit the damage from the real estate and financial crises that continue to play out in his bid for re-election in 2012. While the economy has continued in a precarious state, there is much less panic than in the days when Obama took over from Bush 43. Obama's score is ninth overall. This ranking could easily have been worse, given the state of the economy, but Obama benefits from improvements to a free-falling economy. He also benefits from some positive indicators that are good mainly because the economy is weak but that are conducive to economic recovery.

In the brief Obama record, there are more negatives than positives, which is consistent with his ninth-place ranking. Obama's positives include growth in productivity, an increase in exports, a reduction in budget growth and low taxes as a share of GDP. The high deficits are the largest negative, followed by the high unemployment rate, poor employment growth, the high trade deficit and national debt share of GDP, and the low investment rate.

Obama's Legislative Record

Despite Obama's brief record, he has signed a substantial amount of legislation and has had a number of political battles that have shaped his efforts to extricate the economy from recession:

- Term Asset-Backed Securities Loan Facility (TALF), 2009
- The American Recovery and Reinvestment Act (ARRA), 2009 (stimulus bill)
- Automobile industry bailout, 2009
- Financial reform bill, 2010
- Extension of Bush tax cuts and institution of payroll tax reduction, 2010
- Debt ceiling show-down, 2011
- Potential follow-up stimulus bill and extension of the payroll tax cut

One of the big questions of economic performance early in the Obama presidency is, did the stimulus plan work? Shortly after taking office, Barack Obama pushed through the American Recovery and Reinvestment Act (ARRA), which was comprised roughly of one-third tax cuts, one-third "shovel ready" projects, and one-third payments to the unemployed and the poor. The idea was to have the public sector compensate for the lack of spending by the private sector, which was consistent with economic lessons learned from the Great Depression. This spending would encourage employers to hire people, who then would have more money to spend, and on and on up to higher levels of employment. All 178 House Republicans and all but two Senate Republicans voted against the bill. Republicans have since denounced the bill as a failure.

If the expectation for ARRA was to cure a deep recession that eviscerated not only the U.S. financial sector but also, to a large extent, that of Europe, then the stimulus package definitely came up well short. If one expected the stimulus bill to set the economy on a steady path to lower unemployment, then its record was also weak. But with respect to a more realistic goal of halting the economy's downward spiral, helping to stabilize the economy, and beginning to realize positive economic growth, then it was successful.

One might reasonably question the wisdom of the bill's composition and explore which part of the bill was the most effective. Was it the tax cuts, the transfer payments from government to individuals, or the government projects, like roads and bridges? Given the amount of hoarding of cash by both individuals and businesses, it is unlikely that the tax cuts at top income levels were very helpful. In contrast, the transfers to the unemployed almost certainly were spent, and spending by the government, by definition, is stimulative. However, there is no guarantee that tax cuts will be stimulative. In fact, in a depressed economy, tax cuts focused on those in the more comfortable income brackets are the least stimulative measure that could be implemented.

At the end of 2010, in the waning days of the Democratic majority in the House of Representatives, President Obama disappointed his progressive base by agreeing to extend Bush 43's tax cuts (launched in 2001) that were set to expire at the end of 2010. Obama had preferred to extend the tax cuts to those making less than $250,000 but let the others expire. The Republicans used the economic "argument" that, "It's not a good time to raise anybody's taxes," which apparently seemed economically sensible to enough people.

In addition to extending the Bush 43 tax cuts and despite the emerging funding issue for Social Security and Medicare, Obama proposed and Congress passed a 2 percent temporary reduction in the payroll tax (1 percent for employer and 1 percent for employee). There were also provisions to extend unemployment insurance. It was in every way a budget-busting agreement, but was passed with the hope that the bill would accelerate economic growth. Obama's payroll tax deductions may also have injected some equity into the tax deal as approximately 80 percent of Americans pay more in payroll taxes than they do in federal income taxes. It also restored some of the equity that had been sacrificed over the previous 26 years as the federal government spent the Social Security Trust Fund. Despite the continuation and expansion of tax cuts in December 2010, the federal budget deficit for fiscal year 2011 was $345 billion less than had estimated (though it was still very high at $1.3 trillion).

Obama's health care reform bill will also have an effect on a large sector of the economy (17 percent of the GDP can be traced to the health sector). According to the Congressional Budget Office, its impact on the federal budget is fairly minor, but there will be some winners and losers within the small net budgetary effect. The health care bill will have an increasing input as a number of the key provisions of the bill become effective in 2014.

Context for Obama's Record

Perhaps it is premature to assign a quantitative score to President Obama. He has not had enough "at-bats" to be compared to the other presidents. There are only two years of data on his record, and while that is the same length of time as Gerald Ford, Obama's record is still being built. His record will comprise a minimum of two more years and perhaps six. In his brief record thus far, his performance numbers are not as bad as one might expect. Obama's numbers tell the story that while the economic performance is not good, neither is it in the bottom tier. There are still three presidents who are below his score.

When a president follows a poor economic performance, he usually has an advantage—that is, unless the economy is so damaged and mired in financial turmoil that it takes more than an election cycle to reverse. Unlike Jimmy Carter, Obama received an economy in such shambles that no one really knew the extent of damage, how long it would take to get out of it, or for that matter how to get out of it. The application of Keynesian compensating fiscal policy (see Annex 2) had worked to keep recessions shallow and short ever since the end of WWII. But the Bush administration left Obama and the country with little fiscal room to maneuver, a much worse position than Reagan had encountered when he took office. Obama faced a debt-to-GDP ratio that was almost three times the level that Reagan faced. Also, under Reagan, the top tax rate was 70 percent, so there was plenty of room to lower the rates without being overly generous to the well-to-do. In addition, Obama's economy has had to contend with several waves of real estate foreclosures.

It has been a continuing challenge for Obama to find a way out of the economic fallout from the 2008 crisis. The challenge is compounded by economic turmoil in Europe. Obama cannot count on European economies to pull the U.S. economy forward. Rather, with finances and trade so interconnected between countries, Europe is more likely to be a drag on the United States if Europe cannot solve its economic predicament.

Obama, evidently, has made some progress, but not fully succeeded in the employment-creation phase of the economy. He has also had little co-operation from the opposition party. The financial crisis has proven so deep, so costly, and so pervasive that Obama has had neither the economic tools nor the fiscal maneuvering room to propel the private economy out of its predicament in the short term. And there is no credibility in the claim that we can get out of the crisis by adopting the same tax-cutting, deregulation strategy that laid the groundwork for the crisis in the first place. Such stances ignore the lessons of recent economic history.

10. George H. W. Bush (1989–1993)

George H. W. Bush essentially had to deal with both the fallout from and slowdown of the Reagan economy. The long economic expansion from 1983 to 1989 was subsiding, and there were serious budget issues that were compounded by the S&L crisis. Bush 41's tenth-place finish puts him in the "weak" category of performance.

Bush 41 had a few positives and many negatives, economically speaking. On the positive tally, the inflation rate average was low, exports increased, and taxes as a share of GDP, despite his moderate tax increase, remained low. On the negative side, the core indicators of GDP and employment growth were weak, the investment rate was low, and poverty increased significantly. The deficits increased, and there was a significant increase in the debt share of GDP.

This overall weak record should not be seen as a complete economic failure, however. Bush's economic experience was a kind of reverse of Ford's. In contrast to Ford, the timing of Bush 41's administration in the business cycle was poor. During 1983 through 1989, GDP growth averaged 4.2 percent, well above the period average. The economy had to soften sooner or later.

Repairs of Reaganomics

While he may not have been the most visionary of the 12 presidents, Bush 41 did not let ideology stand in the way of what needed to be done to deal with the federal budget deficit. The Reagan administration, of which he was a central part as vice president, had backed him into a fiscal corner. Bush 41 would have to deal with the negative side of "Reaganomics," which he had referred to as "voodoo economics" in his 1980 campaign against Reagan. Bush 41 was forced to renege on his "no new taxes" pledge and increase taxes to reach the Gramm-Rudman-Hollings deficit targets. The measures did not immediately solve the problem as another round of tax increases was needed under Clinton. Bush 41's cleanup of the S&L crisis (see Chapter 1) also mitigates his low score. Again, Bush had the task of repairing damage caused by a faulty economic model, this time because of inadequate financial regulation.

Finally, Bush 41 left the economy in better shape than many people may recall. Though unemployment was high at 7.5 percent, the GDP growth rate had picked up from the 1991 recession (a −0.2 percent GDP growth rate) to 3.4 percent in the election year of 1992. In 1993, when Clinton took office, the growth rate was 2.9 percent, the average for the period, and the last year of the Bush 41 record.

11. James E. Carter (1977–1981)

Jimmy Carter, despite a number of beneficial long-term initiatives, had a poor economic record and ranks next to last. Whether by his own hand or by the forces of the market and politics, the strong and growing economy that he inherited evolved into the worst "stagflation" in the 66 years of the analysis period.

Despite Carter's low score, his list of significant negatives is not much longer than his list of positives. It is the magnitude of the negatives that brings his score down. On the positive side of his record, savings and investment here high, the national debt share of GDP was the lowest during the 66-year period (32.5 percent), and exports increased. The largest negative by far was inflation, which was followed by high real interest rates, a high tax share of GDP, lower productivity, higher poverty, and a declining stock market.

Appointments of Fed Chairmen

It is not clear what Carter could have done differently other than to have made a better choice initially to lead the Fed. His first choice, William Miller, pursued an interest rate target policy with the idea of keeping interest rates lower to spur investment. Unfortunately, pursuing low interest rates exacerbated inflation. Carter quickly corrected this mistake when Miller stepped down after only one year as chairman, and Carter's next choice of Fed chairman, Paul Volcker, proved highly effective. Volcker was reappointed as Fed chairman by Reagan. Volcker's monetary policy is widely credited with defeating inflation in the early years of the Reagan administration.

Energy Self-Sufficiency

Carter did have vision, particularly when it came to reducing dependency on fossil-fuel through both efficiency measures and substitution of renewable energies. If the United States had followed through on Carter's programs to improve energy efficiency and substitute renewable energy sources for fossil fuel, the nation would be in a much better economic position today.

Nevertheless, Carter left the economy in a bad state with stagflation, high interest rates, and a stock market that had bottomed out. The Reagan record suffered early on until some of the main problems left by Carter were fixed.

12. George W. Bush (2001–2009)

By all measures and all statistical approaches, George W. Bush had the worst economic performance of any of the 12 presidents, significantly worse than his father, Bush 41, and Jimmy Carter. The end of the Bush administration was defined by a financial crisis that had been brewing for most of his presidency. The result was not a mild recession such as the U.S. economy experienced in 1991 or 2001. The 2008 financial crisis (−3.5 percent GDP decline) was worse than the 1982 recession, when GDP fell 1.9 percent and unemployment exceeded 10 percent. The economic damage from the 2008 crisis was extensive. It was a hole dug deep by the mortgage industry, investment banks, the ratings agencies, and the regulators, in particular the Federal Reserve. And it all happened under an economic philosophy of deregulation and weak enforcement.

Bush 43's performance score derives from a very short list of positives and a very long list of negatives. During his administration, inflation did remain low, exports increased, and taxes went down as a share of GDP, consistent with the tax cuts early in his administration and with the declining economy. On the down side, the biggest negatives for Bush 43 were the very low GDP growth and the very large rise in the national debt share of GDP. The next largest negatives were falling employment, a worsening trade deficit, and a rising budget deficit. In addition to these negatives, private investment fell, poverty increased, and the budget growth and share of GDP increased, all by significant to large amounts.

The Bush Tax Cuts

The Bush 43 tax cuts put the United States back on a path of unsustainable deficits. Within three years of taking office, Bush 43 had turned the largest federal budget *surplus* in U.S. history ($236 billion in 2000) into the largest federal budget *deficit* in U.S. history (−$378 billion in 2003). It was perhaps the worst fiscal decision made by a president since WWII. Had Bush not cut taxes unnecessarily, the U.S. government would be in a far better position today. The debt as a percentage of GDP would probably have been less than 50 percent of GDP and perhaps less than 40 percent. Instead, Bush 43's last budget left the debt at 83.4 percent of GDP. The high national debt also jeopardizes key entitlement programs such as Social Security and Medicare because their funding must be viewed in the context of the overall federal budget and national debt.[1]

A Laissez-Faire Economic Philosophy

The most damaging part of Bush 43's record can be traced to the poor regulatory performance that ignored unprecedented levels of financial sector risk. Bush 43 was at the helm and was responsible for setting the economic policy under which the main culprits of the economic crisis were operating. Bush 43 and his advisors, such as Fed Chairman Greenspan and Treasury secretary Paulson, resolutely espoused the doctrinaire economic philosophy of less regulation in a context where more regulation and better enforcement of existing regulations were desperately needed. The result was the worst economic meltdown since the Great Depression.

We cannot blame Bush 43 for all of the greedy excesses and machinations of players like Goldman Sachs and mortgage bankers or the compromised integrity of the ratings agencies. To be fair to Bush 43, human beings have proven to be quite weak at stepping back from risky financial behavior and turning off the golden spigots of speculative income before it is too late, as we also saw under Clinton and Reagan.

However, the signs leading up to financial crises are usually not difficult to identify, and Bush 43 and his economic team ignored them. His economic team also advised that tax cuts were a good idea to begin his administration, and they proved disastrous fiscally and with little or no benefit to growth or employment. Bush 43's desire to expand home ownership proved also to be a failure. The percentage of Americans owning a home in 2009 was below that of 1998, thus erasing a decade of gains. In almost every respect, Bush 43 stands alone as the president with the worst economic performance since WWII.

SUMMARY OF MAJOR FINDINGS AND ECONOMIC LESSONS

In the review of presidents since WWII, several administrations stand out, not necessarily for their scores but for their large long-term impact on the economy. These presidents are the ones with the substantial legislative records and a variety of noneconomic decisions that had strong effects on the economy. Truman, Johnson, Nixon, and Reagan stand out as probably the most significant presidents whose decisions had long-term economic, social, and environmental impacts on the country.

Truman managed a successful transition after WWII, helped set up the international framework for trading, and paid for a large chunk of the costs of both WWII and the Korean War. Johnson created two of the most important government programs, Medicare and Medicaid; followed through on Kennedy's tax cuts; lowered poverty more than any other president; and moved America through some of the most difficult times of the civil rights struggle. Nixon updated the international framework for trade, opened relations with China, signed some of the most important environmental legislation, and ended the Vietnam War, all of which had major economic impacts. Reagan's administration marked the beginning of a number of significant shifts in the economic indicators. He also brought the United States to the end of the Cold War, which paid important budget dividends in reduced defense expenditures. However, his long-term impact also includes substantial negatives.

The Performance of Republicans versus Democrats

Overall Performance

There were 12 presidents in the analysis period, six Republicans and six Democrats. If it was not evident to the reader from earlier chapters, then it should be clear in this chapter: economically speaking, Democratic presidents performed significantly better than Republican presidents. Overall, the three top performances were recorded by Democrats— Truman, Kennedy, and Johnson—while two of the three worst performances were recorded by Republicans, Bush 41 and Bush 43. In addition, four out of the top six performers are Democrats, while four of the bottom six are Republicans.

The Democrats also have the advantage when tallying performance separately in the first and second halves of the 1946 through 2011 period. The comparison of presidents by halves of the analysis period eliminates the advantage of presidents from one party governing in an economically more advantageous time period.

In the first half of the period, again, the top three performances were by Democrats, followed by three Republicans. Nixon, a Republican, had the lowest performance in the first half of the period (but still near the middle overall).

In the latter half of the period, Democrats also have the advantage in performance: Clinton, Obama, and Carter on the Democrat side versus Reagan, Bush 41, and Bush 43 on the Republican side. For the latter period, Clinton (D) had the best performance, followed, in order of performance score, by Reagan (R), Obama (D), Bush 41 (R), Carter (D), and Bush 43 (R). So Democrats ranked first, third, and fifth while Republicans ranked second, fourth, and sixth.

In contemporaneous match-ups, Democrats also edge out Republicans. For example, Johnson scored better than Nixon, and Clinton outscored

Reagan and Bush 43. Truman and Kennedy outscored Eisenhower. The one contemporaneous comparison where Republicans did better was Reagan versus Carter.

Fiscal Performance

The comparison of fiscal performances clearly shows the Democrats to have a much better record overall with respect to both deficits and the debt. With respect to the national debt, five of the six Democratic presidents reduced the national debt as a share of GDP, a total of 75.7 percentage points. Four out of the six Republicans raised the debt, a total of 61.7 percentage points. Only Eisenhower and Nixon actually lowered the debt share, a combined total of 20.1 percentage points. The only Democrat who raised the debt was Obama, and his 13.5 percentage point increase in the debt is in the context of a president who received an economy already spiraling downward. So, despite popular perceptions, Democratic presidents have a far better record of fiscal responsibility.

The Expansion of the Federal Government: Taxes and Spending

The composition of federal expenditures and tax revenues has changed a good deal since 1946 as the United States has mobilized for and demobilized from war and as the population has aged and the social safety net become more extensive. However, for all of the rhetoric about the expanding reach of government, in terms of the share of the economy, the federal government has not grown much since the 1950s. For example, the three-year average federal budget share for 1955 through 1957 under Eisenhower was 16.9 percent. Fifty years later, under Bush during 2005 through 2007 (prior to the economic crisis), the federal budget averaged 19.9 percent of GDP. Yes, government budget share increased, but does it represent a major shift in economic ideology?

The three-percentage-point increase in share of GDP by the federal government really reflects the aging of the U.S. population and the corresponding growth of Social Security and Medicare expenditures. Even after the 2008 crisis, there has been only a minimal increase in the federal government share of GDP outside of Social Security and Medicare. If Social Security and Medicare are taken out of the federal budget, then the share of the federal government of GDP increases from 15.3 percent in 1950 (Medicare did not yet exist) to 17.1 percent in 2011, a mere 1.8 percentage point increase over a 61-year period. Beyond the nation's retirement and elderly medical care programs, it is a pretty tough case to make that "Big Government" programs have taken over the economy.

Given what most Americans want the government to do and the demographic trend in the United States, we should expect an increasing government share over time. The United States continues to get older and has been doing so for the entire period since WWII. Therefore, there will be higher expenditures on Social Security and Medicare, which constitute about one-third of the total federal budget. In addition, as the population grows (the population increased from 141.4 million in 1946 to 311.9 million in 2011), there is a greater need for environmental management of air, water, and other natural resources. Environmental management does not have to entail dramatically higher government budget costs because it is the private sector that will have to implement environmental protection measures. However, it does represent an expansion of government to create incentives for the private sector to behave responsibly with respect to the environment.

Systematic Benefit to Presidents of Earlier Time Periods

Most of the better presidential economic performances occurred in the first half of the 1946 through 2011 time period, that is, before 1978. Clinton was the only exception. If we evaluate economic performance by decade, we also see that the 1960s were the best decade, followed by the 1950s. The 2000s were the worst decade. The U.S. economy was simply performing better, using our set of indicators and methodology, prior to 1978 than it has been since. Is this because the presidents in the first part of the period were better economic managers? Or is it because of advantages that earlier presidents had in terms of a greater abundance of natural resources, less competition, lower cumulative trade and fiscal deficits, along with a younger working-age population? The answer is probably a combination of both. The physical advantages for earlier administrations are undeniable. As to economic management, to the extent that the presidents were guided more by historical lessons, context, and moderation, and less by ideology, the presidents tended to perform better.

One important clarification is in order here. Although earlier presidents had better scores on the economic indicators, it does not mean that the standard of living was higher during the earlier administrations. These earlier presidents no doubt helped the United States build a better standard of living, but the standard of living continued to improve throughout the period. Medical and information technology are light-years ahead of the days of Truman. Americans experience real benefits from these advances every day. Per capita income has increased as well, although income distribution has been more concentrated in recent decades. These trends have dampened the standard-of-living gains across lower income brackets, but, overall, living standards are substantially better in the latter part of the 1946 through 2011 period than in the earlier part. The sustainability of improvements in the living standard, given the United States' lack of attention to environmental priorities, is another question.

Blame for the 2008 Financial Crisis

The Financial Crisis Inquiry Commission (FCIC), which was commissioned to investigate the causes of the 2008 financial crisis, concluded in its 500-page report:[2]

> The captains of finance and the public stewards of our financial system ignored warnings and failed to question, understand, and manage evolving risks within a system essential to the well-being of the American public. Theirs was a big miss, not a stumble. While the business cycle cannot be repealed, a crisis of this magnitude need not have occurred.

There is no question that the forces that caused the 2008 crisis, primarily the investment banks, have a strong grip on both parties. Powerful financial interests influenced policymakers to shirk their fiduciary responsibilities and allowed regulatory agencies to slack off and not hold banks to appropriate risk levels. There were notable players on the Democratic side, including key members of the Clinton economic team such as Robert Rubin and Lawrence Summers—both Treasury secretaries—as well as Democratic members of Congress, who protected Fannie Mae and Freddie Mac though they were in serious financial trouble.

One thing is clear, however. The politicians who were mainly in charge, the people at the very top of the government to whom regulatory agencies were accountable, were the Republicans of the Bush 43 administration. The tolerance for mounting risk was far more in line with the Republican economic philosophy of the free market than it was of the customarily more moderate and pragmatic Democratic approach to the economy. Even after their preeminent contribution to the financial collapse, it has been the Republicans who doggedly oppose current financial reform efforts that would prevent the next financial crisis. It is reasonable, therefore, to apportion the lion's share of the responsibility for the 2008 collapse and its aftermath to the Republican Party.

A President's Record of Appointments

We have seen also how the president can affect the economy by making appointments to key economic positions. Carter initially appointed William Miller as chairman of the Federal Reserve but then replaced him with Paul Volcker. Reagan appointed Alan Greenspan to reform Social Security and, a few years later, to head the Fed. Greenspan was once dubbed "the Oracle" by lawmakers on Capitol Hill and the press for his economic expertise. Later it became apparent that he made some of the most damaging economic policy decisions in the history of the United States, including building the Social Security Trust Fund and then squandering it. An even greater failure by Greenspan was his almost complete abdication of responsibility as the nation's chief financial regulator leading up to the financial collapse of 2008. Had Greenspan not been reappointed by Clinton or Bush 43, a less ideological and more responsible person might have led the Fed, and the 2008 crisis might have been averted. A president's economic power and his performance are also determined by the people he places in key positions.

Economic Policy by History and Context, Not by Ideology

We have seen that tax cuts work only if the context is right. For some people the context is never wrong. That is an ideological approach to economic policy that would only be successful if conditions were always the same. History shows that the context is often not right for tax cuts, and it is a shame that so many Americans waste their time supporting discredited ideological prescriptions for the economy. Ideology has also led presidents down a ruinous path through the deregulation of financial markets. The United States has made valuable progress in the ability of Americans to leverage their assets. But when financial institutions become irresponsible and cease to assess risk, or have no incentive to assess risk, then it is time to abandon the deregulatory mindset and impose regulations to control excessive risk and more strictly enforce existing regulations.

An Economically Proactive President for the Future?

Should the president, as economist, have the economic presence of mind to cast an eye now and then to, for example, Wall Street, and ask his economic advisors, "What are those guys doing over there? Is there anything we should be concerned about in the stock or bond market? Is there a bubble forming that maybe we should take some air out of before it gets too big? Maybe some new regulations, announcements of new policies, tightened standards, better regulatory enforcement?"

What if George W. Bush had asked the Fed, "Is that healthy for banks to be doling out all those subprime mortgages? Could that practice come back to haunt us?" That would seem to be a reasonable and prudent question for the president to ask. And what would Greenspan's answer have been? Should Bush even have needed to ask Greenspan? After all, Greenspan was the revered economic senior statesman who would have seen the danger before anyone else and alerted Bush. But the record shows that neither man took appropriate action. When Bernanke took over for Greenspan, nothing really changed. Still, wouldn't it have been refreshing for a president to be alert and proactive rather than just letting the speculators go wild, piling on layer after layer of risk buried in unregulated derivatives? While Bush was the worst case, he certainly was not the only case. We saw excesses under Reagan with the S&L crisis and under Clinton with the dot.com bubble both of whom experienced the consequences of excessive risk.

The Great Depression, which brewed under Republican president Calvin Coolidge, struck with the stock market crash of 1929. It deepened until 1933, covering Republican president Herbert Hoover's entire administration. The economy did not begin its full recovery until eight years later with the launching of the Second World War. In all, it was 13 years from the time the Depression hit until the time it lifted. Despite the prolonged economic hardship of the 1930s, Americans at that time showed no eagerness to return the Republicans to the White House. There was little evidence at that time that the Republican candidates for president would have done anything different from that which had caused the Great Depression. Republicans opposed Roosevelt's programs and were fixated on controlling the budget deficits as the unemployment rate approached 25 percent of the entire American workforce.

Republicans did not return to the White House for 20 years until Dwight Eisenhower won the presidency in 1952. President Obama will not have that much time to repair the damage of 2008 financial crisis. Realistically, one election cycle working with an opposition party not known for co-operation may not be enough time to fix a crisis that was a deacade in the making.

NOTES

1. Add to that an unfunded prescription drug benefit worth $50-$60 billion annually, and the Medicare program is under even greater stress.

2. Financial Crisis Inquiry Commission (FCIC) Report, January 27, 2011, xvii.

Annex 1

Methodology

RANKING PRESIDENTS BY A SINGLE INDICATOR

Ranking the presidents according to a single indicator does not require any special methodology. It does require a rationale for why we have chosen these particular indicators and the time period over which we rank the presidents.

Indicator Selection

Indicators were selected for partly for their value in capturing economic well-being and partly for attribution to presidential policies. An indicator might be an intermediate in capturing good economic performance. For example, investment leads to good things but is not yet itself a good thing as is higher income (GDP growth) or getting a job (higher employment).

Does the Indicator Measure Something Bad or Something Good?

Another fundamental issue in indicator selection is the degree to which an indicator can be said to be bad or good. For example, debt as a percentage of GDP is generally thought of as a bad thing, but there are instances where debt needs to be increased either to combat an economic downturn or to fund military operations to defend the country. The same is true of taxes; sometimes they need to go up and sometimes they need to go down. In this case, we make the assumption that under normal circumstances (e.g., no wars or economic collapse), higher debt, taxes, and budget expenditures are bad.

Two Types of Indicators

The analysis uses two types of indicators:

Type 1: growth rates (GDP growth, employment growth, stock market growth, etc.)

Type 2: shares (of GDP, of the population, of the labor force, etc.)

Real versus Nominal

Growth rates are always adjusted for inflation to produce the real growth rate of an indicator. That way, the president is neither penalized nor rewarded for indicator changes that are caused by inflation. Inflation is considered separately in the assessment of presidential performance.

CREATING A COMPOSITE INDEX

Combining the indicators into one composite indicator (Chapter 10) requires a number of statistical steps. This composite indicator is the basis for the presidential rankings.

1. Collecting data for each year for each indicator
2. Normalizing the indicators
3. Weighting and aggregating the indicators
4. Creating the final composite ranking with a new scale.

Collecting Observations (Sample Size)

A minimum sample size is necessary to ensure there are enough data to produce meaningful results. There are two samples in effect: the 66 data points for most of the indicators and the 12 presidents. The standard deviations require a minimum sample size of 30 to generate a statistically viable distribution. The min-max approach also used in Chapter 10 does not have this requirement.

Normalization of the Data

The data need to be normalized in some way in order to combine indicators when they are in different units, for example, growth rates and shares of GDP. In this analysis, two methods are used: (1) standardization through the use of standard deviations from the mean, and (2) min-max, where the presidents' performances are expressed as the percentage of the highest presidential value for an indicator minus the lowest presidential value. This latter method also has the advantage of yielding a final score between 0 and 1, which gives a good sense of "groupings" of presidential performance (Excellent, Good, Fair, Poor).

Skewed Data

In some instances there are data points that diverge greatly from the other data. When these data are averaged with other data, they make the differences with the other data look small. There is a statistical method called top coding where the outlier data point is set equal to the next most extreme value so as not to throw off the overall average and/or ranking. However, it was decided not to use this top coding technique and to calculate presidential performance scores on the original data.

Weighting

Weighting is a judgment by the analyst as to how important one indicator is with respect to the others. There are a number of ways to choose weights. One could avoid the issue by just placing equal weights on all of the indicators. Alternatively, one could make a series of subjective judgments on the importance of each indicator.

The weighting structure chosen for this analysis considers a number of factors in assessing how important an indicator is: the degree of influence a president has on the indicator (higher weight), the degree to which the indicator is correlated with one or more of the other indicators (lower weight), the degree of volatility of the indicator (lower weight), and whether the indicator represents intermediate success (e.g.. real interest rate; lower weight) or ultimate success (e.g., GDP or employment growth; higher weight).

If the indicator is volatile, as is the case with most growth rates, then its average is much more important to measuring performance than its trend. This is true of "flow" indicators like GDP growth and stock market growth, which are volatile. Thus, the *change* in their growth rates from the first year to the final year of the administration does not usually say as much about performance as does the *average* growth rate for the indicator that was achieved under a presidential administration. In contrast, for "stock" indicators like debt as a percentage of GDP or the unemployment rate, which do not fluctuate as much, the trend is generally more important than the average.

ANNEX 2

The Great Depression and World War II: Background to the Modern Economy

The Great Depression struck the United States when the stock market crashed on October 29, 1929. An economic decline ensued in which the unemployment rate increased from 3.2 percent in 1928 to 24.9 percent in 1933 and the nation's output fell by 36 percent. Per capita income fell to the level in 1908, thus erasing 20 years of improvement in the nation's standard of living. The economic decline spread across North America and Europe, plunging all industrial economies into depression.

For those who are receptive, this economic tragedy is an opportunity to learn lessons for economic policy. The lessons from the Depression derive from its causes and the way presidents Herbert Hoover and Franklin Roosevelt addressed it and how it was ultimately resolved. There are a number of theories to explain why the economy fell into a depression, including:

- Restrictive monetary and fiscal policies turned a banking crisis into a full-scale financial collapse.
- The Federal Reserve intervened too much, not allowing the money supply to fall to its natural low level, which would allow prices to fall even further, which would have sparked a recovery.
- Increasing concentration of wealth resulted in too high of a savings rate, which along with rising productivity meant that consumer demand could not maintain employment. In addition, the excess wealth of the rich was used in stock market speculation.

- A sudden drop in the return on capital (because of "animal spirits") caused investors to reduce their investments, which led to recession.

The most plausible storyline suggests that the main contributing factors were within the control of policymakers: inappropriate monetary and fiscal policies, as well as a weak regulatory framework. Policymakers desperately wanted to lead the economy out of the depression, but once the depression hit, the wrong policies continued. In 1929, for example, the money supply (M1)[1] was $26.4 billion, but by 1933 it had fallen to $19.8 billion, a 25.0 percent decrease. This is exactly the opposite of what would be prescribed today. The financial crises during this period deepened because of this reduction in the money supply. While deflation was occurring in the economy, the nominal interest rate ranged between 1 and 2 percent. With the high rate of *deflation*, 8 percent, the real interest rate was more than 9 percent, which further depressed investment.

The next step toward a deeper depression occurred when Britain left the gold standard. Other countries were afraid the United States would do the same and started cashing in their dollars for gold. This run on U.S. gold made the Federal Reserve increase the rediscount rate to member banks in an effort to halt the run on gold. This interest rate increase exacerbated the wave of bank failures and plunged the economy ever deeper into depression. We should note that the rediscount rate was also increased in 1933 and 1937, the latter increase contributing to a major recessionary dip in 1938.

On the trade front, countries were desperate to improve the trade balance in order to maintain higher employment. Therefore, there was a strong push for protectionism. In 1930, the Smoot-Hawley Tariff was passed. The curtailment in trade caused by this tariff and by similar measures in other countries prevented any employment relief that could have been achieved through expanded trade.

The third major lesson in how not to deal with a recession was the fiscal policy that was followed in 1932. President Hoover was afraid of ruinous budget deficits. The tax rates were raised to a level that would have doubled tax revenues of a full-employment economy. The tax increase was ineffective in eliminating the deficits, and the economy sank further. Taxes were raised also at the state and local levels, all while the national income had already fallen by 30 percent.

Franklin Roosevelt maintained a similar taxing and spending regime to that of Herbert Hoover throughout the 1930s. Despite Roosevelt's many programs, the federal budget deficits did not exceed 4.4 percent of GDP.

The lowest deficit for the decade occurred in 1938, another year of deep downturn. Government expenditures increased in absolute terms in most, but not all, years, and expenditures as a percentage of GDP ranged mainly between 8 and 11 percent. In 1938, expenditures fell to 7.8 percent of GDP, which may have temporarily lowered the deficit but which also seems to have slowed the weak economy as unemployment increased to more than 19 percent. In addition, to fund his new Social Security program, Roosevelt had to institute a new tax, and in 1936 tax revenues grew faster than expenditures—again, not what would be prescribed for a recession today. The magnitudes of spending that were needed to vault the U.S. economy out of the Depression were not realized until WWII, when government expenditure jumped to more than 40 percent of GDP.

At the height of the Depression in 1933, John Maynard Keynes published his monumental *General Theory of Employment, Interest and Money*. In this book, Keynes proposed the concept of "compensating fiscal policy" as a solution to recession or depression. Compensating fiscal policy aimed to smooth out swings in the business cycle by increasing government spending during recessions and lowering spending during booms. Another important conclusion of Keynes's work was that monetary policy was not effective during a recession. During the Great Depression, some banks hoarded cash, which inhibited investment. This phenomenon became known as the "liquidity trap." Thus, for recessions, the best way out was fiscal stimulus in the form of government spending.

This approach has dominated U.S. economic policy since the end of WWII, and given that the United States has not experienced anything close to the economic collapse of the 1930s, compensating fiscal policy has arguably been very effective. The highest unemployment since WWII was 10.2 percent in 1982, while the peak during the Depression was 24.9 percent in 1933. Many amateur economists appear to have forgotten this historical fact and have vociferously advocated the opposite of compensating fiscal policy, that is, insisting on massive spending cuts during a sluggish and underperforming economy. To be fair, the Democrats also have advocated a procyclical tax increase on the wealthier Americans. There may indeed be room for tax increases if they improve the fiscal balance, but only if they do not impair consumers' willingness to spend.

It is not clear that Keynes was envisioning the magnitude of economic stimulus that ultimately lifted the economy out of depression, but it is clear that the policies of the 1930s, whether under Hoover or Roosevelt, were often at odds with the principle of compensating fiscal policy.

WORLD WAR II

Understanding the economic background from WWII is also important to understanding presidential rankings and the context of economic challenges that we face today. For example, to wage WWII, the federal government increased expenditures to 45.3 percent of the entire economy by 1944. The deficit alone was a quarter of the GDP, compared with today's relatively high 8.9 percent. Even coming on the heels of the recession, 46 percent of the war was paid for by current taxation, leaving 54 percent to be funded by borrowing. The revenue act of 1943 introduced the withholding tax so that taxes could be collected throughout the year. Tax collection costs were reduced because employers became the tax collectors. The borrowing was mainly through bonds sold to the public and the banking system. The ability of the economy to absorb both the level of taxation and the level of borrowing is impressive, given that it had been in the doldrums for the previous 12 years. Paying taxes and buying bonds were also viewed as a patriotic duty to support those fighting overseas.

The effects on the economy were radical. Unemployment that had stood at 19.0 percent as recently as 1938 fell to 9.9 percent in 1941, the lowest in 12 years. The unemployment rate fell to 4.7 percent in 1942 and to 1.9 percent in 1943. It was clear that massive deficit spending had hauled the economy out of the Depression.

The institutions and programs that sprang out of the Depression remain cornerstones of our economy. New Deal initiatives including Social Security, the Federal Deposit Insurance Corporation, and the Securities and Exchange Commission were all established to reduce the risks inherent in a free enterprise system. The Glass-Steagall Act was passed in 1933 to prohibit commercial banks from engaging in investment activities. These initiatives had the common objective of preventing or easing the negative byproducts of free market activity. Without these institutions functioning effectively, the United States may very well find itself back in a 1930s-style depression. A World War III–related stimulus would likely be an even less appealing solution than was WWII. With painful lessons learned in the Depression, an upgraded regulatory system based on those lessons, and the newly strengthened U.S. manufacturing sector, the United States was ready to assume leadership of the world economy.

RELEVANCE TO THE 2008–2009 AND PRIOR RECESSIONS

Since WWII, policymakers have successfully employed macroeconomic policies based on lessons learned from the Great Depression to keep recessions from becoming depressions. One of the most important lessons from the Great Depression is that when the private economy falters, the public sector should step in with a significant stimulus, mostly through spending, even if large fiscal deficits are likely. We learned from the Depression that it is a bad idea to further restrict the economy through spending cuts or tax increases. Debt can be paid off when the economy is growing steadily again, which we also learned after WWII. Unfortunately, many antigovernment politicians loudly contest the lessons learned from the Depression. They vigorously pursue spending cuts, which are proven to further weaken a struggling economy, particularly when private-sector business is unwilling to hire more workers and private-sector consumers cannot or will not spend.

NOTE

1. M1 is the narrowest definition of the money supply and includes mainly cash in circulation and transactions deposits.

Annex 3

Statistics

Table A.1 GDP and Productivity Statistics

Year	GDP Current Prices ($ billion)	GDP Constant 2005 Prices ($ billion)	GDP Growth Rate (%)	Productivity Index: Non-Farm Business Sector (1992 = 100)	Productivity Growth Rate (%)
1945	223.0	2,011.4	−1.1		
1946	222.2	1,792.2	−10.9		
1947	244.1	1,776.1	−0.9	37.1	
1948	269.1	1,854.2	4.4	38.2	2.8
1949	267.2	1,844.7	−0.5	39.4	3.3
1950	293.7	2,006.0	8.7	42.1	6.7
1951	339.3	2,161.1	7.7	43.2	2.7
1952	358.3	2,243.9	3.8	44.0	1.8
1953	379.3	2,347.2	4.6	45.0	2.3
1954	380.4	2,332.4	−0.6	45.8	1.9
1955	414.7	2,500.3	7.2	47.8	4.2
1956	437.4	2,549.7	2.0	47.4	−0.7
1957	461.1	2,601.1	2.0	48.7	2.6
1958	467.2	2,577.6	−0.9	49.7	2.2
1959	506.6	2,762.5	7.2	51.6	3.8
1960	526.4	2,830.9	2.5	52.2	1.2
1961	544.8	2,896.9	2.3	53.9	3.1

(*continued*)

Table A.1 (continued)

Year	GDP Current Prices ($ billion)	GDP Constant 2005 Prices ($ billion)	GDP Growth Rate (%)	Productivity Index: Non-Farm Business Sector (1992 = 100)	Productivity Growth Rate (%)
1962	585.7	3,072.4	6.1	56.3	4.5
1963	617.8	3,206.7	4.4	58.2	3.5
1964	663.6	3,392.3	5.8	59.9	2.9
1965	719.1	3,610.1	6.4	61.8	3.1
1966	787.7	3,845.3	6.5	64.0	3.6
1967	832.4	3,942.5	2.5	65.1	1.7
1968	909.8	4,133.4	4.8	67.3	3.4
1969	984.4	4,261.8	3.1	67.5	0.2
1970	1,038.3	4,269.9	0.2	68.5	1.5
1971	1,126.8	4,413.3	3.4	71.2	4.0
1972	1,237.9	4,647.7	5.3	73.6	3.3
1973	1,382.3	4,917.0	5.8	75.8	3.1
1974	1,499.5	4,889.9	−0.6	74.6	−1.6
1975	1,637.7	4,879.5	−0.2	76.7	2.8
1976	1,824.6	5,141.3	5.4	79.2	3.3
1977	2,030.1	5,377.7	4.6	80.5	1.6
1978	2,293.8	5,677.6	5.6	81.6	1.3
1979	2,562.2	5,855.0	3.1	81.2	−0.4
1980	2,788.1	5,839.0	−0.3	81.0	−0.3
1981	3,126.8	5,987.2	2.5	82.1	1.4
1982	3,253.2	5,870.9	−1.9	81.2	−1.1
1983	3,534.6	6,136.2	4.5	84.8	4.4
1984	3,930.9	6,577.1	7.2	86.5	2.0
1985	4,217.5	6,849.3	4.1	87.9	1.6
1986	4,460.1	7,086.5	3.5	90.6	3.1
1987	4,736.4	7,313.3	3.2	90.9	0.3
1988	5,100.4	7,613.9	4.1	92.3	1.6
1989	5,482.1	7,885.9	3.6	93.1	0.8
1990	5,800.5	8,033.9	1.9	94.7	1.8
1991	5,992.1	8,015.1	−0.2	96.2	1.5
1992	6,342.3	8,287.1	3.4	100.0	4.0
1993	6,667.4	8,523.4	2.9	100.6	0.6
1994	7,085.2	8,870.7	4.1	101.6	1.0
1995	7,414.7	9,093.7	2.5	102.0	0.4
1996	7,838.5	9,433.9	3.7	104.7	2.6
1997	8,332.4	9,854.3	4.5	106.2	1.5

Table A.1 (continued)

Year	GDP Current Prices ($ billion)	GDP Constant 2005 Prices ($ billion)	GDP Growth Rate (%)	Productivity Index: Non-Farm Business Sector (1992 = 100)	Productivity Growth Rate (%)
1998	8,793.5	10,283.5	4.4	109.3	2.9
1999	9,353.5	10,779.8	4.8	112.9	3.3
2000	9,951.5	11,226.0	4.1	116.8	3.4
2001	10,286.2	11,347.2	1.1	120.1	2.9
2002	10,642.3	11,553.0	1.8	125.7	4.6
2003	11,142.1	11,840.7	2.5	130.2	3.6
2004	11,853.3	12,246.9	3.4	133.7	2.6
2005	12,623.0	12,623.0	3.1	135.9	1.6
2006	13,377.2	12,958.5	2.7	137.1	0.9
2007	14,028.7	13,206.4	1.9	139.1	1.5
2008	14,291.5	13,161.9	−0.3	140.0	0.6
2009	13,939.0	12,703.1	−3.5	143.2	2.3
2010	14,526.5	13,088.0	3.0	149.1	4.1
2011	15,087.7	13,313.4	1.7	150.1	0.7

Table A.2 Inflation, Interest Rates, and Money Supply Statistics

Year	CPI-U Index (1982–1984 = 100)	CPI-U Inflation Avg.-Avg. Annual Rate %	Bank Prime Interest Rate % (Nominal)	Bank Prime Interest Rate % (Real)	Money Supply, M2, Seasonally Adjusted ($ billion)	Annual Growth Rate %
1945	18.0	2.3	1.5	−0.8		
1946	19.5	8.3	1.5	−6.3		
1947	22.3	14.4	1.5	−11.3		
1948	24.1	8.1	1.8	−5.8	174.9	
1949	23.8	−1.2	2.0	3.2	177.0	1.2
1950	24.1	1.3	2.2	0.9	184.7	4.4
1951	26.0	7.9	2.5	−5.0	195.7	5.9
1952	26.5	1.9	3.0	1.1	208.3	6.5
1953	26.7	0.8	3.2	2.4	218.7	5.0
1954	26.9	0.7	3.1	2.3	232.4	6.2
1955	26.8	−0.4	3.2	3.6	243.9	5.0

(*continued*)

Table A.2 (continued)

Year	CPI-U Index (1982–1984 = 100)	CPI-U Inflation Avg.-Avg. Annual Rate %	Bank Prime Interest Rate % (Nominal)	Bank Prime Interest Rate % (Real)	Money Supply, M2, Seasonally Adjusted ($ billion)	Annual Growth Rate %
1956	27.2	1.5	3.8	2.2	254.6	4.4
1957	28.1	3.3	4.2	0.9	265.8	4.4
1958	28.9	2.8	3.8	1.0	287.1	8.0
1959	29.1	0.7	4.5	3.8	297.8	3.7
1960	29.6	1.7	4.8	3.1	312.3	4.9
1961	29.9	1.0	4.5	3.5	335.5	7.4
1962	30.2	1.0	4.5	3.5	362.7	8.1
1963	30.6	1.3	4.5	3.2	393.2	8.4
1964	31.0	1.3	4.5	3.2	424.8	8.0
1965	31.5	1.6	4.5	2.9	459.2	8.1
1966	32.4	2.9	5.6	2.7	480.0	4.5
1967	33.4	3.1	5.6	2.5	524.3	9.2
1968	34.8	4.2	6.3	2.0	566.8	8.1
1969	36.7	5.5	8.0	2.3	587.9	3.7
1970	38.8	5.7	7.9	2.1	626.5	6.6
1971	40.5	4.4	5.7	1.3	710.3	13.4
1972	41.8	3.2	5.3	2.0	802.3	13.0
1973	44.4	6.2	8.0	1.7	855.5	6.6
1974	49.3	11.0	10.8	−0.2	902.4	5.5
1975	53.8	9.1	7.9	−1.1	1,016.6	12.7
1976	56.9	5.8	6.8	1.0	1,152.6	13.4
1977	60.6	6.5	6.8	0.3	1,271.1	10.3
1978	65.2	7.6	9.1	1.4	1,366.9	7.5
1979	72.6	11.3	12.7	1.2	1,474.7	7.9
1980	82.4	13.5	15.3	1.6	1,600.4	8.5
1981	90.9	10.3	18.9	7.8	1,756.1	9.7
1982	96.5	6.2	14.9	8.1	1,911.2	8.8
1983	99.6	3.2	10.8	7.4	2,127.8	11.3
1984	103.9	4.3	12.0	7.4	2,311.7	8.6
1985	107.6	3.6	9.9	6.1	2,497.4	8.0
1986	109.6	1.9	8.3	6.3	2,734.0	9.5
1987	113.6	3.6	8.2	4.4	2,832.8	3.6
1988	118.3	4.1	9.3	5.0	2,995.8	5.8
1989	124.0	4.8	10.9	5.8	3,159.9	5.5
1990	130.7	5.4	10.0	4.4	3,279.1	3.8
1991	136.2	4.2	8.5	4.1	3,379.8	3.1

Table A.2 (continued)

Year	CPI-U Index (1982–1984 = 100)	CPI-U Inflation Avg.-Avg. Annual Rate %	Bank Prime Interest Rate % (Nominal)	Bank Prime Interest Rate % (Real)	Money Supply, M2, Seasonally Adjusted ($ billion)	Annual Growth Rate %
1992	140.3	3.0	6.3	3.2	3,434.0	1.6
1993	144.5	3.0	6.0	2.9	3,487.4	1.6
1994	148.2	2.6	7.2	4.4	3,502.0	0.4
1995	152.4	2.8	8.8	5.9	3,649.1	4.2
1996	156.9	3.0	8.3	5.1	3,823.9	4.8
1997	160.5	2.3	8.4	6.0	4,046.6	5.8
1998	163.0	1.6	8.4	6.6	4,373.4	8.1
1999	166.6	2.2	8.0	5.7	4,632.9	5.9
2000	172.2	3.4	9.2	5.6	4,913.2	6.1
2001	177.1	2.8	6.9	4.0	5,428.6	10.5
2002	179.9	1.6	4.7	3.0	5,775.2	6.4
2003	184.0	2.3	4.1	1.8	6,064.1	5.0
2004	188.9	2.7	4.3	1.6	6,407.8	5.7
2005	195.3	3.4	4.9	1.5	6,673.1	4.1
2006	201.6	3.2	8.0	4.6	7,065.2	5.9
2007	207.3	7.8	8.1	0.2	7,493.8	6.1
2008	215.3	−0.9	5.1	6.1	8,245.1	10.0
2009	214.5	−0.4	3.3	3.6	8,528.7	3.4
2010	218.1	1.7	3.3	1.5	8,796.4	3.1
2011	224.9	3.2	3.3	0.1	9,640.1	9.6

Table A.3 Employment Statistics

Year	Civilian Noninstitutional Population > 16 yrs (000)	Civilian Labor Force Total (000)	Participation Rate %	Number Employed (000)	Annual Employment Growth %	Unemployed Total (000)	Unemployment Rate %
1945	90,373	53,138	58.8	53,137		1,020	1.9
1946	98,998	56,749	57.3	56,747	6.8	2,227	3.9
1947	101,827	59,350	58.3	57,039	0.5	2,311	3.9
1948	103,068	60,621	58.8	58,345	2.3	2,276	3.8
1949	103,994	61,286	58.9	57,649	−1.2	3,637	5.9
1950	104,995	62,208	59.2	58,920	2.2	3,288	5.3
1951	104,621	62,017	59.3	59,962	1.8	2,055	3.3
1952	105,231	62,138	59.0	60,255	0.5	1,883	3.0
1953	107,056	63,015	58.9	61,181	1.5	1,834	2.9
1954	108,321	63,643	58.8	60,111	−1.7	3,532	5.5
1955	109,683	65,023	59.3	62,171	3.4	2,852	4.4
1956	110,954	66,552	60.0	63,802	2.6	2,750	4.1
1957	112,265	66,929	59.6	64,070	0.4	2,859	4.3
1958	113,727	67,639	59.5	63,037	−1.6	4,602	6.8
1959	115,329	68,369	59.3	64,629	2.5	3,740	5.5
1960	117,245	69,628	59.4	65,776	1.8	3,852	5.5
1961	118,771	70,459	59.3	65,745	0.0	4,714	6.7
1962	120,153	70,614	58.8	66,703	1.5	3,911	5.5
1963	122,416	71,833	58.7	67,763	1.6	4,070	5.7
1964	124,485	73,091	58.7	69,305	2.3	3,786	5.2

Table A.3 (continued)

Year	Civilian Noninstitutional Population > 16 yrs (000)	Civilian Labor Force Total (000)	Participation Rate %	Number Employed (000)	Annual Employment Growth %	Unemployed Total (000)	Unemployment Rate %
1965	126,513	74,455	58.9	71,089	2.6	3,366	4.5
1966	128,058	75,770	59.2	72,895	2.5	2,875	3.8
1967	129,874	77,347	59.6	74,372	2.0	2,975	3.8
1968	132,028	78,737	59.6	75,920	2.1	2,817	3.6
1969	134,335	80,734	60.1	77,902	2.6	2,832	3.5
1970	137,085	82,771	60.4	78,678	1.0	4,093	4.9
1971	140,216	84,382	60.2	79,366	0.9	5,016	5.9
1972	144,126	87,034	60.4	82,152	3.5	4,882	5.6
1973	147,096	89,429	60.8	85,064	3.5	4,365	4.9
1974	150,120	91,949	61.3	86,793	2.0	5,156	5.6
1975	153,153	93,775	61.2	85,846	−1.1	7,929	8.5
1976	156,150	96,158	61.6	88,752	3.4	7,406	7.7
1977	159,033	99,009	62.3	92,018	3.7	6,991	7.1
1978	161,910	102,251	63.2	96,049	4.4	6,202	6.1
1979	164,863	104,962	63.7	98,825	2.9	6,137	5.8
1980	167,745	106,940	63.8	99,303	0.5	7,637	7.1
1981	170,130	108,670	63.9	100,397	1.1	8,273	7.6
1982	172,271	110,204	64.0	99,526	−0.9	10,678	9.7
1983	174,215	111,550	64.0	100,833	1.3	10,717	9.6

(continued)

199

Table A.3 (continued)

Year	Civilian Noninstitutional Population > 16 yrs (000)	Civilian Labor Force Total (000)	Participation Rate %	Number Employed (000)	Annual Employment Growth %	Unemployed Total (000)	Unemployment Rate %
1984	176,383	113,544	64.4	105,005	4.1	8,539	7.5
1985	178,206	115,461	64.8	107,149	2.0	8,312	7.2
1986	180,587	117,834	65.3	109,597	2.3	8,237	7.0
1987	182,753	119,865	65.6	112,440	2.6	7,425	6.2
1988	184,613	121,669	65.9	114,968	2.2	6,701	5.5
1989	186,393	123,869	66.5	117,341	2.1	6,528	5.3
1990	189,164	125,840	66.5	118,793	1.2	7,047	5.6
1991	190,925	126,346	66.2	117,718	−0.9	8,628	6.8
1992	192,805	128,105	66.4	118,492	0.7	9,613	7.5
1993	194,838	129,200	66.3	120,260	1.5	8,940	6.9
1994	196,814	131,056	66.6	123,060	2.3	7,996	6.1
1995	198,584	132,304	66.6	124,900	1.5	7,404	5.6
1996	200,591	133,943	66.8	126,707	1.4	7,236	5.4
1997	203,133	136,297	67.1	129,558	2.3	6,739	4.9
1998	205,220	137,673	67.1	131,463	1.5	6,210	4.5
1999	207,753	139,368	67.1	133,488	1.5	5,880	4.2
2000	212,577	142,583	67.1	136,891	2.5	5,692	4.0
2001	215,092	143,734	66.8	136,933	0.0	6,801	4.7
2002	217,570	144,863	66.6	136,485	−0.3	8,378	5.8
2003	221,168	146,510	66.2	137,736	0.9	8,774	6.0
2004	223,357	147,401	66.0	139,252	1.1	8,140	5.5

Table A.3 (continued)

Year	Civilian Noninstitutional Population > 16 yrs (000)	Civilian Labor Force Total (000)	Participation Rate %	Number Employed (000)	Annual Employment Growth %	Unemployed Total (000)	Unemployment Rate %
2005	226,082	149,289	66.0	141,710	1.8	7,579	5.1
2006	228,815	151,409	66.2	144,418	1.9	6,991	4.6
2007	231,867	153,123	66.0	146,050	1.1	7,073	4.6
2008	233,788	154,322	66.0	145,370	−0.5	8,951	5.8
2009	235,801	154,189	65.4	139,888	−3.8	14,301	9.3
2010	237,830	153,885	64.7	139,070	−0.6	14,815	9.6
2011	239,618	153,616	64.1	139,873	0.6	13,743	8.9

Table A.4 Savings, Investment, Poverty, the Stock Market and Trade Statistics

Year	NIPA Personal Savings Rate %	Private Investment Share of GDP %	Population below Poverty Line % of total	Dow Jones Year-End Values (Nominal)	Dow Jones Year-End Values (Real)	Real Growth in Dow Jones Industrial Averages %	Exports as a Share of GDP %	Trade Balance Percent of GDP
1945	20.4	4.8	N.A.	192.91	1071.72		3.0	−0.3
1946	9.6	14.0	N.A.	177.20	908.72	−15.2	6.4	3.2
1947	4.3	14.3	N.A.	181.16	812.38	−10.6	7.7	4.4
1948	6.9	17.9	N.A.	177.30	735.68	−9.4	5.8	2.0
1949	4.9	13.8	N.A.	200.13	840.88	14.3	5.4	2.0
1950	7.1	18.4	N.A.	235.41	976.80	16.2	4.2	0.3
1951	8.4	17.7	N.A.	269.23	1035.50	6.0	5.0	0.7
1952	8.3	15.1	N.A.	291.90	1101.51	6.4	4.6	0.3
1953	8.2	14.9	N.A.	280.90	1052.06	−4.5	4.0	−0.2
1954	7.5	14.1	N.A.	404.39	1503.31	42.9	4.2	0.1
1955	6.9	16.6	N.A.	488.40	1822.39	21.2	4.3	0.1
1956	8.5	16.5	N.A.	499.47	1836.29	0.8	4.9	0.5
1957	8.4	15.3	N.A.	435.69	1550.50	−15.6	5.2	0.9
1958	8.5	13.8	N.A.	583.65	2019.55	30.3	4.4	0.1
1959	7.5	15.5	22.4	679.36	2334.57	15.6	4.5	0.1
1960	7.2	15.0	22.2	615.89	2080.71	−10.9	5.1	0.7
1961	8.4	14.4	21.9	731.14	2445.28	17.5	5.1	0.8
1962	8.3	15.0	21.0	609.18	2017.15	−17.5	5.0	0.6
1963	7.8	15.2	19.5	767.21	2507.22	24.3	5.0	0.7
1964	8.8	15.4	19.0	874.13	2819.77	12.5	5.3	0.9

Table A.4 (continued)

Year	NIPA Personal Savings Rate %	Private Investment Share of GDP %	Population below Poverty Line % of total	Dow Jones Year-End Values (Nominal)	Dow Jones Year-End Values (Real)	Real Growth in Dow Jones Industrial Averages %	Exports as a Share of GDP %	Trade Balance Percent of GDP
1965	8.6	16.4	17.3	969.26	3077.02	9.1	5.2	0.6
1966	8.2	16.7	14.7	785.69	2424.97	−21.2	5.2	0.4
1967	9.4	15.4	14.2	905.11	2709.91	11.8	5.2	0.3
1968	8.4	15.5	12.8	943.75	2711.93	0.1	5.3	0.0
1969	7.8	15.9	12.1	800.36	2180.82	−19.6	5.3	0.0
1970	9.4	14.7	12.6	838.92	2162.16	−0.9	5.7	0.2
1971	10.0	15.8	12.5	890.20	2198.02	1.7	5.6	−0.1
1972	8.9	16.8	11.9	1020.02	2440.24	11.0	5.7	−0.4
1973	10.5	17.7	11.1	850.86	1916.35	−21.5	6.9	0.1
1974	10.7	16.6	11.2	616.24	1249.98	−34.8	8.4	−0.3
1975	10.6	14.1	12.3	852.41	1584.41	26.8	8.5	0.8
1976	9.4	16.0	11.8	1004.65	1765.64	11.4	8.2	−0.3
1977	8.7	17.8	11.6	831.17	1371.57	−22.3	7.9	−1.3
1978	8.9	19.1	11.4	805.01	1234.68	−10.0	8.1	−1.3
1979	8.8	19.2	11.7	838.74	1155.29	−6.4	9.0	−1.0
1980	9.8	17.2	13.0	963.99	1169.89	1.3	10.1	−0.7
1981	10.6	18.3	14.0	875.00	962.60	−17.7	9.8	−0.5
1982	10.9	15.9	15.0	1046.54	1084.50	12.7	8.7	−0.7
1983	8.7	16.0	15.2	1258.64	1263.69	16.5	7.8	−1.6

(continued)

Table A.4 (continued)

Year	NIPA Personal Savings Rate %	Private Investment Share of GDP %	Population below Poverty Line % of total	Dow Jones Year-End Values (Nominal)	Dow Jones Year-End Values (Real)	Real Growth in Dow Jones Industrial Averages %	Exports as a Share of GDP %	Trade Balance Percent of GDP
1984	10.2	18.7	14.4	1211.57	1166.09	-7.7	7.7	-2.8
1985	8.2	17.5	14.0	1546.67	1437.43	23.3	7.2	-2.9
1986	7.6	16.7	13.6	1895.95	1729.88	20.3	7.2	-3.1
1987	6.5	16.6	13.4	1938.83	1706.72	-1.3	7.7	-3.2
1988	6.9	16.1	13.0	2168.57	1833.11	7.4	8.7	-2.2
1989	6.6	16.0	12.8	2753.20	2220.32	21.1	9.2	-1.7
1990	6.5	14.8	13.5	2633.66	2015.04	-9.2	9.5	-1.4
1991	7.0	13.4	14.2	3168.80	2326.58	15.5	10.0	-0.5
1992	7.3	13.6	14.8	3301.11	2352.89	1.1	10.0	-0.6
1993	5.8	14.3	15.1	3754.09	2597.99	10.4	9.8	-1.1
1994	5.2	15.5	14.5	3834.44	2587.34	-0.4	10.2	-1.4
1995	5.2	15.4	13.8	5117.12	3357.69	29.8	10.9	-1.3
1996	4.9	15.8	13.7	6448.27	4109.80	22.4	11.1	-1.3
1997	4.6	16.7	13.3	7908.25	4927.26	19.9	11.5	-1.3
1998	5.3	17.2	12.7	9181.43	5632.78	14.3	10.8	-1.9
1999	3.1	17.5	11.9	11497.10	6901.02	22.5	10.6	-2.8
2000	2.9	17.8	11.3	10786.85	6264.14	-9.2	11.0	-3.8
2001	2.7	16.2	11.7	10021.50	5658.67	-9.7	10.0	-3.6
2002	3.5	15.5	12.1	8341.63	4636.81	-18.1	9.4	-4.0
2003	3.5	15.5	12.5	10453.92	5681.48	22.5	9.3	-4.5
2004	3.6	16.6	12.7	10783.01	5708.32	0.5	10.0	-5.2

Table A.4 (continued)

Year	NIPA Personal Savings Rate %	Private Investment Share of GDP %	Population below Poverty Line % of total	Dow Jones Year-End Values (Nominal)	Dow Jones Year-End Values (Real)	Real Growth in Dow Jones Industrial Averages %	Exports as a Share of GDP %	Trade Balance Percent of GDP
2005	1.5	17.2	12.6	10717.50	5487.71	-3.9	10.3	-5.7
2006	2.6	17.4	12.3	12463.15	6182.12	12.7	11.0	-5.8
2007	2.4	16.4	12.5	13264.82	6104.38	-1.3	11.8	-5.1
2008	5.4	14.6	13.2	8776.39	4076.35	-33.2	12.9	-5.0
2009	5.1	11.1	14.3	10428.05	4861.56	19.3	11.4	-2.8
2010	5.3	12.4	15.1	11577.51	5308.35	9.2	12.7	-3.6
2011	4.4	12.7	N.A.	12217.56	5431.50	2.3	13.8	-3.8

Table A.5 Federal Expenditure, Revenue and Debt Statistics

Year	Total Federal Outlays ($ billion)	Total Tax Receipts ($ billion)	Federal Budget Deficit/Surplus ($ billion)	Federal Outlays Share of GDP %	Growth Rate of Federal Outlays %	Tax Receipts Share of GDP %	Federal Deficits Percent of Budget %	Debt as a Percent of GDP %
1945	92.7	45.2	−47.6	41.9	6.5	20.4	−51.3	117.5
1946	55.2	39.3	−15.9	24.8	−40.5	17.6	−28.9	121.7
1947	34.5	38.5	4.0	14.8	−43.4	16.5	11.6	110.3
1948	29.8	41.6	11.8	11.6	−18.5	16.2	39.6	98.2
1949	38.8	39.4	0.6	14.3	34.8	14.5	1.5	93.1
1950	42.6	39.4	−3.1	15.6	5.5	14.4	−7.3	94.1
1951	45.5	51.6	6.1	14.2	8.7	16.1	13.4	79.7
1952	67.7	66.2	−1.5	19.4	49.6	19	−2.2	74.3
1953	76.1	69.6	−6.5	20.4	4.1	18.7	−8.5	71.4
1954	70.9	69.7	−1.2	18.8	−10.0	18.5	−1.6	71.8
1955	68.4	65.5	−3.0	17.3	−6.6	16.6	−4.4	69.3
1956	70.6	74.6	3.9	16.5	−1.7	17.5	5.6	63.9
1957	76.6	80.0	3.4	17.0	3.2	17.8	4.5	60.4
1958	82.4	79.6	−2.8	17.9	1.6	17.3	−3.4	60.8
1959	92.1	79.2	−12.8	18.8	7.6	16.1	−14.0	58.6
1960	92.2	92.5	0.3	17.8	−0.3	17.9	0.3	56.0
1961	97.7	94.4	−3.3	18.4	3.1	17.8	−3.4	55.2
1962	106.8	99.7	−7.1	18.8	9.0	17.6	−6.7	53.4
1963	111.3	106.6	−4.8	18.6	−0.3	17.8	−4.3	51.8
1964	118.5	112.6	−5.9	18.5	5.1	17.6	−5.0	49.3

Table A.5 (continued)

Year	Total Federal Outlays ($ billion)	Total Tax Receipts ($ billion)	Federal Budget Deficit/Surplus ($ billion)	Federal Outlays Share of GDP %	Growth Rate of Federal Outlays %	Tax Receipts Share of GDP %	Federal Deficits Percent of Budget %	Debt as a Percent of GDP %
1965	118.2	116.8	−1.4	17.2	−1.6	17	−1.2	46.9
1966	134.5	130.8	−3.7	17.8	11.2	17.4	−2.7	43.5
1967	157.5	148.8	−8.6	19.4	14.2	18.3	−5.5	42.0
1968	178.1	153.0	−25.2	20.5	9.0	17.7	−14.1	42.5
1969	183.6	186.9	3.2	19.4	−3.3	19.7	1.8	38.6
1970	195.6	192.8	−2.8	19.3	0.7	19	−1.5	37.6
1971	210.2	187.1	−23.0	19.5	0.3	17.3	−11.0	37.8
1972	230.7	207.3	−23.4	19.6	2.5	17.6	−10.1	37.1
1973	245.7	230.8	−14.9	18.7	0.8	17.7	−6.1	35.6
1974	269.4	263.2	−6.1	18.7	0.9	18.3	−2.3	33.6
1975	332.3	279.1	−53.2	21.3	11.9	17.9	−16.0	34.7
1976	371.8	298.1	−73.7	21.4	3.7	17.2	−19.8	36.2
1977	409.2	355.6	−53.7	20.7	1.8	18	−13.1	35.8
1978	458.7	399.6	−59.2	20.7	5.3	18	−12.9	35.0
1979	504.0	463.3	−40.7	20.1	1.0	18.5	−8.1	33.2
1980	590.9	517.1	−73.8	21.7	6.0	19	−12.5	33.4
1981	678.2	599.3	−79.0	22.2	3.5	19.6	−11.6	32.5
1982	745.7	617.8	−128.0	23.1	2.5	19.2	−17.2	35.3
1983	808.4	600.6	−207.8	23.5	3.2	17.5	−25.7	39.9

(continued)

Table A.5 (continued)

Year	Total Federal Outlays ($ billion)	Total Tax Receipts ($ billion)	Federal Budget Deficit/Surplus ($ billion)	Federal Outlays Share of GDP %	Growth Rate of Federal Outlays %	Tax Receipts Share of GDP %	Federal Deficits Percent of Budget %	Debt as a Percent of GDP %
1984	851.8	666.4	−185.4	22.2	0.1	17.3	−21.8	40.7
1985	946.3	734.0	−212.3	22.8	7.4	17.7	−22.4	43.8
1986	990.4	769.2	−221.2	22.5	2.0	17.5	−22.3	48.2
1987	1,004.0	854.3	−149.7	21.6	−1.7	18.4	−14.9	50.4
1988	1,064.4	909.2	−155.2	21.3	2.9	18.2	−14.6	51.9
1989	1,143.7	991.1	−152.6	21.2	3.6	18.4	−13.3	53.1
1990	1,253.0	1,032.0	−221.0	21.9	6.3	18	−17.6	55.9
1991	1,324.2	1,055.0	−269.2	22.3	0.9	17.8	−20.3	60.7
1992	1,381.5	1,091.2	−290.3	22.1	0.5	17.5	−21.0	64.1
1993	1,409.4	1,154.3	−255.1	21.4	−0.7	17.5	−18.1	66.1
1994	1,461.8	1,258.6	−203.2	21.0	1.8	18	−13.9	66.6
1995	1,515.7	1,351.8	−164.0	20.6	0.9	18.4	−10.8	67.0
1996	1,560.5	1,453.1	−107.4	20.2	0.5	18.8	−6.9	67.1
1997	1,601.1	1,579.2	−21.9	19.5	0.5	19.2	−1.4	65.4
1998	1,652.5	1,721.7	69.3	19.1	2.2	19.9	4.2	63.2
1999	1,701.8	1,827.5	125.6	18.5	1.6	19.8	7.4	60.9
2000	1,789.0	2,025.2	236.2	18.2	2.6	20.6	13.2	57.3
2001	1,862.8	1,991.1	128.2	18.2	1.6	19.5	6.9	56.4
2002	2,010.9	1,853.1	−157.8	19.1	6.2	17.6	−7.8	58.8
2003	2,159.9	1,782.3	−377.6	19.7	4.7	16.2	−17.5	61.6
2004	2,292.8	1,880.1	−412.7	19.6	3.2	16.1	−18.0	63.0

Table A.5 (continued)

Year	Total Federal Outlays ($ billion)	Total Tax Receipts ($ billion)	Federal Budget Deficit/Surplus ($ billion)	Federal Outlays Share of GDP %	Growth Rate of Federal Outlays %	Tax Receipts Share of GDP %	Federal Deficits Percent of Budget %	Debt as a Percent of GDP %
2005	2,472.0	2,153.6	−318.3	19.9	4.0	17.3	−12.9	63.6
2006	2,655.0	2,406.9	−248.2	20.1	3.7	18.2	−9.3	64.0
2007	2,728.7	2,568.0	−160.7	19.7	0.0	18.5	−5.9	64.6
2008	2,982.5	2,524.0	−458.6	20.8	5.4	17.6	−15.4	69.7
2009	3,517.7	2,105.0	−1,412.7	25.2	17.4	15.1	−40.2	85.2
2010	3,456.2	2,162.7	−1,293.5	24.1	−3.3	15.1	−37.4	94.2
2011	3,603.1	2,303.5	−1,299.6	24.1	2.9	15.4	−36.1	98.7

Selected Bibliography

Bernanke, Ben. "Lessons of the Financial Crisis for Banking Supervision." Speech before the Federal Reserve Bank of Chicago Conference on Bank Structure and Competitive Change, May 7, 2009. http://www.federalreserve.gov/newsevents/speech/bernanke 20090507a.htm.

Bucks, Brian K., Arthur B. Kennickell, Traci L. Mach, and Kevin B. Moore. "Changes in U.S. Family Finances from 2004 to 2007: Evidence from the Survey of Consumer Finances." *Federal Reserve Bulletin* 95 (February 12, 2009). http://www.federalreserve.gov/pubs/bulletin/2009/pdf/scf09.pdf.

Curry, Timothy, and Lynn Shibut. "The Cost of the Savings and Loan Crisis: Truth and Consequences." *FDIC Banking Review* 13, no. 2 (December 2000). http://www.fdic.gov/bank/analytical/banking/2000dec/brv13n2_2.pdf.

Family and Medical Leave Act of 1993. Pub. L. No. 103-3 (1993). http://www.dol.gov/whd/regs/statutes/fmla.htm.

Financial Crisis Inquiry Commission. "Financial Crisis Inquiry Report: Final Report of the National Commission on the Causes of the Financial and Economic Crisis in the United States, Official Government Edition." Washington, DC: U.S. Government Printing Office, 2011. http://fcic.law.stanford.edu/report/.

Geller, Martinne. "U.S. Soft Drink Sales Volume Falls More in '07." Reuters, March 12, 2008.

Heflin, Jay. "Financial Crisis Cost Households $17 trillion, Treasury Official Says." *On the Money: THE HILL's Finance and Economy Blog*, May 3, 2010. http://thehill.com/blogs/on-the-money/801-economy/ 95689-financial-crisis-cost-households-17-trillion-treasury-official-says.

Jackson, Jill, and John Nolen. "Health Care Reform Bill Summary: A Look at What's in the Bill." *CBS News*, March 21, 2010. http:// www.cbsnews.com/8301-503544_162-20000846-503544.html.

Jacobe, Dennis. "In U.S., 54% Have Stock Market Investments, Lowest since 1999." Gallup, April 20, 2011. http://www.gallup.com/poll/ 147206/stock-market-investments-lowest-1999.aspx.

Joint Select Committee on Deficit Reduction. 2011.

Lewis, Michael. *The Big Short: Inside the Doomsday Machine*. New York: W.W. Norton and Company, 2011.

The Miller Center. http://millercenter.org/.

Morgensen, Gretchen, and Joshua Rosner. *Reckless Endangerment*. New York: Henry Holt & Co., 2011.

Office of Management and Budget. "Budget Concepts and Budget Process." http://www.whitehouse.gov/sites/default/files/omb/ budget/fy2012/assets/concepts.pdf.

Pro Publica. "Bailout Recipients." http://projects.propublica.org/bailout/ list.

Recovery.gov. http://www.recovery.gov/pages/default.aspx.

Reich, Robert."Washington and Wall Street: The Revolving Door." Review of *Reckless Endangerment* by Gretchen Morgensen and Joshua Rosner. *New York Times*, May 27, 2011, Sunday Book Review. http://www.nytimes.com/2011/05/29/books/review/book -review-reckless-endangerment-by-gretchen-morgenson-and-joshua -rosner.html.

Seskin, Eugene P., and Robert P. Parker. "A Guide to the NIPA's." *Survey of Current Business* (March 1998). http://www.bea.gov/scb/ account_articles/national/0398niw/maintext.htm.

Stiglitz, Joseph. *Freefall: America, Free Markets, and the Sinking of the World Economy.* New York: W.W. Norton and Company, 2010.

U.S. Bureau of Economic Analysis. "Concepts and Methods of the U.S. National, Income and Product Accounts." November 2010. http:// www.bea.gov/national/pdf/NIPAhandbookch1-7.pdf.

U.S. Bureau of Economic Analysis. "Methodology Papers: Descriptions of the methodologies used to prepare BEA's National, Industry, Regional, and International Accounts Data." http://www.bea.gov/ methodologies/index.htm.

U.S. Census Bureau. "Historical Poverty Tables—People." http://www
.census.gov/hhes/www/poverty/data/historical/people.html.

U.S. Census Bureau Census. "Income Inequality." http://www.census
.gov/hhes/www/income/data/historical/inequality/index.html.

U.S. Department of Labor, Bureau of Labor Statistics. http://www.bls
.gov/data/.

U.S. Department of Labor, Bureau of Labor Statistics. "Consumer Price
Index All Urban Consumers—(CPI-U)." 2011. ftp://ftp.bls.gov/
pub/special.requests/cpi/cpiai.txt.

U.S. Department of Treasury. "Major Foreign Holders of Treasury Securities." http://www.treasury.gov/resource-center/data-chart-center/
tic/Documents/mfh.txt.

U.S. Environmental Protection Agency. "CERCLA Overview: The Comprehensive Environmental Response, Compensation, and Liability
Act (CERCLA), Act by Congress on December 11, 1980." http://
www.epa.gov/superfund/policy/cercla.htm.

U.S. Social Security Administration. "Actuarial Publications." http://
www.ssa.gov/OACT/STATS/index.html.

U.S. Social Security Administration. "Report of the National Commission
on Social Security Reform." January 1983. http://www.ssa.gov/
history/reports/gspan.html.

Index

About the Author

Richard J. Carroll is an economist, evaluation specialist, and financial analyst who has published several books and articles about the U.S. economy that cover a range of issues focusing on lessons for current policy. He has extensive international economic experience including work with the World Bank and other international and bilateral organizations in more than 40 countries, providing economic and financial expertise for economic policies and international investment projects. He specializes in evaluating economic programs and investments. He holds a BA and MA in economics from Georgetown University, an MBA from the Wharton School, University of Pennsylvania, and was a Fulbright Scholar in Germany.